Guide to

BOSTON'S BEST
RESTAURANTS

PHANTOM GOURMET

Guide to
BOSTON'S BEST RESTAURANTS

St. Martin's Griffin ⚟ New York

www.stmartins.com

Book design by rlf design

Library of Congress Cataloging-in-Publication Data

Phantom Gourmet.
   The Phantom Gourmet guide to Boston's best restaurants / The Phantom
Gourmet.—1st St. Martin's Griffin ed.
      p. cm.
   ISBN-13: 978-0-312-34959-2
   ISBN-10: 0-312-34959-9
   1. Restaurants—Massachusetts—Boston Region—Guidebooks. 2. Boston
Region (Mass.)—Guidebooks. I. Title.

   TX907.3.M42P43 2006
   647.95744'61—dc22

   2006001202

First Edition: June 2006

10 9 8 7 6 5 4 3 2 1

This book is dedicated to the owners, managers, and employees of the restaurant industry. You risk your money and time; you devote your talent and effort; you build and create businesses that make all our lives better. I admire what you do, and I hope that you find the following pages worthy of your noble industry.

Contents

"Great Ates" by Location

PHANTOM GOURMET'S HANDY PRICE INDEX*

$	**Cheap**	**Under $15**
$$	**Moderate**	**About $20**
$$$	**Expensive**	**$25 and up**

*based on average entrée price

Acknowledgments

I've never met most of these people, but I know that each of them helped make this book possible:

Dan Andelman
Dave Andelman
Eddie Andelman
Mike Andelman
Phil Balboni
Evan Berenson
Peter Christie
Monica Collins
Dale Dorman
Kim Driscoll
Gayle Fee
Sean Finley
Ed Goldman
Bob Howard
Lou Imbriano
Claire Jones
Ted Jordan
Kenny Lawrence
Patrick Lyons
Julio Marenghi

Pete Masucci
Tom Mercer
John Mitchell
Joe O'Donnell
Chris Palermo
The PhanClub
Jim Priest
Pat Purcell, Jr.
Ramiro and Pebbles
Laura Raposa
Jerry Remy
Eric Sherman
Cory Silva
Paul Sullivan
George Tobia
Mark Viveiros
Morgan White, Jr.
The Wong Family
Zito and Jen

Without all of you, I might be forced to get a real job.

North End Restaurants

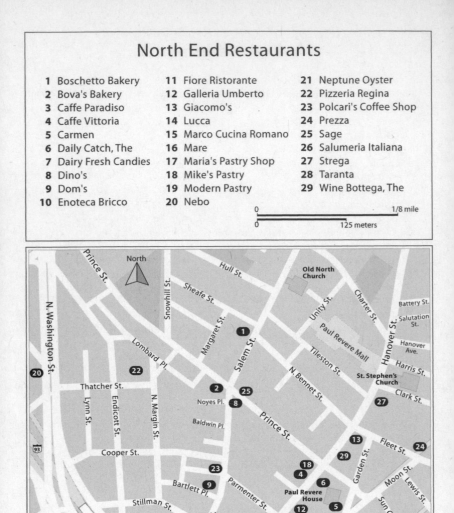

0   1/8 mile

0   125 meters

Introduction

As the Phantom Gourmet, Boston's most trustworthy restaurant critic, I've guarded my top-secret identity like a sacred family recipe. I always dine in disguise; I have enough aliases to fake out the CIA; and I never leave a crumb of evidence in my path. Because I'm so mysterious, I get no special treatment. The experience I have is the same as you'll have when you dine at the restaurants in this book.

Thanks to my boss, I've been on a belly-busting eating spree for the last decade. I've converted all that caloric energy into writing reviews for *The Phantom Gourmet* TV show on UPN-38, the CBS-4 News, WBZ News Radio 1030-AM, and the *Boston Herald*. Millions of people see, hear, and read my reports on the dining scene, then post their comments in the FEEDback Forum on www.PhantomGourmet.com.

The thing I hear more often than the clanging of pots is the pressing need for a restaurant guide "to go." The market is flooded with all-you-can-read buffets on where to eat out, but this book is the ultimate menu of the most "Phan-tastic" restaurants in Boston and beyond. I've compiled a Great Ate list for every major food group (yes, French fries ARE part of the Phantom food pyramid) and neighborhood. Eight of my favorite places are singled out for each delicious category like Fried Clams, Fine Dining, and the Theater District. If you're hungry for a certain something, I'll tell you my eight favorite places to get it. If you're headed to a particular neighborhood, city, or region, I'll point you to the area's eight greatest dining destinations.

Forget aimless searching; this guide gets to the point so you can eat what you want. You can still search the A-to-Z index for your favorite spots and the page on which they're listed.

I spend more time eating out than most people spend even thinking about food during their everyday lives, and I've got the gut to prove it. A big THANKS goes out to all you masters of the kitchen, for keeping me employed. To my "Phans," I give a super-sized salutation. And to anyone who operates a restaurant, treat every customer like a critic . . . because you never know which one could be THE PHANTOM GOURMET. Until I've eaten my way through every restaurant in the land, consider me out to lunch.

—*The Phantom Gourmet*
Mysterious Restaurant Critic

Deep, Dark, Delicious
Restaurant Secrets

As the executive producer and maître d' for the *Phantom Gourmet* TV show, I've spent the last 10 years visiting restaurants, talking to chefs and owners, booking guests, writing scripts, and watching thousands of hours of videotape of the best food in New England. Basically, my job is to produce such a hunger-inducing television show that viewers will want to lick their flatscreens. At times, it's absolute torture to spend the entire day staring at pictures of big, fat burgers, crispy fried clams, lobster, and juicy sirloins.

Now, before you get the wrong idea, let me make the following very clear: I am *not* the Phantom Gourmet.

However, I work more closely with the Mysterious Critic than anybody else on Earth (all via e-mail, of course, to protect his identity). He's taught me a great deal about getting the most out of the dining experience. Drawing on my experience, I've compiled the following list of tips and tricks to keep in mind when you're eating out at a restaurant.

Make a List

There are thousands of restaurants in New England. In this book alone, there are nearly 500 restaurants listed as Great Ate winners. With all that delicious information overload, you need to make a list of MUST VISIT restaurants. Keep your own Great Ate list on hand. Scribble it on a sauce-stained napkin, keep it in your Palm Pilot, or tattoo it on your tummy. That way, the next time somebody asks where you want to eat, you'll know exactly where to go.

Skip Amateur Night

Ask any chef or restaurateur, and they'll tell you a dark secret: Friday and (especially) Saturday dinners are known as "amateur night" in the restaurant industry. Everybody goes out to eat on the weekends, the dining rooms are packed, reservations are tough, and kitchens are slammed during peak dining hours. If you want a more relaxed and refined dining experience, try another night of the week. Mondays and Tuesdays are the slowest, but the executive chef is usually running the show on Wednesdays and Thursdays.

How to Get In

Even Phantom has trouble making reservations at some hot restaurants (he knows all the tricks of the trade, but he can't request a table for Mr. P. Gourmet). Sometimes the best way to get in is simply to show up and ask for a table. Restaurants typically set aside a few seats for VIPs and high-end hotel concierges. Of course, a host always appreciates the "Vegas Handshake," where you fold a $20 bill and DISCREETLY slip it into his hand when the rest of hungry herd isn't looking.

What Not to Order

People are always asking servers for recommendations and inquiring about the best dish on the menu. But sometimes waiters are trained to respond with the most expensive entrée. Try going the other route, and ask about the worst thing on the menu. Most of the time, you'll get a laugh and a more honest answer, and you'll extrapolate a much better dining decision.

How to Complain

Don't yell, don't scream, and don't blame the server for bad food. Most important, DON'T MAKE A PUBLIC SCENE. If you have a disappointing dining experience, pay your bill, pay your tip, and politely ask to see a manager. If that doesn't work, a thoughtful letter to the restaurant owner or general manager almost always results in a generous response, an invitation for a free dinner, or at least a little closure.

Tip 20 Percent

Sorry, but 15 percent just doesn't cut it anymore. Waiters, waitresses, and bartenders have the toughest job in the world. They make almost nothing in terms of salary, so they really survive on gratuities. You should always tip at least 20 percent, which absolutely includes the total from tax and wine. If you don't get great service, still tip the full amount. Seek retribution by exercising your right not to return.

Most important: dine out frequently, visit a healthy variety of restaurants, and constantly challenge yourself by trying new foods, new flavors, and new neighborhoods. The more you eat, the more you learn. Now *that's* food for thought.

—Dan Andelman
  Executive Producer/Maître D'
  Phantom Gourmet, Inc.

Message from the CEO

When I started Phantom Gourmet in 1993, the idea was simple. Compared to sports, politics, and even cooking, restaurants were "underserved." I wanted to give them the media attention they deserved. I needed a food critic to be the heart and soul of the enterprise, but I felt strongly that he must remain incognito since others in the field seemed completely tainted by special treatment. So the Phantom Gourmet was born (actually, hired). The show's aim was to be fun and informative, while covering everything from fine dining to fast food.

Turns out that it really is better to be lucky than good. Boston restaurants exploded like Phantom's waistline, and along with them, Phantom's fame. From the show's humble roots on cable, it's grown to a full hour-long television program on UPN-38 with a feature on the CBS-4 *Evening News*, a spot on WBZ News Radio 1030-AM, and a page in the *Boston Herald*. Phantom has his own Phantom Gourmet Gift Card and hosts Boston's best restaurant and food event (The Phantom Gourmet Food Festival) each fall next to Fenway Park.

How did the Phantom phenomenon happen? Adults now eat more than half their meals outside the home, and it's arguable that dining out is America's number-one hobby. Decades from now, preparing your own food may well be like gardening, building your own house, or making your own clothes . . . something you do for relaxation rather than economic sense. If you don't believe me, think back a couple of centuries, when almost every American was a farmer.

If put to proper use, this book should be covered in ketchup, duck sauce, and cocktails within the next year. To those who own and operate restaurants, I really admire what you do. Keep up the great work. And remember to treat each customer like a critic . . . because you never know which one could be the Phantom Gourmet.

—*Dave Andelman, CEO*
Phantom Gourmet, Inc.

"GREAT ATES"
by Category

All-Time Phantom Favorites

GREAT ATE

Phantom dines at hundreds of restaurants every year in search of unforgettable dining rooms. Some candidates were obvious winners for their top-rated scores. Others stood out for memorable meals and a truly unique take on the spirit of dining out. From fine dining to take-out, only the 8 GREATEST eateries make it into Phantom's all-time favorites

THE GREATEST: Fine! Fine! Fine! Dining

Arrows $$$
Berwick Rd., Ogunquit, Maine, (207) 361-1100,
www.arrowsrestaurant.com

When there's a $50 per person cancellation fee, you know you're either being taken for a ride or you're in for something special. Arrows is the current record holder for Phantom's all-time highest restaurant rating, making it well worth the trip to Maine. Set amidst dense woods and gorgeous gardens, this eighteenth-century farmhouse is highly romantic. Dressed-up diners duck into the wood-and-glass-encased porch, where a sprawling birch tree and square lanterns illuminate a woodland scene. The playful menu changes daily, with 90 percent of the restaurant's produce grown on the grounds. They cure their own hams and fish, and each entrée is actually four mini creations. Seasonal inspirations might include red wine and honey-poached beef or cedar plank salmon with rosemary rhubarb candy.

THE GREATEST: Sushi

Oishii Sushi Bar $$
612 Hammond St., Chestnut Hill, Mass., (617) 277-7888

Oishii is a snug sushi bar with ten coveted counter seats where customers can watch the sushi experts slice and roll. It's a bare-basics closet of a room, but there's no better dressed fish in town (or out of town)! Chef Ting crafts generous portions of tasty, superbly fresh fish. Phantom goes for the toro, which is the most fantastically fatty part of the tuna. At Oishii, the salmon shimmers, the red clam comes paper thin, and the spicy scallop hand rolls are sublime. Hot entrées are equally outstanding, with udon noodles and stone-grilled selections. There's a second, more spacious location in Sudbury.

THE GREATEST: Exotic Flavors

Oleana $$$
134 Hampshire St., Cambridge, Mass., (617) 661-0505,
www.oleanarestaurant.com

For Phantom's adventurous palate, Oleana is in a flavor-filled league of its own. The Middle Eastern–influenced menu swirls exotic spice into Mediterranean dishes like sea scallops with tangerine butter. The only difficulty is deciding between fried mussels with hot peppers or za'atar lemon chicken with Turkish pancakes. Not to worry, you can order pre-appetizer bread spreads (Armenian bean & walnut pâté, anyone?) while making up your mind. Equally outrageous desserts include baked Alaska with passion fruit caramel and chocolate hazelnut baklava. The pretty dining room is intimate and rustic with stone tiling and colorful North African artifacts, and there's a garden patio in warmer weather.

THE GREATEST: Tamales, Tostadas, & Tacos

Taqueria Cancun $$
192 Sumner St., Boston, Mass., (617) 567-4449

You won't need much cash at this East Boston taqueria, where the tamales, tostadas, and tacos are awesome. The menu is Mexican meets Salvadoran, which means lots of tortillas, rice, and beans. Phantom especially loves their enchiladas piled with spicy pork, guacamole, pico de gallo, and sour cream. The pupusas, or ground corn cakes stuffed with meat and beans, make a tasty appetizer, and the Montanero plate is a feast of flank steak, a runny fried egg over rice, and glistening pork rinds. Definitely save room for desserts like the gushing sweet plantain empanadas.

THE GREATEST: Rare Cheeses & Gourmet Grocery

Formaggio Kitchen $$
244 Huron Ave., Cambridge, Mass., (617) 354-4750,
www.formaggiokitchen.com

Formaggio Kitchen is a gourmet grocer with the best cheese counter in the entire country. Phantom has eaten extensively through France and Italy, so he knows a good Roquefort or pecorino when he smells it. FK's 400 varieties of funky fromage include 20 kinds of chèvre and rare artisan finds from across the globe. There's a cheese cave in the basement for proper storing, and samples are spread around the store. The boutique space is packed to the picture windows with imported jams, oils, wine, unpasteurized olives, farm fresh eggs, and uncommon produce. Phantom could subsist on their house-made granola and cinnamon bread alone; their charcuterie specialist makes the best chicken liver mousse in town; and the kitchen takes creative license with tasty sandwiches and take-out dinners.

THE GREATEST: Tapas

Dali $$

415 Washington St., Somerville, Mass., (617) 661-3254,
www.dalirestaurant.com

Dali has an exotic, eclectic atmosphere that's like a nonstop party in a surrealistic flea market. It's a highly ornamented, social space, but there's plenty of potential for romantic dining due to sexy Latin music, recessed alcoves, and beaded curtains. The fruit-infused sangria pairs magically with Spanish tapas like roast duckling in berry sauce. Phantom also enjoys the sautéed Iberian sardines and the fried cheese with caramelized onions and honey. Dali's signature is the fresh catch of the day baked in coarse salt, which they debone and fillet tableside. Birthdays are celebrated festively, with waiters singing in Spanish and blowing bubbles over the celebrant's head.

THE GREATEST: Classy Comfort Food

Union Bar and Grille $$$

1357 Washington St., Boston, Mass., (617) 423-0555,
www.unionrestaurant.com

Union Bar and Grille turns out urban comfort food for the stylish soul. The menu is nonethnic, yet on the forefront of creativity with dishes like the 10K tuna with a coriander crust and candied red peppers. The grilled BBQ ribs come with smoked sea salt, and every table starts off with skillet cornbread. Almost every one of their delicious desserts is capped with homemade ice cream in wild flavors like Marcona almond, ginger, or blood orange. The gothic-meets-urban scene combines massive wrought-iron chandeliers and black leather banquettes, and the dark lounge is framed in floor-to-ceiling glass and slanted mirrors.

THE GREATEST: Clay Oven Flatbread

Flatbread Company $$

5 Market Sq., Amesbury, Mass., (978) 834-9800,
www.flatbreadcompany.com

The Flatbread Company supports local farms, using organic and natural ingredients. Their mission is commendable, but Phantom saves his loudest applause for the flatbreads themselves, fired in a massive, dome-shaped clay oven right in the dining room. The free-form crust is made from wheat, cake yeast, and spring water, resulting in chewiness and slim structure. Yummy flatbreads include Nitrate-Free Pepperoni with cauldron tomato sauce, Cheese & Herb with garlic oil, and Maple Fennel Sausage with caramelized onions. The earthy setting was converted from an old mill, so it's easy to watch your kids while they run around the cavernous room. Additional Flatbread locations include Portland, Maine; North Conway, New Hampshire; and Portsmouth, New Hampshire.

Bakeries
GREAT ATE

Bakeries help Phantom get through the day with hot breakfast pastries, sugary afternoon treats, and fresh-baked breads at dinner. Phantom gets his chocolate-frosted, fruit-topped fill at the 8 GREATEST bakeries.

TASTY TIP Day-old bread is great for making French toast, but when it comes to sandwiches, fresh is the only way to roll. Ask your neighborhood bakery for its oven schedule.

THE GREATEST: Tarts

Flour $

1595 Washington St., Boston, Mass., (617) 267-4300,
www.flourbakery.com

Flour Bakery is a refreshingly calm café with soothing sky-blue walls, blond wood tables, and a gorgeous gourmet spread of pastries, breads, pizza, and quiche. The blackboard wall is chalked with the day's specials, the weather forecast, and a quote of the day. In the morning, Phantom goes for chocolate brioche, sticky buns, and sour cream coffee cake. By lunch it's time for an upscale BLT featuring applewood-smoked bacon. Their dainty little tarts come in four darling sizes with flavors like lemon lust, ooey-gooey caramel nut, fresh fruit, and chocolate truffle. They also bake delicate cookies like meringue clouds and Scharffen Berger chocolate chip.

THE GREATEST: Greek Pastry

Athan's Bakery $

1621 Beacon St., Brookline, Mass., (617) 734-7028,
www.athansbakery.com

Athan's Bakery makes the most mouth-watering Greek pastry, including an impressive assortment of baklava. Ten different versions line up in honey-drenched bundles, including a traditional phyllo triangle, a threadlike haystack funneled with almonds, and a phyllo box folded around a juicy prune. Athan's has an old-world, café atmosphere and a handful of tables where customers can enjoy their purchases on the spot. Marble counters, wooden bins of cookies, and copper baking molds decorate the room, and bakery clerks follow shoppers around to bag the sweet treats. Athan's also whips up intricate European pastries like the cherry-ganache Jamaica and the genoise citron cake with luscious lemon curd. Athan's has a second bakery and café on Washington Street in Brighton.

THE GREATEST: Cupcakes

Party Favors $
1356 Beacon St., Brookline, Mass., (617) 566-3330,
www.partyfavorsbrookline.com
Party Favors is a party planner's paradise, offering a full line of party supplies and
just-baked sweets. Every inch of the store is crammed with colorful piñatas and in-
flated balloons, with a constant aroma of pastries, cookies, and cakes wafting
through. The store whips up rich, smooth, beautiful buttercream frosting, which is
lovingly lavished on four sizes of vanilla and chocolate cupcakes. There are one-
bite tea cupcakes, swirl cupcakes with rainbow confetti, regular cupcakes, and
jumbo cupcakes crowned with an individual flower or an adorable farm animal.
The kitchen also turns out a chocolate espresso torte of yellow cake soaked with
espresso syrup, white chocolate espresso mousse, and mocha beans.

THE GREATEST: Pie

Petsi Pies $
285 Beacon St., Somerville, Mass., (617) 661-PIES
Petsi Pies is a small storefront turning out perfect pies from a two-oven kitchen.
Their secret is in the rich, flaky crust warmed to a golden hue. There's awesome apple pie, pecan pie, and even whoopie pie. The house specialties are all southern, including sweet potato pie, delicately spiced with a touch of honey and brown sugar.
Phantom loves the peach blueberry pie bursting with ripe fruit and the potato mushroom tart layered with roasted red potatoes and Gruyère cheese.

THE GREATEST: European Pastry

Truly Jörg's $
126 Broadway (Route 1), Saugus, Mass., (781) 231-5888,
www.trulyjorgs.com
Outfitted with antique baking equipment, Truly Jörg's is Phantom's favorite patis-
serie for artsy, tasty treats. The Swiss-trained chef has cooked for presidents and
movie stars but feels most at home in his Saugus kitchen, turning out European pastry for an appreciative public. The sweet smell of brioche, buttery croissants, and
tea cookies permeates the room, and customers linger on the couch to read the paper and eat yummy stuff. Delicate desserts include éclairs, fruit tarts, tiramisu,
miniature marzipan figures, and crispy Napoleons. They also teach classes on top-
ics like bread-baking, cake-decorating, fruit-carving, wine education, and cooking.
Sessions take place almost every Tuesday, Wednesday, and Thursday, and they're
all posted on their Web site.

THE GREATEST: Rustic Bread

Iggy's Bread of the World $
130 Fawcett St., Cambridge, Mass., (617) 924-0949,
www.iggysbread.com
Iggy's Bread of the World is a bakery with a serious respect for the environment.
Their mission to produce high-quality breads includes a commitment to community
service, organic farmers, and recycling. Naturally leavened, hearth-baked loaves
are crafted twice daily, using all-natural grains and flour. Iggy's is especially
known for four affordable staples: country sourdough, whole wheat sourdough,
francese, and seedless white rye. Lunchtime highlights include baguette sandwiches, fashioned into gourmet combinations like eggplant and cheese; arugula,
tuna, and tomato; or Brie, tomato, and basil. Iggy's bread is often found in area
restaurants and grocery stores like Shaw's and Whole Foods.

THE GREATEST: Fresh-Baked Selection

White's Pastry $
1041 Pearl St., Brockton, Mass., (508) 584-5100
White's Pastry displays an assortment of more than 200 sweets in a giant dessert
case. Among their icing-sheathed treats, Phantom favors the Oreo cheesecake with
a cookie crumb crust, all heaped with whipped cream, caramel, ganache, and Heath
Bar bits. The Pavarotti is a dense chocolate cake with chocolate filling and chocolate curls on top, and the lemon mousse is a yellow cake laced with fluffy lemon
filling. All of their sizeable cakes are available by the slice, too. Additional locations include Hingham, Braintree, and Canton.

THE GREATEST: Doggie Bakery

Polka Dog Bakery $
256 Shawmut Ave., Boston, Mass., (617) 338-5155,
www.polkadog.com
Polka Dog is spilling over with baked goods and pastries. But take a closer look,
and you'll understand why your dogs are barkin'. All the cookies, cupcakes, and
cannoli are created exclusively for your pooch. The all-natural treats contain no
added salt or sugar, so Fluffy can safely indulge. Liver's Lane is made with beef
liver and Parmesan cheese, and the Treatza Pizza uses tomato paste and Italian
herbs. Even the worst doggy breath subsides with some parsley-flecked After Dinner Mints. On Sundays, Polka Dog does brunch with Pupcakes and Blueberry
Woofles. It's also fashion central for Fido, stocked with rhinestone collars, designer
leashes, and disco ball bowls.

Barbecue
GREAT ATE

Southerners and Midwesterners both claim the best ribs and brisket in the country, but there are plenty of pit masters up North that know how to smoke and sauce. Instead of sticking to one regional style, Boston barbecue embraces the full range of flavors and sauces: vinegary Carolina style, tomato-based Kansas City style, Memphis style dry rubs, and spicy Texas style. Phantom got plenty of protein picking the 8 GREATEST barbecue joints.

TASTY TIP Paper towels are good. Wet Naps are better. But if you don't want to stink of smoke and sauce, the best way to clean up after a big barbecue meal is simply to shower or jump in a lake.

THE GREATEST: Regional Barbecue

RedBones $$
55 Chester Ave., Somerville, Mass., (617) 628-2200,
www.redbonesbbq.com

Covering the full sweep of the barbecue belt, RedBones has the best regional renditions. Texas beef, St. Louis ribs, and Georgia pulled pork top the list. Tantalizing appetizers include sausage du jour, hush puppies, buffalo shrimp, and corn fritters. An eclectic crowd of bikers, families, and singles packs the psychedelic neon den downstairs, while barflies buzz about the 24 daily changing microbrews on tap. Cyclists take note: RedBones offers a complimentary, first-in-the-nation bicycle valet.

THE GREATEST: BBQ Sandwiches

Blue Ribbon Bar-B-Q $
908 Massachusetts Ave., Arlington, Mass., (781) 648-7427,
www.blueribbonbbq.com

Blue Ribbon Bar-B-Q does Phantom's favorite meaty sandwiches, full of pit-smoked specialties like Texas Sliced Beef Brisket, Kansas City Burnt Ends, and Memphis Dry-Rubbed Barbecued Ribs. The oversized offerings come with baked beans, slaw, and homemade pickles. They'll even put together a feedbag for four or supper for six. Most customers blow through like tumbleweed and get it to go, but the colorful, chrome-lined digs are done up with vintage signs and license plates. There's a second Blue Ribbon in West Newton.

THE GREATEST: **Pit Master**

Pit Stop Barbeque $
888 Morton St., Dorchester, Mass., (617) 436-0485
Pit Stop Barbeque is so tightly spaced that customers can hardly see through the take-out window. In fact, it's cramped to the point that the grill master has to sit on the floor. The cash register is on one side, the prep area is on the other, and the middle houses an old-fashioned brick pit where the cook tends to mouthwatering ribs, sausage, and chicken. The meaty menu has all the barbecue staples, plus side dishes like candied yams, collard greens, mac & cheese, and sweet potato pie.

THE GREATEST: **BBQ Fixins**

Memphis Roadhouse $$
383 Washington St. (Route 1), South Attleboro, Mass., (508) 761-5700,
www.memphisroadhouse.com
At Memphis Roadhouse, there's only one place to sit: the smoking section (and we're not talking tobacco)! Following the BBQ bible, they cook low and slow over a hickory wood-smoked pit. The huge selection of hearty fixins includes creamy slaw, BBQ pit beans, collard greens, and country cornbread. They're all prepared in-house daily, along with MR's specialty sauces: Original BBQ, Carolina Style BBQ, and Carolina Vinegar. Southern specialties range from New Orleans catfish étouffée and oyster po-boys to Texas chili. It's a gingham tablecloth and neon-lit scene surrounded by jazz legend portraits, tin torpedo lamps, and blues in the background.

THE GREATEST: **Soulful Atmosphere**

Bob's Southern Bistro $$
604 Columbus Ave., Boston, Mass., (617) 536-6204,
www.bobssouthernbistro.com
Formerly known as Bob the Chef's, Bob's Southern Bistro joins stick-to-your-ribs southern fare and classy atmosphere with soulful success. Bob's juicy "glorifried" chicken is the ultimate golden fried poultry, with gnarly, knotted batter jacked up on Cajun spice. Other down-South specialties include collard greens, corned beef hash, BBQ ribs, fried catfish, and sweet potato pie. Bob ups the soul food ante with live jazz, and there's a stone bar for cocktails while you wait. On Sundays you can get your grits at the all-you-can-eat buffet brunch.

THE GREATEST: Ribs

Uncle Pete's Hickory Ribs $$
72 Squire Rd., Revere, Mass., (781) 289-7427,
www.unclepetes.com

Get your rib fix at Uncle Pete's, recently transplanted from East Boston to Revere. The meaty mecca is an interesting intersection of Thai food and southern BBQ infused with hickory, oak, and applewood smoke. The wicked pork ribs are remarkably tender thanks to the three-day cooking procedure. The massive caramelized Texas beef ribs are steeped in rich spices, and the smoky pulled pork forgoes vinegar in favor of sweet BBQ sauce. Phantom also loves their Asian peanut slaw and the mango salsa served with fried tortillas.

THE GREATEST: Barbecue Sauce

Firefly's Bar-B-Que $$
350 E. Main St., Marlborough, Mass., (508) 357-8883,
www.fireflysbbq.com

Firefly's is a fun barbecue house where the low and slow cooking is as appealing as the colorful decor. Hickory, cherry, and applewood smoke the meats, which are packed with flavor from spice-filled dry rubs. For added zest, the condiment bar includes five saucy sauces (North or South Carolina, Memphis, spicy Beelzebar, and Texas), assorted pickles, and 40 radical hot sauces. The Phantom Platter served on a purple pupu plate combines ribs, wings, brisket, catfish fingers, and homemade chips. Phantom also loves the cracklin' bread, grilled with onions and smoked mozzarella. There's a second Firefly's in Framingham.

THE GREATEST: Pulled Pork

Muddy River Smokehouse $$
21 Congress St., Portsmouth, N.H., (603) 430-9582,
www.muddyriver.com

The Muddy River Smokehouse is a comfortable barbecue and blues house where the arts of smoking, grilling, and saucing are taken seriously. The pulled pork is slow-smoked for 15 hours, shredded by hand, and mixed with secret barbecue sauce. Other highlights are the moist, flavorful ribs that are first rubbed with spices and then slow-smoked over hickory logs for 12 hours. There's baby back, meaty St. Louis, and the massive Texas ribs, big enough to knock over Fred Flinstone's car.

Breakfast
GREAT ATE

When the sun comes up, Phantom bolts out of bed for sticky-sweet maple syrup, sizzling sausage, and a steaming cup of joe. The 8 GREATEST breakfast spots impressed Phantom with their mastery of the basics.

TASTY TIP

Never let a waiter top off your cup of coffee, it throws off the ratio of brew to cream to sugar. To avoid computing percentages and fractions over breakfast, finish your entire cup and wait patiently for a complete refill.

THE GREATEST: Blueberry Pancakes

Mike's City Diner $
1714 Washington St., Boston, Mass., (617) 267-9393
Mike's City Diner ladles out the city's best blueberry pancakes, layered in fat, fluffy, bronze-topped short stacks with sweet-tart patches of fruit. The American breakfast menu sizzles with eggs, waffles, and smokin' pork sausages. The heart-attack homemade hash mixes potato cubes with beefy corned beef under two runny fried eggs. Black-and-white-checked tabletops fill the luncheonette; counter stools overlook the griddle kitchen; and oldies twist and shout overhead.

THE GREATEST: Bargain Breakfast

Brookline Lunch $
9 Brookline St., Cambridge, Mass., (617) 354-2983
Ironically, Brookline Lunch is Phantom's favorite place to get breakfast in *Cambridge*. There's no better bargain than their dirt-cheap eggs and pancake basics. Every omelet is piled high with skillet home fries and grilled veggies, plus hot sauce, toast, and homemade jam. The small nook is big on charm, with weathered paint and a mishmash of cheery colors splashed from the open kitchen to the tall wooden booths. Lunch offerings show a glimpse of the owners' Middle Eastern heritage, including kebobs, hummus, falafel, and stuffed grape leaves.

THE GREATEST: Hash

Charlie's Sandwich Shoppe $
429 Columbus Ave., Boston, Mass., (617) 536-7669
No one feeds a hash fix like Charlie's Sandwich Shoppe. Forget the beef, this jumbo cake of ground turkey and potatoes is ribboned with onions and carrots and

buried beneath two fried eggs. Charlie's serves up breakfast all day from behind a long, swivel-stool counter. The greasy spoon, old-school decor includes historic Boston photos, glass domes covering gorgeous pies, and communal tables where you might meet a longtime Charlie's loyalist. With heaping plates and cheap prices, it's no wonder this coffee shop is such a success.

THE GREATEST: French Toast

Zaftigs $$

335 Harvard St., Brookline, Mass., (617) 975-0075,
www.zaftigs.com

Zaftigs is THE hot brekky spot in the Boston area for French toast. They whip up a thick, gooey banana-stuffed version made with bourbon-vanilla batter that's finished with glorious date butter. Dieters need not apply! This Jewish-style restaurant makes mean Reuben sandwiches, pastrami on rye, and toasted bagels loaded with lox. They also dish out cheddar apple omelets, noodle kugel, knishes, and chopped liver. Wooden floors and bright paintings make the expansive space homey, and customers in the know can call ahead to get their names on the wait list.

THE GREATEST: Omelet

Arthur & Pat's $

239 Ocean Street, Marshfield, Mass., (781) 834-9755

Arthur & Pat's flips and folds Phantom's favorite omelets, like the lobster specialty loaded with fresh seafood, spinach, and cheese sauce. Their biggest strengths are 26 years of family-run tradition and reliable creativity from the chef. Two hundred menu selections are posted all over the walls like a mouthwatering collage. The potato pancakes stack smoked salmon and poached eggs, and kids go crazy for the banana Belgian waffle with warm vanilla bean sauce and glazed pecans. Arthur & Pat's is only open seasonally from April to October.

THE GREATEST: Eggs Benny

Terrie's Place $

676 E. Broadway, South Boston, Mass., (617) 268-3119

At Terrie's Place, the Irish influence is in the atmosphere and on the menu. The eggs Benedict are done the traditional way with hollandaise, poached eggs, Canadian bacon, and English muffins. But breakfast "Phanatics" like Phantom won't ever get bored, thanks to six variations on the original. Multiple makeovers and ingredient stand-ins include crusty corned beef hash, Irish bacon, spinach, and sausage. Terrie's also serves some tasty banana nut French toast. Green vinyl booths and counter stools brighten the modest decor, and there's a quirky coffee mug collection on display.

THE GREATEST: **Belgian Waffles**

Sound Bites $
708 Broadway, Somerville, Mass., (617) 623-8338
Sound Bites may be a hole in the wall with pushy service, long lines, and a "no newspapers" rule, but Phantom can't resist their Belgian waffles. Whole-grain squares are topped with whipped cream and a mountain of exotic fresh fruit like papaya, kiwi, blueberries, strawberries, banana, and mango. Additional standouts include grilled blueberry muffins, "NoPlaceLikeHomeFries," and omelets like the Art, Tom & Jack, which is filled with tomatoes, jack cheese, and artichokes. While waiting for a table, customers can get started at the self-service coffee bar.

THE GREATEST: **Southern Breakfast**

Keith's Place $
469 Blue Hill Ave., Dorchester, Mass., (617) 427-7899
Keith's Place is a bright, casual morning spot serving new versions of old southern favorites. They don't serve pork products, but early-morning plates promise butter-milk biscuits, porgies and stick-to-your-ribs grits, home fries, and stuffed three-egg omelets. Phantom loves their signature light and fluffy sweet potato pancakes spiced with cinnamon, nutmeg, and ginger. Stick around for lunch to sample soul food like smothered chicken, mac & cheese, and sweet candied yams.

Brunch
GREAT ATE

There's nothing like a big, fat brunch of mimosas and eggs Benedict to top off the weekend. Boston brunches are mostly a Sunday-only event, with a few Saturday exceptions. Except for high-end establishments and hotel dining rooms, most places don't take reservations. Phantom finds the best of breakfast AND lunch at the 8 GREATEST brunch spots.

TASTY TIP If you want to "beat the brunch buffet," skip the breads, pastries, muffins, and bagels at the front of the line. The "high rent district" (omelets, carving stations, etc.) sits at the end of the buffet.

THE GREATEST: Pajama Brunch

Tremont 647 $$
647 Tremont St., Boston, Mass., (617) 266-4600,
www.tremont647.com

Tremont 647 is known for its unusually delicious food, but every Saturday and Sunday the stylish space transforms into a wickedly fun pajama brunch. Customers and servers roll out of bed and sport their sleepwear right into the dining room. The daring menu dishes out pepper-rimmed Bloody Mary's with pickled green beans, along with chocolate chip pancakes, breakfast pizza, and Andy's signature MoMos (pork-ginger dumplings). Some waitresses have been known to get a little risqué with their bedtime attire, and there have even been reports of a certain large someone sporting purple silk PJs.

THE GREATEST: Gourmet Buffet

Henrietta's Table $$$
The Charles Hotel, 1 Bennett St., Cambridge, Mass., (617) 661-5005,
www.henriettastable.com

Henrietta's Table in the Charles Hotel is a charming country kitchen with a spectacular, if pricey Sunday brunch. From noon to 3 p.m., gobs of gorgeous food are laid out on beautiful spreads and in huge cast-iron pans for an all-you-can-eat feast of locally farmed fare. The gluttonous, high-end cuisine includes fresh fruit, grilled veggies, salads, shucked oysters, jumbo shrimp, smoked fish, seven kinds of pâté, cheese, eggs, roasts, waffles, pastries, and a 10-dessert smorgasbord. Fresh-squeezed orange juice flows freely, and the rustic-themed dining room is outfitted with over-sized cupboards and harvest photos.

THE GREATEST: Beautiful Brunch

Sonsie $$$
327 Newbury St., Boston, Mass., (617) 351-2500,
www.sonsieboston.com

Debut your designer threads at Sonsie, where you'll never before have seen such beautiful brunchers. The scene-seeking crowd packs into marble café tables with a front-row view of the Newbury Street sidewalk. Phantom goes for the eclectic cuisine. Lime crab cakes and open-face steak sandwiches give way to huevos rancheros, brick oven pizzas, and banana rum French toast. Even if you split your leather pants, don't pass on insanely good desserts like baby éclairs and blackberry sorbet with citrus curd. After all, you can always buy a replacement pair of trousers at the luxe boutiques next door.

THE GREATEST: Jazz Brunch

Johnny D's Uptown $
17 Holland St., Davis Square, Somerville, Mass., (617) 776-2004,
www.johnnyds.com

Johnny D's Uptown is Phantom's favorite jazz brunch. Rocking out on Saturday and Sunday, the band plays from 10 a.m. to 2 p.m. The atmosphere is down-to-earth friendly, and the menu strikes a melodious tune with Cajun-influenced food. The old-fashioned oatmeal comes with plump raisins and a side of maple sugar to add as needed. They also serve sweet cheese blintzes, an andouille sausage scramble, pecan granola, cheddar grits, and fried catfish with eggs. The Belgian waffles pack a sugary punch with candied nuts, strawberries, bananas, and whipped cream. Seven nights a week, Johnny D's is a hopping live music venue, with an eclectic range of bluegrass, Latin, and swing.

THE GREATEST: Brunch with a View

Skyline Sunday Brunch $$
Museum of Science, Science Park, Boston, Mass., (617) 723-2500,
www.mos.org

Little galaxy gazers who visit Boston's Museum of Science are sure to work up an appetite. On Sunday, you're guaranteed a successful experiment at the sixth-floor Skyline brunch. Wolgang Puck Catering puts together the menu, ranging from the omelet station to the carving block, and desserts like chocolate almond cake. In between, there's applewood smoked bacon, ricotta-stuffed French toast, and goodies like BBQ shrimp. No other eggs in town come with a museum pass and an unforgettable view of the city's silhouette. At a discounted price you can get a package involving a Mugar Omni Theater ticket, admission to the main exhibits, and free parking. The self-service meal includes juice, coffee, tea, cereal, a carving station, French toast, sausage, banana nut muffins, and raspberry Danish.

THE GREATEST: Dim Sum

China Pearl $
9 Tyler Street, Boston, Mass., (617) 426-4338
www.chinapearlrestaurant.com
The wait at China Pearl can be horrendous; the multi-level Chinatown favorite is cramped; and you often have to eat with strangers. But once you secure a seat, your sweet reward starts rolling in, literally. Dim sum is a Chinese brunch tradition in which bamboo steamers are stacked on wobbly carts and wheeled around the room. Dainty dumplings stuffed with shrimp make the rounds, along with BBQ pork buns, spring rolls, spare ribs, taro cakes, and sesame balls. Customers motion when they spot something they want, and the servers make a little mark on the table's running tally. Don't sweat the translation; it's hard to spend more than $10 per person.

THE GREATEST: Eclectic Brunch

Blue Room $$$
1 Kendall Sq., Cambridge, Mass., (617) 494-9034,
www.theblueroom.net
The Blue Room puts together eclectic offerings for the adventurous Sunday bruncher. Forget omelets and bagels; the spread here is dedicated to organic produce and loaded with global flavor. Favorites include Moroccan chicken, five spice ribs, and hot salted shrimp. The buttermilk pancakes are THE best in Boston, and a dozen hot and cold dishes line the buffet bar. There's also a separate table of pastries and dessert like gingerbread, pineapple upside-down cake, and Persian rice pudding. The textural, artsy space displays exposed brick, wood beams, and zinc tables, and the chefs work from an open kitchen to keep everything replenished.

THE GREATEST: Funky Brunch

Julian's $
318 Broadway, Providence, R.I., (401) 861-1770,
www.juliansprovidence.com
Julian's is a vintage bistro with a starving-artist style that captures the softer side of punk. The exposed brick space brings together a huge disco ball, LEGO art, and a brass cappuccino machine that won't quit. Twenty-three omelet options make the menu, along with five kinds of eggs Benedict like the Desperado with avocado and

salsa. There's a huge list of pancakes with nuts, chocolate, fruit, spices, or rainbow sprinkles that can be cooked in the batter or added on top. Julian's makes a mean blue cheese hash, and you can kick brunch up a notch with six different mimosas. The kitchen stays open for dinner, too, and Scrabble Night gets going every Monday at 7 p.m.

Burger
GREAT ATE

Sinking his teeth into a big, juicy burger is Phantom's favorite all-American pastime. The best beef on a bun is thick through the middle (to preserve the juices) with good marbling (for flavor). When he's on the hunt for the absolute best beef on a bun, the Caped Critic heads to one of the 8 GREATEST burger joints.

Pressing down on a patty with a spatula results in a dry, flavorless burger. Seek out the grill cooks who leave their plump burgers to sizzle and stay juicy.

THE GREATEST: Burger Selection

Bartley's Burger Cottage $
1246 Massachusetts Ave., Cambridge, Mass., (617) 354-6559,
www.mrbartleys.com
Bartley's Burger Cottage is nearly part of the Harvard curriculum, with dormlike decor and modest plastic patio seating. Their incredible hamburger selection includes dozens of celebrity-named creations. The Viagra rises to the occasion with blue cheese and bacon, while the New England Patriots burger stacks cheddar and guacamole. The creepy Stephen King is mysteriously delicious with Muenster cheese, and the Arnold Schwarzenegger is jacked up on 14 ounces of double Swiss cheeseburger. Sweet potato fries and a peppermint patty frappe are required, not elective.

THE GREATEST: 20-Minute Burger

R. F. O'Sullivan's Pub $
282 Beacon St., Somerville, Mass., (617) 492-7773
Phantom heads to R. F. O'Sullivan's Pub for thick, juicy, mouthwatering burgers at their jaw-breaking best. Each belly-busting beast is a half pound of ground sirloin that requires 20 minutes on the grill. O'Sullivan's is also one of the only restaurants that will actually serve a burger the way Phantom likes it—RARE! The menu lists two dozen burgers like the Black and Blue, coated in fresh-ground black pepper and topped with blue cheese.

THE GREATEST: Gigantic Burger

Eagle's Deli & Restaurant $
1918 Beacon St., Brighton, Mass., (617) 731-3232
Eagle's Deli is a hole-in-the-wall grill with one heck of a he-man burger. Named after a regular with a mammoth appetite, the Reilly burger is a serious stacking of six half-pound patties topped with 12 slices of cheese, all held together by a wooden teriyaki stick. It comes with five pounds of fries and unlimited fountain soda. Ask the guys behind the greasy griddle what you'll get for eating the whole thing, and they'll tell you. Indigestion!

THE GREATEST: Buns & Toppings

Fuddruckers $
Route 1 North, Saugus, Mass., (781) 233-6399,
www.fuddruckersNE.com
At Fuddruckers, burgers come in four different-sized patties that reach up to a whole gigantic pound. But, hey, size doesn't matter. It's the toppings that make these burgers special. There's a complimentary produce bar loaded with everything from lettuce, tomato, and onion to nacho cheese, salsa, and jalapeños. Smoked bacon, homemade chili, and guacamole are a little extra. The house-baked buns are fluffy, buttery, and awesome. After throwing back a coffee, Oreo, or mocha shake and a human-head-sized burger, no one leaves Fuddruckers hungry. Two other Fuddruckers location are on Route 114 West in North Andover, Mass., (978) 557-1100, and at Jordan's Furniture, 50 Walker's Brook Dr., in Reading Mass., (781) 942-4891.

THE GREATEST: Angus Beef Patties

Wild Willy's $
46 Arsenal St., Watertown, Mass., (617) 926-9700
Wild Willy's is a cowboy-themed burger joint filled with ten-gallon hats, spurs, and painted landscapes of the West. Customers can sidle up to the counter and order some big ol' charbroiled Angus burgers on buttery grilled buns. The tangy Bubba Burger wears barbecue sauce, crispy bacon, pickles, onion, and cheddar, while the Rio Grande includes roasted green chiles from New Mexico. Sweet frappes and floats finish off the feast. The York, Maine, location shows off a talking cowboy mannequin, and there's an outpost in Rochester, New Hampshire, too.

THE GREATEST: **VIP Burger**

The Bristol $$

200 Boylston St., Boston, Mass., (617) 338-4400,
www.fourseasons.com/boston/dining.

The Bristol in the distinguished Four Seasons Hotel may seem like last place you'd order a burger, but their $17 VIP version takes old-school comfort food to luxury levels. The juicy half-pound sirloin patty is neatly wrapped in aged Vermont cheddar on a toasted poppy seed bun. There's also a double-smoked bacon burger and a black truffle burger on brioche. The sprawling denlike setting displays red leather sofas, fireplaces, and a grand piano at the bar.

THE GREATEST: **Retro Hamburger**

Johnny Rockets $

www.johnnyrockets.com

Bursting with feel-good Americana, Johnny Rockets is a '50s-themed diner chain decked out in red vinyl booths with a soda bar ringed with stools and tabletop jukeboxes. The all-American menu is a salute to the red, white & blue featuring retro hamburgers formed into ⅓-pound patties. They're hand pressed and grilled, topped with cheddar, mushrooms, onions, and bacon. Chili fries make a fine side, and Johnny Rockets also serves hand-dipped shakes, soda pop, and apple pie. Soda jerks bop around in bow ties and little white caps, singing and dancing to the oldies into ketchup bottle "mics."

THE GREATEST: **Mini Burgers**

Stockyard $$

135 Market St., Brighton, Mass., (617) 782-4700,
www.stockyardrestaurant.com

The Stockyard sits on the site of North America's very first cattle yard, so it's no surprise that they have such a beefy following today. The original landowner and cattle rancher even sold some of his meat to George Washington in 1775. The centuries-old stockyard eventually moved to Littleton, making way for the present-day Stockyard. The in-house butchers work their meaty magic into Phantom's favorite mini burgers, served in sets of four called Stockyard Sliders. The chopped sirloin Stockburger is equally delicious, topped with turkey, Swiss cheese, and bacon. The collectibles decor is stylishly dated, displaying antique cigarette machines, gas lamps, and sports signs.

Candy & Chocolate
GREAT ATE

Yummy gumdrops, lollipops, taffies, and chocolates are the sticky-sweet things that keep Phantom on the hunt for superior sugars. Pre-packed treats are accessible and nostalgic, but they fall flat against the complexities and lingering finish you'll find in a fresh, handmade chocolate. The Mysterious Critic says it's worth the extra mileage to feel like a kid again in the 8 GREATEST candy stores.

 TASTY TIP **Die-hard chocoholics may think they've melted and gone to heaven on The Old Town Trolley Boston Chocolate Tour. Trolley conductors offer up mouth-watering morsels of chocolate trivia while making several tasting stops in the city's best chocolate kitchens. The tour runs on Saturdays and Sundays from January to April. See www.trolleytours.com/chocolatetour for more details.**

THE GREATEST: Novelties

Sugar Heaven $
218 Newbury St., Boston, Mass., (617) 266-6969,
www.sugarheaven.us
Think you've died and gone to Sugar Heaven? It's possible at this wild retro store where bins of colorful candy are crammed between a sky-blue ceiling and a plastic grass floor. Customers shop until midnight for candy novelties like spun-to-order cotton candy and make-your-own Pixie Sticks with flavors of bubble gum, orange cream, and fruit punch. The M&M Colorworks machine dispenses 21 bold, beautiful shades of milk chocolate at the push of a lever.

THE GREATEST: Hot Chocolate

L. A. Burdick Chocolate $
52-D Brattle St., Cambridge, Mass., (617) 491-4340,
www.burdickchocolate.com
Burdick Chocolate turns out the most delicious chocolate treats, but their hot chocolate is the best Phantom has ever had. Poured into giant mugs, the not-too-sweet, intoxicating drink is like a liquefied candy bar with steamed milk. Their dainty chocolate mice deserve special praise, too. The tasty treats consist of a ganache body covered in chocolate, a painted chocolate face, almond ears, and a

ribbon tail. Other creative chocolate combinations include the downright decadent dessert cakes, fruit tartlets, and tea cookies. The flagship café is in Walpole, New Hampshire, with an additional shop in Northampton, Massachusetts. All three locations are cozy European-style cafés bejeweled in antique mirrors, dainty lamps, and marbled floors.

THE GREATEST: Old-Fashioned Candy

Yummies $
Route 1, Kittery, Maine, (207) 439-5649,
www.yummies.com
For the ultimate kid-in-a-candy-store sugar high, head to Yummies. Ten thousand pounds of candy and nuts pack the shelves, with barely enough aisle room for Phantom to squeeze through. They've got every mouthwatering morsel imaginable, from the fun and unusual to the nostalgic and old-fashioned. Hard-to-find goodies include Bit-o-Honey, Jawbreakers, Candy Buttons, and Mary Janes. Yummies stocks every current PEZ character, gourmet jelly beans, tons of hard candy, and homemade fudge.

THE GREATEST: Sweet Sloop

Harbor Sweets $
85 Leavitt St., Salem, Mass., (978) 745-7648,
www.harborsweets.com
Harbor Sweets produces the most divine butter crunch ever conceived. Their signature Sweet Sloop is a nutty almond slab molded into the shape of a sailboat, covered in white and dark chocolate and splashed with crushed pecans. The secret recipe is whipped up in copper pots on an assembly line that's visible from the shop. Like a museum of chocolate, the room also displays tasty signs explaining the candy-making process. Free samples are offered to browsing customers.

THE GREATEST: Candy-Infused Ice Cream

Hilliard's House of Candy $
316 Main St., North Easton, Mass., (508) 238-6231,
www.hilliardscandy.com
Hilliard's House of Candy is Phantom's favorite for seasonal sweets. Along with marshmallow pumpkins at Halloween come deliciously sticky chocolate caramel apples. Thanksgiving brings a cornucopia of roasted nuts, followed by ribbon candy at Christmas, chocolate bunnies at Easter, and fudge in July. Summertime ushers in Hilliard's homemade ice cream (Easton location only), packed with their very own handmade candies like cashew turtles and cherry cordials. No matter the

month, locations in Easton, Canton, and Hanover turn out sensational soft centers, caramel nut patties, and pecan crackle.

THE GREATEST: Chocolate-Dipped Fruit

Chocolate Dipper $
Chestnut Hill Mall, 199 Boylston St., Chestnut Hill, Mass., (617) 969-7252,
www.thechocolatedipper.com
The Chocolate Dipper specializes in chocolate-dipped fresh fruit. Their extravagant assortment includes jumbo glazed Australian apricots, kiwi slices, blueberries, green grapes, raspberries, bananas, and the ever-popular strawberry. Aside from fruit, they offer chocolate-dipped cookies, pretzels, truffles, caramels, nuts, and brownies. Luscious milk chocolate is mixed in 100-pound tanks, and skilled chocolatiers make the premium goodies in full view of the customer. They have another location at Downtown Crossing.

THE GREATEST: Mints

Ye Olde Pepper Companie $
122 Derby St., Salem, Mass., (978) 745-2744,
www.yeoldepeppercandy.com
Established in 1806, Ye Olde Pepper Companie is America's oldest candy company. In fact, the country's very first manufactured sweet treat was the Gibralter. This pure sugar confection has a smooth, dissolving texture similar to after-dinner mints and comes in tasty batches of lemon or peppermint. It's hand-pulled on a hook, much like taffy. The stretching gives it stripes before the wad is cut with scissors into diamond-shaped pieces. Other old-fashioned specialties include molasses Black Jacks, Sassafras Slugs, and Root Beer Barrels.

THE GREATEST: Fudge

Winfrey's $
42 Newburyport Turnpike, Rowley, Mass., (978) 948-7448,
www.winfreys.com
At Winfrey's the major draw is the 20-odd flavors of decadent, melt-in-your-mouth fudge. This velvety cream-and-butter concoction is given flavors that surpass the ordinary chocolate, peanut butter, and vanilla standbys; at Winfrey's, you can order rocky road, Kahlua mudslide, or cranberry walnut. The sweet shop also displays saltwater taffy and 100 kinds of fabulous, dainty chocolates in streamlined glass cases. Winfrey's fudge is also sold at stores in Beverly, Stoneham, and Newburyport.

Local Chains
GREAT ATE

A handful of cookie-cutter concepts give chain restaurants a bad rap, but some select homegrown versions dish out real value and tasty plates. Phantom shares a particular pride in local business with the 8 GREATEST local chains.

TASTY TIP **Some of the biggest players in the restaurant industry got their start in New England, including Dunkin' Donuts, Friendly's, Legal Sea Foods, Bruegger's Bagels, The Capital Grille, and (of course) Boston Market.**

THE GREATEST: Chocolate Orgasm Brownie

Rosie's Bakery $
www.rosiesbakery.com
Rosie's Bakery whips up superb desserts with pure butter, fresh cream, and loads of sugar. The Chocolate Orgasm is a rich square of brownie perfection that's moist and chocolaty with shiny fudge frosting that sticks to the roof of your mouth. Rosie's brews a robust cup of coffee, which you can also taste in the coffee butter-cream icing on the Harvard mocha cake. The ovens are in a constant flurry of activity, turning out raspberry Snow Queen cakes, Boston cream pies, and a dozen kinds of cookies and tarts. Rosie's has locations in Cambridge, Chestnut Hill, Lexington, South Station, and Wellesley.

THE GREATEST: Suburban Chain

Not Your Average Joe's $$
www.notyouraveragejoes.com
At Not Your Average Joe's, customers can get city-standard food without battling the traffic or shelling out a fortune. The affordable chain is located in suburban neighborhoods like Arlington, Watertown, Randolph, and Beverly. Booth seating keeps it casual, but the snazzy atmosphere combines colorful retro lights, wrought iron, and oversized mirrors. All tables get a heaping basket of Tuscan bread, plus a spicy olive oil dip infused with parmesan and garlic. The global menu includes pasta, pizza, salads, and sandwiches. Phantom's favorites are the Voodoo Shrimp and the Black Angus sirloin meat loaf with garlic mashed potatoes.

THE GREATEST: Upscale Pizza Chain

Figs $$
www.toddenglish.com

The Figs chain is Todd English's creation—a cross between a European bistro and a pizzeria. Servers in jeans and T-shirts deliver Italian entrées, and thin-crust pizza is the signature item. Propped on an upside-down cookie sheet, the free-form pizza pies are crispy with bold flavored toppings. Phantom favors the sauceless Bianco, piled with caramelized sweet onions and balsamic drizzled arugula. The fig and prosciutto pie has a rosemary crust; the spicy shrimp is topped with avocado and tomato relish; and the Italian sausage pizza includes charred eggplant and torn basil. Figs locations include Charlestown, Beacon Hill, and Wellesley.

THE GREATEST: Family Style

Vinny T's $$
www.vinnyts.com

Vinnie T's is the best of the local chain establishments that serve family-style Italian food. Every dish is huge, so Phantom rounds up his big-bellied friends to pass around platters of fried calamari, lasagna, fettuccine carbonara, penne alla vodka, and veal Marsala. Appetizers and entrées come in two sizes, and parties of six can opt for the four-course prix fixe. The atmosphere is boisterous, packed with people and pictures of famous Italian Americans. No one leaves hungry or empty-handed!

THE GREATEST: Bagel Chain

Finagle A Bagel $
www.finagleabagel.com

The "Bagel Buzz Saw" for cutting bagels gets a lot of attention, but it's the tasty bagels themselves that help Finagle A Bagel make its mark. They now have 19 retail locations in and around Boston. Every step of the bagel-making process is done in full view of the customers, from boiling and baking the dough to cooling and preparing the final product. The bagel lineup includes 17 varieties with traditional flavors like plain, onion, marble, and 100 percent whole wheat. Crazier concoctions include apple caramel, triple chocolate chip, and jalapeño cheddar.

THE GREATEST: Cape Cod Cooking

Hearth 'n Kettle $
www.hearthnkettle.com

Located on the main streets of towns in Cape Cod and Southeastern Mass, Hearth 'n Kettle serves three affordable meals a day with straightforward simplicity. The rustic dining rooms feature wooden beams, high-backed booths, and working fire-places. For lunch and dinner, their mantra is "Cape Cod Fresh," as the kitchen uti-lizes local seafood and day boat haddock and sea scallops. But Phantom's favorite meal at the H 'n K is breakfast. All of their awesome breads, muffins, and pastries come hot out of the oven at their Centerville bakery. For a true taste of the Cape, start the day with the thick sweet potato and cranberry pancakes with walnuts.

THE GREATEST: Boneless Buffalo Wings

Ninety Nine Restaurant & Pub $$
www.99restaurants.com

The Ninety Nine Restaurant chain claims to have invented the boneless Buffalo wing, which is the perfect finger food along with a tall, frosted mug of Sam Adams. Juicy tenders of chicken breast are battered by hand, fried to golden perfection, covered in spicy sauce, and served in traditional fashion with blue cheese dressing and celery sticks. The Ninety Nine also offers Gold Fever Wings dripping in honey mustard BBQ sauce and honey BBQ wings with a tangy sauce smeared over every boneless inch. The kitchen is truly all-American with entrées like grilled sirloin, 10-ounce Steakburgers, and fish & chips.

THE GREATEST: Brick-Oven Pies

Bertucci's $$
www.bertuccis.com

Bertucci's turns out brick-oven pizza pies in a fun, family environment. Kids can even get a ball of raw dough to play with, so the parents can sit back and relax. The atmosphere is always loud and lively, and the open kitchen puts on quite a show shoveling food in and out of an 850-degree old-fashioned brick oven. As for the pizza, the light crust is crackly, and fancy toppings include caramelized onions, roasted peppers, zucchini, pesto, rosemary ham, and smoked bacon. Enjoyed at big wooden farmhouse tables, the pies taste rustically delicious.

National Chains
GREAT ATE

Though many culinary critics ignore chains, Phantom appreciates finding familiar food at affordable prices while traveling across the country. When Phantom is in a no-surprises kind of mood, he heads to the 8 GREATEST chains.

TASTY TIP Curbside pickup is the latest innovation in the lazy world of takeout. When you pull into the parking lot, a camera spots your car and sends your order out with a server. Now that's some delicious technology!

THE GREATEST: Fresh-Baked Bread

Panera $
www.panera.com
Panera Bread is a perky lunch place built around handcrafted artisanal breads. Rarely do chains bake from scratch on-site, but that's Panera's pledge for every loaf, muffin, and pastry. Sandwiches are stacked on thick slices of honey wheat, rosemary walnut, and kalamata olive bread. Even the heart-warming soups like chicken noodle, baked potato, and broccoli cheddar are ladled into sourdough bread bowls. To top it all off, Panera is the kind of place that makes you want to linger, complete with winter fireplaces, free Wi-Fi access, and café charm.

THE GREATEST: Wild Atmosphere

Rainforest Café $$
75 Middlesex Turnpike, Burlington, Mass., (781) 272-7555,
www.rainforestcafe.com
The Rainforest Café is a wild place to shop and eat. Families embark on a mealtime safari under a lush canopy of synthetic trees. The jungle atmosphere covers every inch of the dining room, with lifelike butterflies, animated alligators, chest-pounding gorillas, fish tanks, running waterfalls, and mock thunderstorms. While their little explorers run around, adults can sip fruity, tropical drinks. The global menu carries exotic flair, filled with fun rainforest facts and dishes like Leaping Lizard Lettuce Wraps and Caribbean coconut shrimp. At dessert, don't miss the Sparkling Volcano, which leans warm brownie slabs against a mountain of ice cream, "erupting" with molten caramel lava and chocolate sauce.

THE GREATEST: **Waterfront Chain**

Chart House $$
60 Long Wharf, Boston, Mass., (617) 227-1576,
www.chart-house.com

The Chart House is a national chain that only opens locations on waterfront property. You can count on a great view at every one, but each is distinctive for its locally inspired architecture and locally influenced food. Boston's Long Wharf Chart House is on the harbor in the rustic Gardiner Building where John Hancock had his offices. The charming eighteenth-century setting is very inviting with loft seating, huge candelabras, and a maze of pulleys tucked up in the peaked ceiling. The seafood-rich menu lists native and imported delicacies, like the gorgeous tower of lump crabmeat, avocado, and mango.

THE GREATEST: **Steakhouse**

The Capital Grille $$$
359 Newbury St., Boston, Mass., (617) 262-8900,
www.thecapitalgrille.com

The Capital Grille dry-ages its beef for two weeks in temperature- and humidity-controlled meat lockers. The extra effort achieves incredibly flavorful steaks like the juicy rib eye and the tender filet mignon. The atmosphere is just as striking with dark wood, red leather banquettes, marbled lamps, and gold-framed art crowding every inch of wall. Well-groomed guests flaunt their expense accounts while perusing the staggering 300-vintage-long wine list. Locations include the Back Bay, Chestnut Hill, and Providence.

THE GREATEST: **Eat & Play**

Dave & Busters $$
Providence Place Mall, Providence, R.I., (401) 270-4555,
www.daveandbusters.com

Dave & Buster's is a great place for the kid in everyone. Where else can you roam a whirling arcade of simulators, skee ball, billiards, and firing ranges while hailing cocktails from the bar? Of-age customers can chaperone up to three children. After working up an appetite from all that activity, you can take a time-out for full-service dining amidst palm trees and stained glass. American pub grub is smothered in cheese and sour cream, with winners like poblano quesadillas, chicken cheesesteaks, and Jack Daniel's BBQ burgers.

THE GREATEST: Bloomin' Onion

Outback Steakhouse $$
www.outback.com

Outback Steakhouse is fearlessly cheesy with an Aussie atmosphere including boomerangs and surfboards. The meaty chain is also dependable for flavorful steaks, fun menu names like Jackeroo Chops, and oversized "Aussie-Tizers." Competitors have tried to imitate the Bloomin' Onion, but none comes close to the spicy floral-cut spread of the original batter-dipped fried onion. Other Outback favorites include the Gold Coast Coconut Shrimp and cheese fries obscured by massive amounts of Monterey Jack, cheddar, and bacon. Call-ahead seating and curbside takeaway make the Outback an unbeatable Down Under deal.

THE GREATEST: Deep-Dish Pizza

Uno Chicago Grill $$
www.unos.com

Uno Chicago Grill is THE deep-dish authority. As the inventor of the ultra-thick pie, Uno has perfected its deliciously chewy crust and crispy edges. The toppings go beyond the old standbys with options like chicken portabella and garlic Spinoccoli (layered with spinach and broccoli). Having recently reinvented itself, Uno goes beyond pizza with a neighborhood grill menu of steak, ribs, seafood, and pasta. Phantom swears they have the most underrated wings of all chain restaurants! The company even hires a full-time antique hunter who does nothing but travel the country in search of Chicago memorabilia for the walls.

THE GREATEST: Drinks & Appetizers

TGI Friday's $$
(800) FRIDAYS,
www.tgifridays.com

TGI Friday's is Phantom's favorite chain for finger foods and "bevvies." The pub grub appetizers find the right proportions between grease and gooey cheese. Steamy starters like pork pot stickers, Tuscan spinach dip, and loaded potato skins only get better with one of Friday's specialty drinks like the Fireworks Colada, the Candy Cane, and the Lone Star Jalapeño Mary. Their expert mixologists embrace the blender with frozen favorites like the ultimate mudslide, Peach Slush, and Bourbon Blizzards. Underagers can slurp to their heart's content, too, with Coke floats, strawberry milkshakes, and other ice cream concoctions.

Cheap Eats
GREAT ATE

Edible bargains and outrageous meal deals can be found all around this expensive town. Whether it's happy hour (free filet mignon sandwiches at Morton's), late-day discounts (Au Bon Pain's early evening bake sale), or prix-fixe menus (lunchtime at Sel de la Terre or Upstairs on the Square), you just need to know where to look. Phantom barely breaks a five at the 8 GREATEST cheap eats.

TASTY TIP Over 100 of Boston's best restaurants take part in Restaurant Week at the end of August. For just over $20 at lunch and $30 at dinner, you get a complete three-course prix fixe meal.

THE GREATEST: Bargain Lunch

Bukowski Tavern $
50 Dalton St., Boston, Mass., (617) 437-9999
Bukowski Tavern boasts the best midday bargain in the city, with a Steal of a Meal Lunch Deal every weekday. From noon to 8 p.m., burgers and hot dogs cost just $1.69 ($1 more for cheese). Bukowski is also known for uncommonly good pub grub and an impressive beer menu that includes 100 different bottled brews. The margarita fries are sprinkled with lime, salt, sugar, and cilantro, and the White Trash Cheese Dip is a gooey, guilty pleasure. They also make a mean bacon blue cheese burger and corkscrew mac & cheese with broccoli, chorizo, and garlic toast. Named after the famous poet, Bukowski features pictures of departed authors lining the wall. There's a second, more stylish location in Inman Square, Cambridge.

THE GREATEST: Dinner Deal

Dok Bua Thai Kitchen $
411 Harvard St., Brookline, Mass., (617) 277-7087,
www.dokbuathai.com
Part grocery store and part restaurant, Dok Bua is 100 percent dirt cheap. When your tummy starts grumbling in the aisles filled with exotic Asian imports, you can settle into the kitschy dining area for authentic Thai food. From 5 p.m. to 11 p.m., the unbeatable $8.95 dinner special includes an entrée like crispy pork, pad-si-ew noodles, or coconut curry, plus sides of rice, soup, Thai crispy rolls, and dumplings. The $6.50 lunch special (11 a.m. to 5 p.m.) includes two sides. The menu comes with a photo album of high-quality dishes so you see what *som-tom*

(papaya salad), *poo-nim* (crispy soft-shell crab), and whole steamed fish look like before you place your order.

THE GREATEST: Affordable Family Outing

Mendon Twin Drive-In $
35 Milford St. (Route 16), Mendon, Mass., (508) 473-4958,
www.mendondrivein.com
Mendon Twin Drive-In is one of the few remaining outdoor movie theaters in New England. With two screens and a capacity of 800 vehicles, this place shows first-run movies every night during the summer. At $20 per carload, you can stuff as many people as possible in your car for a back-to-back, two-movie show! The sound is broadcast over AM/FM stereo, and patrons are welcome to toss Frisbees in the grassy drive-in field. The atypical snack bar is decorated in '50s memorabilia and serves impressive finger foods along with Mexican selections. Cheese dogs, mozzarella sticks, and popcorn chicken make an expected appearance, with tasty cameos by tacos, nachos, and jalapeño poppers.

THE GREATEST: $1 Tapas

Masa $$
439 Tremont St., Boston, Mass., (617) 338-8884,
www.masarestaurant.com
Masa is the exception to the rule in the swank South End, offering bargain food and a hot and spicy scene. The copper bar is inviting for cocktails, and you can also score $1 Southwest tapas from Sunday to Thursday (5–11 p.m.) and Friday and Saturday after 9:30 p.m. Of the 10 options on the tapas menu, Phantom favors the steak and guacamole, chorizo with cranberry chutney, chicken taquitos, shrimp ceviche, and empanadas. For extra savings and an all-around sampling, order the $15 combo platter, which includes a pitcher of sangria. Masa has a selection of over 60 tequilas, which pair well with the strong Latin flavors in the food.

THE GREATEST: Price Buster Menu

Halfway Café $$
174 Washington St., Dedham, Mass., (781) 326-3336,
www.thehalfwaycafe.com
The Halfway Café lives up to its "good food cheap" slogan, with nearly every menu item ringing up at less than $10. They even sweeten the pot with a daily Price Buster meal for just $7.99. The featured entrée is steak tips on Monday, turkey tips on Tuesday, stuffed shells and country fried chicken on Wednesday, pot roast on Thursday, and fried clam strips on Friday. The regular menu includes pizza, burg-

ers, salads, steamers, and sandwiches. The café has a comfortable feel with wooden tables and booths, a stocked bar, and scores of framed sports photos on the walls. Locations include Dedham, Marlboro, Watertown, and Canton.

THE GREATEST: Cheap Chinese

King Fung Garden $
74 Kneeland St., Boston, Mass., (617) 357-5262
King Fung Garden may be a closet-sized hole-in-the-wall, but their ridiculously cheap Chinese dishes include legendary Peking ravioli. They come pan-fried and steamed, served with soy and fiery chili sauce. The crispy wontons are just as delicious, with more doughy heft around a pork nugget. Mongolian fire pots are also a house specialty, along with rice cakes, pea pod stems, and the three-course Peking duck that requires a 24-hour notice to prepare. Just remember to bring cash; credit cards are not accepted.

THE GREATEST: Inexpensive Italian

Galleria Umberto $
289 Hanover St., Boston, Mass., (617) 227-5709
Galleria Umberto is hit hard during lunch, which is the only meal served. The doors of the cafeteria-style eatery stay open until the food runs out, but you can call in your order before you go. Although the menu is limited, you won't find better Sicilian specialties anywhere. Phantom likes to line up early for four kinds of calzones filled with combinations of ricotta, mozzarella, spinach, salami, and sausage. Square Sicilian-style slices of cheese pizza come on a thick crust, and deep-fried arancini rice balls hide a cache of peas and gravy. The price is right, with every item costing less than $4. You can also order tiny Dixie cups of table wine.

THE GREATEST: Late-Night Menu

McCormick & Schmick's $$
34 Columbus Ave., Boston, Mass., (617) 482-3999,
www.mccormickandschmicks.com
McCormick & Schmick's is a seafood and steakhouse with outrageously cheap happy hour food. Theatergoers can swing by before the show until 6:30 p.m. (weekdays) and afterward from 10 p.m. to midnight for the $1.95 social hour menu at the bar. In addition to half-pound cheeseburgers with fries, changing selections include steamed mussels in garlic chili broth, clam shooters, cheese quesadillas, chicken wings, bruschetta, and oysters on the half shell. Phantom likes to position himself at the bar with a stiff drink and to put his purple chompers on autopilot. The same great deals are available at their location in Faneuil Hall.

Chicken
GREAT ATE

Second to no other white meat, chicken is a dinner champion that's not afraid to show a little leg. Whether it's baked, broiled, roasted, sautéed, fried, or grilled, this versatile staple is a lean, tasty protein. No matter which way it's cooked, the goal is always the same: moist, juicy meat. Phantom cries "Fowl!" at the 8 GREATEST chicken eateries.

 TASTY TIP **White breast meat is the most popular cut of chicken in America. But around the world, the chicken thigh is the king of clucks. Sure it has a little extra fat, but thigh meat is much more flavorful.**

THE GREATEST: Roast Chicken

Hamersley's Bistro $$$
553 Tremont St., Boston, Mass., (617) 423-2700,
www.hamersleysbistro.com
Hamersley's Bistro is a homey French eatery serving the most exquisite slow-roasted chicken. It's utterly juicy, surrendering garlic, lemon, and parsley with every single bite. Gordon Hamersley can usually be seen sporting his signature Red Sox cap from the open kitchen, where European cuisine comes together in astoundingly delicious dishes. For starters, try the crispy duck confit with couscous and fig salad. For an entrée, you can't go wrong with the seared sea scallops and lemony endives with pistachios. Pale brick walls, wrought-iron candelabras, and wooden ceiling beams reinforce the refined country setting.

THE GREATEST: Wings

Buff's Pub $
317 Washington St., Newton, Mass., (617) 332-9134
The large buffalo head mounted on the wall is the first clue that Buff's Pub is serious about wings. Made only from farm fresh chicken that's never been frozen, the outstanding finger food would probably take flight if not grounded in heavenly sauce. The traditional BBQ wings are extra-thick through the middle and deep-fried to render the joints crunchy. Slightly sweeter versions include honey hot and honey BBQ. Other pub grub includes deep-dish potato skins and beef soft tacos. As an all-American watering hole, Buff's is lined with beer ads and bar stools, and there are plenty of brews on tap. Phantom prefers the Blueberry Ale and a house exclusive called Buff's Pale Ale.

THE GREATEST: **Chicken Under a Brick**

Caffè Umbra   **$$**
1395 Washington St., Boston, Mass., (617) 867-0707,
www.caffeumbra.com
You won't find a better bird under a brick than at Caffè Umbra, where country European fare shows rustic French and Italian influences. It might seem odd to use building materials in the kitchen, but this Tuscan technique provides the necessary weight to form a deeply browned, crispy-crackly skin that holds in the moisture. Phantom also enjoys their signature dessert of sticky toffee pudding with vanilla bean ice cream and toffee sauce. The streetside bar has a great view of the Holy Cross Cathedral, and the simply decorated room is marked by rough brick walls and snug tables.

THE GREATEST: **Chicken Pie**

Harrows Chicken Pies   **$**
126 Main St., Reading, Mass., (781) 944-0410,
www.chickenpie.com
Harrows Chicken Pies has a phenomenal 60-year-old recipe for their namesake specialty. What was once a full-service restaurant is now strictly a take-out business. The cars line up for soul-satisfying pies packed with huge chunks of chicken, homemade gravy, carrots, and potatoes in a golden, freshly baked crust. They're available in four sizes that range from individual portions to the mammoth six-person pie. The all-natural delicacies are available cold or hot, along with mashed potatoes and veggie sides. Phantom likes to order extra chicken gravy and then to follow his meal with blueberry pie for dessert.

THE GREATEST: **White Meat Menu**

Chicken Lou's   **$**
50 Forsyth St., Boston, Mass., (617) 859-7017
Chicken Lou's is a ridiculously cheap sub shop in the heart of Northeastern's campus. There are picnic tables outside, but friendly counter service and hot-off-the-grill bargains make for a convenient quick stop. They also have the most extensive white meat menu around. The makeshift space is lined with a collage of sandwich descriptions, each creatively named. Whether you opt for the Chicken Cordon Lou, the Buffa'Lou Popcorn Chicken, or Lou's Portion #9, you'll be clucking happy. They even serve up Phantom Strips! U.S.D.A.'s Choice Sub (a teriyaki cheesesteak topped with grilled onions) was named for Phantom Gourmet CEO Dave Andelman, who ate there incessantly during law school.

THE GREATEST: Rotisserie Chicken

Boston Market $
www.bostonmarket.com
It may come as a surprise for such a wide-reaching chain, but Boston Market turns
out one heck of a rotisserie chicken. Plump birds spin and roast over flames, re-
quiring little added fat since they self-baste in their own juices. Half and quarter
portions can be ordered in tummy-tempting flavors like spicy Tuscan or double
marinated sweet garlic. Other white meat standouts include roasted turkey, the
Chicken Carver sandwich with creamy Dijon, and chicken drumsticks for the kids.
The focused menu allows customers to mix and match home-style entrées with all
the fixin's, like savory stuffing, mac & cheese, garlic dill potatoes, coleslaw, hot
cinnamon apples, and sweet potato casserole.

THE GREATEST: Berched Chicken

Ma Glockner's $$
151 Maple St., Bellingham, Mass., (508) 966-1085,
www.maglockners.com
Ma Glockner's berched half chicken is at the top of the coop. The super-moist suc-
culence comes from a novel preparation of parboiling the birds in special seasoning
and finishing them on a flattop grill. The unique, brittle-crisp skin acts as a steam
shield around the deliciously moist poultry. It's been the mainstay of the menu since
1937, and the unconventional delicacy is still served with Ma's tantalizing cinnamon
buns. The restaurant has an astounding 400-person capacity, and chicken-themed
decorations are stashed around the rooms. Seniors, families, and KENO fanatics
crowd into and around the booths, low tables, and spacious cocktail lounge.

THE GREATEST: Chicken Parm

Red Sauce $$
174 Sylvan St., Danvers, Mass., (978) 750-4949,
www.nakedfish.com/red_sauce_info.htm
Red Sauce makes the "Ferrari of chicken parmesan." This golden-brown version of
the classic dish covers juicy poultry in a buttery coating, cooks it to a crisp, and
tops it with gooey cheese and sweet, creamy tomato sauce. Pizza, pasta, and grilled
meats fill the menu, and everything including the wine is affordably priced. The
bruschetta trio includes three separate variations: garlicky mushroom, tomato and
basil, and roasted peppers with mozzarella. Tasty fried calamari comes with roasted
tomato sauce and hot cherry pepper pesto, and the steamed mussels are smothered
in fragrant tomato broth. The atmosphere features a large, open space with high
ceilings, gorgeous chandeliers, and servers in—what else—red tuxedo jackets.

Chinese
GREAT ATE

Boston's Chinatown is a sure bet for Asian eats, but Phantom has discovered scrumptious stir-fries and pupu platters scattered all over the Boston area and around New England. With a lifetime of duck sauce under his belt, Phantom salutes the 8 GREATEST Chinese restaurants.

TASTY TIP New Year's Eve is the busiest night of the year for Chinese restaurants. If you want to make sure you're chowing down on chow mein when the ball drops, make sure you fax your order by Christmas.

THE GREATEST: Upscale Chinese

Golden Temple $$$
1651 Beacon St., Brookline, Mass., (617) 277-9722
Where else can you get fine Chinese food while putting back the strongest Mai Tais on the eastern seaboard? The Golden Temple is one of the most beautiful restaurants in all of New England, with a modern mix of architecture, lighting, and music. The high-end cuisine comes at a price, but luxurious dishes like the Chardonnay chicken and batter-fried lobster are worth a few extra bucks. This Brookline institution is always innovating, and the bar scene sizzles at night with a house DJ and dancing.

THE GREATEST: Chinese & Sushi

Billy Tse $$
240 Commercial St., Boston, Mass., (617) 227-9990
What's a Pan-Asian restaurant doing in Boston's Italian North End? Just serving some of the area's most sophisticated Chinese and Japanese cuisine. Billy Tse brings a sense of style to the modern atmosphere and surprisingly light cuisine. Businessmen and neighborhood residents add to the pleasant atmosphere of the bar, the dining room, and the sushi bar. Phantom loves digging his chopsticks into the sesame chicken, Taipei fried rice, and coconut shrimp. Imaginative sushi rolls include the East maki with shrimp, avocado, and cucumber. The original Billy Tse is in Revere.

THE GREATEST: **Spare Ribs**

Chinatown $$
103 Sharon St., Stoughton, Mass., (781) 297-3886
Residents of the South Shore need not venture all the way to Boston's Chinatown since their very own Chinatown serves authentic Asian food in Stoughton and Brockton, too. The restaurant's massive kitchen is visible from the dining room through glass walls, and one glimpse of the master chefs proves these guys know how to work a wok. The delectable chicken scrolls have moist meat inside every crunchy bite. The regular spare ribs are delicious, but for the ultimate appetizer indulgence, try the meaty Chinatown special ribs that are even bigger and more tender with superior sweetness.

THE GREATEST: **Ultimate Asian Complex**

Kowloon $$
948 Broadway (Route 1 North), Saugus, Mass., (781) 233-0077,
www.kowloonrestaurant.com
It's almost impossible to describe the Kowloon to anyone who's never experienced this Asian food and entertainment complex firsthand. Owned and operated by the Wong family since 1950, the Kowloon has evolved into a legendary landmark on Route 1 in Saugus. With seating for nearly 1,200 customers, it's a mind-boggling operation featuring famous Chinese food, a Thai kitchen, a sushi bar, and the Comedy Connection upstairs. Phantom's favorite dishes include the garlicky Saugus Wings, Eddie Andelman Lo Mein with chicken and shrimp, and lobster with ginger and scallions.

THE GREATEST: **Food Court Alternative**

Bernard's $$
Chestnut Hill Mall, 199 Boylston St., Chestnut Hill, Mass., (617) 969-3388
Bernard's is a delightful stir-fried surprise in the Chestnut Hill Mall. This unlikely location is no indication of the spectacular food and excellent service inside. The dining room is decked out in bamboo shades and features a jade-colored wall etched in jungle scenes. It's always full of regulars who come for the tempting menu of Chinese, pan-Asian, and healthy "spa" selections. Phantom's purple chopsticks head straight for the sautéed shrimp with roasted black beans or the grilled sirloin steak over steamed jade broccoli.

THE GREATEST: Late-Night Lounge

Peking Tom's $$
25 Kingston St., Boston, Mass., (617) 482-6282,
www.pekingtom.com

Bringing a nostalgic twist to Boston's cool cocktail crowd, Peking Tom's Longtang
Lounge is as fun as it is funky. The ultra-hip bar mixes up a colorful list of special-
ties including updated versions of Fog Cutters, Mai Tais, and Scorpion Bowls. The
food is delectably sharable, like the seafood Peking dumplings, Szechuan salt and
pepper squid, and kung pao chicken lettuce wraps. Peking Tom's is always jumping
after work and after hours, when festive dining and imbibing kick into high gear.

THE GREATEST: Suburban Chinese

China Sky $$
11 Forest St., Wellesley, Mass., (781) 431-2388,
www.chinaskyrestaurant.com

Who said you have to go urban for decent Chinese? China Sky takes Szechuan and
Cantonese specialties to the edge . . . the suburbs, that is. Challenging the culinary
limits of the genre and cuisine, this upscale outpost is a pricier, more elegant eatery
where reservations are the norm. Smoky blue walls are marked with sizzling red
characters; Japanese dishes (including sushi) diversify the menu; and the sliding-
door Tea Ceremony Room is perfect for private parties. Phantom's favorites also
include steamed pork dumplings, lobster soong lettuce wraps, and incredibly crispy
General Tso's chicken. Lunch specials include a choice of soup and rice for less
than $10.

THE GREATEST: Pupu Platters

Quan's Kitchen $$
652 East Washington St., North Attleboro, Mass., (508) 699-7826,
www.quanskitchen.net

Quan's Kitchen is a completely unexpected delight in a North Attleboro strip mall.
The stylish interior is modern with ruby-red walls and sleek light fixtures. Even the
pupu platters have style. Instead of a flaming presentation on a wooden tray, the
boneless spare ribs, egg rolls, and beef teriyaki are laid out geometrically on a
white porcelain platter. General Gau himself would go to war over this rendition of
the sweet and spicy recipe, and the sushi chefs slice and dice in full view of the din-
ing room. Quan has a second (takeout and delivery only) kitchen in Mansfield.

Coffee
GREAT ATE

Aside from its stimulating caffeine power and warming effect, coffee creates the perfect excuse for afternoon snacks. Brews range in depth and color, from the lighter American roast to the darker French roast. Of the *robusta* and *arabica* species (the two most common beans), the Caped Critic prefers the more complex flavor of the latter. Phantom gets his daily dose at the 8 GREATEST coffee shops.

TASTY TIP Anyone can order a cup of java, but using the proper buzz words will get you just enough cream and sugar. "Half-caf" means half decaf; "skinny" means skim milk; "cake in a cup" means double cream, double sugar; and "wet" means more milk than usual.

THE GREATEST: Bean Selection

Polcari's Coffee Shop $
105 Salem St., Boston, Mass., (617) 227-0786

Polcari's is the best place in town to buy roasted coffee beans. The old-world North End shop is lined with creaky, wooden floors and 30 different options that they'll grind on the spot or bag as whole beans. They also sell an impressive range of rice, grains, tea, and dried beans. Polcari's is also a dried herb and spice emporium, stocking 100 different varieties like Greek oregano and licorice root. There's even authentic Italian lemon slush right outside the door, where you scoop it yourself and pay by the honor system.

THE GREATEST: Box O' Joe

Dunkin' Donuts $
www.dunkindonuts.com

Dunkin' Donuts is the master of the quickest and most consistent cup of coffee. They dump any brew older than 18 minutes, ensuring a fresh pour every time. Their portable 10-serving Box O' Joe comes with plenty of cups and lots of cream and sugar, making it perfect for meetings, parties, and heavy coffee consumers. Of their 52 baked goods, Phantom prefers the glazed and chocolate-covered donuts, which go down so smooth with an icy-cold Coffee Coolatta.

THE GREATEST: Coffeehouse Culture

Diesel Café $
257 Elm St., Somerville, Mass., (617) 629-8717,
www.diesel-cafe.com

When Phantom wants to chill in a coffeehouse all afternoon, Diesel Café is the java
hut of choice. It's inviting up front, with a glass garage door that opens to the sidewalk on sunny days. But you can get lost in the never-ending back room or the
diner-style middle section complete with retro booths and two pool tables. An alternative crowd settles in for earthy eats like the turkey-avocado Monkey Wrench
sandwich. High-octane beverages are also in evidence, from typical espresso to
specialties like sweet Vietnamese coffee. Diesel premiums include the Eight Ball
(ice cream and coffee), the Solid Six (six shots of espresso!), and Tuck's Turtle
(hot chocolate, caramel, hazelnut, and whipped cream).

THE GREATEST: Ethiopian Coffee

Addis Red Sea $$
544 Tremont St., Boston, Mass., (617) 426-8727,
www.addisredsea.com

Addis Red Sea is a transporting Ethiopian experience. Adventurous customers eat
with their hands on squat stools around a tiny woven table. After digging into sam
busa tarts filled with beef and lentils, the meal turns to spicy stews and fried meats
that are scooped up with thin, spongy flatbread called *injera*. A grand finale of Har-
rar coffee is the way to go, since Ethiopia is the motherland of the original bean-
yielding plant. The dark, smooth brew is deliciously aggressive, infused with
cardamom.

THE GREATEST: Spiked Coffee

The Castle $$$
1230 Main St. (Route 9), Leicester, Mass., (508) 892-9090,
www.castlerestaurant.com

Surrounded by a moat, the Castle is so imaginatively medieval, you almost expect
King Arthur to pop in and join you at the round table. Many dishes and drinks are
prepared tableside, including the Café Espanol. Kahlúa and Spanish brandy are
flambéd, mixed with hot coffee, and topped with whipped cream. The rim of the
glass is coated with lemon and sugar and caramelized to lend citrus flavor to every
sip. Tall wooden chairs make everyone feel like royalty, surrounded by armor,
shields, and swords. The Crusader Room is casual, while the Camelot Room offers
fine dining over dishes like lobster Thermidor, Châteaubriand King Henry VIII,
and Filet Mignon Guinevere.

THE GREATEST: Specialty Java Drinks

Café Algiers $

40 Brattle St., Cambridge, Mass., (617) 492-1557

The fairly hidden Café Algiers is well known to Harvard bookworms in search of a cozy study nook. Toting laptops and notebooks, they keep the candles burning at both ends with the area's best Arabian coffee. The thick, complex flavors are brewed into piping-hot, unusual specialties like mint coffee and espresso frappes. You can also count on authentic Turkish coffee, known for its fierce strength and notes of cinnamon, nutmeg, and cardamom. The exotic environs capture the coffeehouse culture of the Middle East with intricate patterns, octagonal tables, and lanterns. Maps of the Middle East adorn the walls, and velvet curtains complete the look. There's also a full menu of kebabs, falafel, and hummus.

THE GREATEST: Cappuccino

Caffe Vittoria $

296 Hanover St., Boston, Mass., (617) 227-7606

Caffe Vittoria is an authentic European café, appropriately located in the North End. It's easy to get lost in the multilevel expansion, but don't disappear without one of their awesome cappuccinos. Frothed from an old-fashioned espresso machine, it arrives at the table piping hot with a sugary chocolate dusting. Marble-topped tables pack the house, and old black-and-white photos spread clear across the walls. If you're up for something sweet, there are plenty of tempting treats like cannoli, biscotti, and gelato. The service can be abrupt and lightning-fast, but they encourage customers to lounge around and pass the time.

THE GREATEST: Coffee Alternative

Tealuxe $

0 Brattle St., Cambridge, Mass., (617) 441-0077,
www.tealuxe.com

When Phantom is overcaffeinated and looking for an herbal infusion, he puts a hold on the java huts and heads straight for his favorite coffee alternative. Tealuxe has 100 loose-leaf selections at all three locations (Harvard Square, the Back Bay, and Providence). Cool jazz sets the mood, along with copper tables, and wooden bins of tea lined up like a card catalog. The teatender helps customers pick from a range of green, black, oolong, and herbal options. Customers with tea indecision can take the Tea Questionnaire or peruse the Top Ten List for suggestions like Irish cream, China white peach, lemongrass, vanilla jasmine, and passion fruit rooibos.

Comfort Food

GREAT ATE

Whether reminiscent of Mom's cooking or just a feel-good meal, comfort food helps us all slow down and smell the bacon. This culinary category includes all the foods you loved when you were a kid and still love today. They're heartwarming, feel-good foods like chicken noodle soup, spaghetti and meatballs, or a big bar of chocolate. Phantom gets nostalgic nourishment from the 8 GREATEST comfort food eateries.

TASTY TIP — **Beware of quotation marks! If you see a comfort food favorite flanked by quotes on a trendy menu, chances are it won't be what you expect. Lasagna is very different from "Lasagna" (the former is an old-school Italian classic, the latter is a free-form experiment that will probably cost more than it's worth).**

THE GREATEST: Mac & Cheese

Zon's $$
2 Perkins St., Jamaica Plain, Mass., (617) 524-9667,
www.zonsjp.com
Zon's has a magnetizing deep-red dining room with funky candelabras and an updated version of old-school comfort. Their mac & cheese is an over-the-top, fromage-filled entrée that comes in three gooey versions. The basic recipe mixes bow-tie-shaped farfalle pasta with a luxurious cheese blend of sharp farmhouse cheddar and creamy, nutty fontina. There's also the Mac Daddy with garlicky grilled chorizo sausage or the mac, cheese & peas. Phantom also loves their radical burgers and brioche bread pudding.

THE GREATEST: Grilled Cheese

The Paramount $$
44 Charles Street, Boston, Mass., (617) 720-1152
The Paramount is a neighborhood coffee shop turned yuppie, with cafeteria-style service and one heck of a grilled cheese. Hot off the griddle, this chewy-crusted one-hander displays a tie-dye of golden sizzle marks, a double dose of American cheese, and tomato slices inside. Along with breakfast all day, The Paramount does burgers, fancy salads, and greasy griddle grub. It's stylish and modern with patches of brick, gallery art, and silver-lined seats. The mood turns upscale by night with dressed tables and full service.

THE GREATEST: New England Classics

Durgin Park $$
5 Faneuil Hall Market Pl., Boston, Mass., (617) 227-2038,
www.durgin-park.com
Durgin Park is a Boston institution with pack-'em-in feeding rooms crammed with communal checkered tables. Generations of customers make a regular pilgrimage to the place for classic New England fare served at fair price. Hearty menu staples include clam chowder, Indian pudding, Boston baked beans, tons of seafood, cornbread, and Yankee pot roast. Sassy waitresses fall somewhere between witty and crass, but it's all in the name of good, laughable fun.

THE GREATEST: Stone Hearth Cooking

The Fireplace $$
1634 Beacon St., Brookline, Mass., (617) 975-1900,
www.fireplacerest.com
The Fireplace is a cozy nest of a neighborhood restaurant tending to comfort food in the stone hearth. Paired with New England microbrews and American wines, the rotisserie dishes include spit-roasted chicken with sage brown butter. Phantom also enjoys the Maine mussels steamed in lemon garlic broth and any of the wood-smoked specialties. As the name implies, the copper and wrought-iron space revolves around a roaring fireplace, where bimonthly "chats" include themed tastings.

THE GREATEST: Gastro-Pub

The Publick House $
1648 Beacon St., Brookline, Mass., (617) 277-2880,
www.thepublickhousebrookline.com
The Publick House lives up to its hops hype as the gastro-pub Boston has been thirsty for. "Shots: Don't sell 'em," declares the menu. But you won't care about Cuervo once you've glanced at the handpicked beer list with 100 diamond-in-the-rough selections. Their 27 taps are the cleanest in town, and each highly selective microbrew is served at the proper temperature in the appropriate glassware. Sophisticated pub grub is often infused with porters, Pilsners, and other brews. Try the pulled pork marinated in Arrogant Bastard or the sautéed littlenecks in Allagash White broth. The gothic interior shows lots of beer pride posters, dueling fireplaces, and Red Sox on the big screen.

THE GREATEST: Cocktail-Friendly Comfort Food

Anthem $$

138 Portland St., Boston, Mass., (617) 523-8383,
www.anthemboston.com

Located near North Station, Anthem turns out comfort food for the cocktail crowd. Chef Robert Fathman takes a whimsical approach to American bistro food by offering unique creations like fried Twinkies with berry coulis. In addition to mango martinis and blood orange cosmos, the fearless, flamboyant menu lists a pupu platter with fried tuna maki, seaweed salad, sweet & spicy braised pork ribs, and tempura fried shrimp. The dressed-up atmosphere comes together with velour and beaded curtains, plush couches, a mahogany bar, and rich colors in the stylish downstairs lounge.

THE GREATEST: Lobster Macaroni & Cheese

The Loft Steak and Chop House $$

1140 Osgood St. (Rt. 125), North Andover, Mass., (978) 686-0026,
www.loftsteakandchophouse.com

Located in a 160-year-old wooden barn, The Loft Steak and Chop House is authentically old school. Exposed posts and beams set the tone for the classic New England tavern atmosphere. Although the kitchen turns out high-class entrées like steak au poivre and chicken piccata, Phantom always orders off the "Old Time Favorites" menu. It's almost impossible to pass up comfort foods like chopped sirloin and American chop suey. Their lobster macaroni and cheese is made with four cheeses, rotini pasta, and big chunks of seafood, all baked until the top is golden-brown. The Loft has a sister seafood restaurant named Joe Fish, which is conveniently located next door.

THE GREATEST: Bread Pudding

Stephanie's on Newbury $$

190 Newbury St., Boston, Mass., (617) 236-0990,
www.stephaniesonnewbury.com

Stephanie's on Newbury is a delicious oasis from a long day of shopping. If you can tear yourself from the fireplace, there's a homey bistro setting where you can sink into a cozy banquette. But when the weather heats up, there's nothing hotter than Stephanie's high-profile sidewalk seating. Stylish comfort food dishes include meat loaf with caramelized onions or Phantom's favorite bread pudding sweetened on candied apples, caramel, and vanilla ice cream. It's food for the people, but you won't mind slipping into your newly purchased threads for the occasion.

Date Places
GREAT ATE

Money can't buy love, but it can buy a romantic meal, a secluded nosh, a wine & dine dinner, or a hot night on the town. When contemplating the proper venue, concentrate on mood lighting and a strong wine list; there's nothing like a little bubbly to stimulate conversation! When Phantom's in the mood for amour, he heads to one of the 8 GREATEST date places.

TASTY TIP Do a dry run before a big date! Test-run your driving route, check the parking situation, confirm the reservation, request a secluded table, and check the reservation list to make sure none of your exes will be sitting at the booth next to you.

THE GREATEST: Cozy Nook

Taberna de Haro $$
999 Beacon St., Brookline, Mass., (617) 277-8272
Taberna de Haro serves some of the tastiest tapas this side of Madrid. If the sunshine-colored walls could talk, their breath would smell intensely of sweet garlic. A traditional brick oven infuses the fragrant bulb into every other dish, which does wonders for the palate but could prove problematic for a first kiss! Dried chili peppers and baskets of lemons overflow from the open kitchen. Spanish bar foods are divided into small snack-sized plates and larger casseroles, while Rioja and sherry occupy the wine list. For canoodling couples, the undersized wooden tables practically force you to eat off each other's plates.

THE GREATEST: Sophisticated Romance

Sel de la Terre $$$
255 State St., Boston, Mass., (617) 720-1300,
www.seldelaterre.com
Drenched in earthy colors, Sel de la Terre looks like it was carved right out of the ground. Southern French cooking is the focus, with extra attention to the rustic country fare of Provence. Aromatic herbs are harvested from their garden and worked into ratatouille, bouillabaisse, olive-crusted lamb, and the signature rosemary pommes frites. The chef is also proud of his artisinal breads, for which he uses organic grapes as a starter. The crusty baguettes are the best in the city, and there's even an annexed boulangerie where early risers can pick up croissants, currant scones, and French pastries.

THE GREATEST: Fun First Date

Ascari Café at F1 Boston $$
290 Wood Rd., Braintree, Mass., (781) 848-2300,
www.f1boston.com

Ladies and gentlemen, rev your romantic engines! F1 Boston is Phantom's favorite
pit stop AND first date destination. At the area's only indoor go-kart racetrack, you
can work up an appetite for pub grub (and love) while zipping into a full-costume
red jumpsuit, capped with a helmet. Phantom likes to order up some nachos and
burgers at the trackside Ascari Café while strategizing over the next go-round.
They also have a full bar for post-race cocktails. Pictures of famous drivers help
break the ice and fuel conversation while you're placing bets about the cars below.
Phantom suggests racing before you eat, since a big dinner can weigh you down in
the fast lane.

THE GREATEST: Fabulous Food

Olives $$$
10 City Square, Charlestown, Mass., (617) 242-1999,
www.toddenglish.com

Now that Olives is accepting reservations, the only risk of dining here is if you're
on a blind date. In which case, you'll have plenty to talk about thanks to the open
kitchen, where flames jump up off the grill. Todd English designed Olives to be
comfortably rustic with candlelight and hardwood floors. The menu highlights
country Mediterranean cuisine and tasty pastas. Think black truffle flan, chestnut
agnolotti, Kobe beef flatbread, and spice market lamb. If the night is going well,
keep it going over a decadent dessert like the vanilla bean soufflé.

THE GREATEST: Date on a Budget

The Dish $$
253 Shawmut Ave., Boston, Mass., (617) 426-7866,
www.southenddish.com

The dish on The Dish is that it's stylish and intimate enough for a date, but it won't
wound your wallet. Large mirrors give the clever illusion of a roomier space while
showing off red votives, exposed brick, and framed chalkboards highlighting daily
specials. The menu is mostly Mediterranean with yummy sharables like garlicky
hummus and warm country olives. Phantom loves the Cajun meat loaf and the
wood-oven pizzas, which are decked out in exciting toppings like red bliss pota-
toes, caramelized onions, blue cheese, and bacon.

THE GREATEST: Nightlife

Tiki Room $$
1 Lansdowne St., Boston, Mass., (617) 351-2580,
www.tikiroomboston.com

Firing up Boston's nightlife with a wacky tropical twist, the Tiki Room is decked
out in coconuts, tiki torches, and Polynesian statues, with cheesy Elvis movies
playing on the television. Customers get into the mood by slinging colorful leis
around their necks, while cocktail umbrellas jazz up the drinks and reggae music
sets the mood for festive communal dining. The mix-and-match pupu platters let
guests pick six of their skewered snacks like egg rolls, spicy peanut chicken, and
potato skins. You can also order up a 60-ounce scorpion bowl and roast your own
s'mores.

THE GREATEST: Beautiful Food, Beautiful People

Mistral $$$
223 Columbus Ave., Boston, Mass., (617) 867-9300,
www.mistralbistro.com

With the strength of its namesake winds (and exquisite Mediterranean fare), Mistral sweeps diners off their feet. Every bite goes down smoothly in this soaring
space that's reminiscent of a farmhouse, but made over with city style. Terra-cotta
floors and mini cypress trees add a dramatic edge, while Boston's hottest beefcakes
and cupcakes meet and mingle at the bar. Seafood, olive oil, tomatoes, and garlic
are worked into unbelievable dishes, and thin grilled pizzas are the signature appetizer, served with smoky chili oil.

THE GREATEST: Dinner and a Movie

Chunky's Cinema Pub $
150 Bridge St., Pelham, N.H., (603) 635-7624,
www.chunkys.com

For dinner and a movie, Chunky's Cinema Pub is one-stop shopping. The theater
shows first-run movies and doubles as a full-service restaurant. Groups can gather
at tables and kick back in the comfort of Lincoln Town Car seats while hailing
drafts by the pitcher from the waiters. They also serve wine, and an extensive food
menu features dishes named after movie stars and blockbusters. Dine before or during the show on Lord of the Onion Rings, Kevin Bacon burgers, or a half-pound
Steak Out. Another Chunky's location can be found in Haverhill, Massachusetts.

Dessert
GREAT ATE

In all their chocolate-coated, fruit-filled wonder, desserts bring a sweet ending to any meal. Restaurants that are serious about dessert usually hire a pastry chef (look for credits at the bottom of the menu); it's not a sure-fire guarantee, but there's a good chance that such desserts will be worth their weight in calories. Phantom skips the apps and entrées at the 8 GREATEST dessert places.

TASTY TIP

Sure, it might take 20 minutes to make a properly puffy soufflé. But when a restaurant requires pre-ordering desserts along with entrées, they're usually just upselling customers before they get full.

THE GREATEST: Dessert Menu

Finale $$
One Columbus Avenue, Boston, Mass., (617) 423-3184,
www.finaledesserts.com

Defying the mantra of mothers everywhere, Finale insists that dessert comes first. The elegant desserterie serves light meals and hot toddies but it's the artfully stunning cookies, cakes, and chocolates that entice most diners. They're open late for the post theater crowd, perfecting signature dishes like molten chocolate cake and crème brûlée. Phantom flips for the Manjari mousse and the tiny little fruit tartlets. Both locations in Boston's Park Plaza and Harvard Square feature open kitchens where customers can watch on as desserts are assembled. Strategically angled mirrors ensure that even the tables at the back of the room get a great view.

THE GREATEST: Whoopie Pie

Wicked Whoopies $
5 Mechanic St., Gardiner, Maine, (877) 447-2629,
www.wickedwhoopies.com

Wicked Whoopies is THE authority on making whoopie. Whoopie pies, that is! Just when you thought the original recipe of whipped cream between devils food cake couldn't get any better, Isamax has redefined the pie with 20 flavors and variations. Phantom's favorites include strawberry, chocolate chip, and raspberry & cream. There's also a whopping five-pound Wicked Whoopie and a chocolate-dipped Whoop-de-Doo that's like a gourmet Ring Ding. They roll out 5,000 pies daily, which you can buy online or at the tiny, bright retail shop in Gardiner, Maine.

THE GREATEST: Cheesecake

Cheesecake Factory $$
115 Huntington Ave. Suite 181, Boston, Mass., (617) 399-7777,
www.thecheesecakefactory.com

The Cheesecake Factory showcases three dozen kinds of rich, creamy cheesecake. The atmosphere screams family fun with Egyptian-style columns and potted palms. The novel-length menu is packed with oversized entrées, but Phantom goes for their signature desserts chock full of candies, fruit, and sweets. Flavors worth a try include chocolate chip cookie dough, pumpkin, white chocolate raspberry truffle, key lime, and Snickers. Boston-area locations include the Prudential Center, CambridgeSide Galleria, and Chestnut Hill's Atrium Mall.

THE GREATEST: Baked Alaska

Oleana $$$
134 Hampshire St., Cambridge, Mass., (617) 661-0505,
www.oleanarestaurant.com

Oleana has really perfected one corner of the dessert category with their baked Alaska. The wispy, hot-cold creation has a core of coconut ice cream covered in crunchy meringue, which is perched on a chunky macaroon surrounded by passion fruit caramel. Besides dessert, the Middle Eastern–0influenced menu swirls exotic spice into Mediterranean dishes like sea scallops with tangerine butter. Plus, you can order pre-appetizer bread spreads while perusing the entrée options. Oleana has a rare treasure of a dining room that's pretty and intimate with rustic stone tiling, colorful North African artifacts, and a garden patio in warmer weather.

THE GREATEST: Cream Puffs

Beard Papa's $
1 Faneuil Hall Marketplace, Boston, Mass., (617) 570-9070,
www.muginohousa.com

Beard Papa's is a Japanese chain making the world's best cream puffs. Quincy Market customers can watch the treats as they're made and assembled on the spot. It starts with choux pastry baked in a special two-layer shell that's crispy on the outside and super-soft on the inside. The puffs are filled to order and finished with powdered sugar. Whipped vanilla custard made from Madagascar vanilla beans is Beard Papa's signature, but additional flavors include Belgian chocolate and strawberry. They can also be piped into a chocolate éclair.

THE GREATEST: **Boston Cream Pie**

Parker's $$$
Omni Parker House, 60 School St., Boston, Mass., (617) 227-8600,
www.omnihotels.com/hotels/default.asp?topic=dining&h_id=20
As the birthplace of the Boston cream pie, Parker's is THE place to order this New
England classic. It's not really a pie at all, but a gloriously messy recipe of cushy
sponge cake and thick custard topped with chocolate glaze. Heaping slices are
served up at the Omni, which is steeped in nineteenth-century history. Politicians
and celebrities have long loved the hotel, appointed with bronze, American oak,
and ostentatious chandeliers. Settling into the over-the-top extravagant dining
room, you'll dine well on local fare like clam chowder and baked Boston scrod.

THE GREATEST: **Chocolate Buffet**

Café Fleuri $$$
Langham Hotel Boston, 250 Franklin St., Boston, Mass., (617) 451-1900,
www.langhamhotels.com/langham/boston
Every Saturday from September to June, the local chapter of chocoholics anony-
mous meets at the gorgeous Café Fleuri for a special support group. The 12-step
program consists of gorging on an extravagant all-you-can-eat chocolate bar buffet. The irresistible spread lines up every imaginable form of cocoa, including
éclairs, cakes, tortes, cookies, and ice cream. There's dark chocolate mousse, light
chocolate mousse, and even a spicy cinnamon chocolate version. The house signature is the chocolate croissant pudding; also notable is the dark rum banana dac-
quoise.

THE GREATEST: **Fruit Tart**

Pastiche Fine Desserts $
92 Spruce St., Providence, R.I., (401) 861-5190,
www.pastichefinedesserts.com
Pastiche Fine Desserts is a tantalizing dessert café, turning out Phantom's favorite
fruit tarts. To make the tarts, they fill a butter pastry shell with vanilla custard and
top it off with concentric circles of jewel-like kiwi, blueberries, strawberries, and
orange. The space is warm and inviting with small, intimate tables, a working fireplace, and sophisticated European character. Pastiche is stocked with other superb
sweets like orange chocolate Bavarian cake, Russian teacakes, biscotti, rugelach,
and chocolate walnut truffle cookies. Their many beverage options include deluxe
coffee concoctions, tea, chai, and hot chocolate.

Diners
GREAT ATE

In all their chrome-plated glory, diners deliver good, honest food to real people. The very first "night lunch wagon" was launched in Providence in 1872, but the industry really took off in Worcester in the 1880s. Diner culture is still concentrated in its New England birthplace, and Phantom ate a lot of pie to find the 8 GREATEST diners.

TASTY TIP According to diner expert Randy Garbin, the first thing you should do when you walk into a diner is to look up at the ceiling. If the staff takes the time to wipe down and clean off the ceiling, chances are they're keeping the kitchen spic-and-span, too.

THE GREATEST: Baked Ham

Dream Diner $
384 Middlesex Rd., Tyngsboro, Mass., (978) 649-7097,
www.dreamdiner.com
Dream Diner is a spirited retro scene decorated with a vintage Coca-Cola motif, red vinyl booths, counter stools, and antique convertibles out front. Nothing says nostalgia better than their chocolaty, creamy whoopie pie. Breakfast is served all day, with sweet potato pancakes and three dozen omelets named after original diner car companies. Top-notch lunch plates include the spinach and feta Greek burger and the crock of chicken pot pie sealed in puff pastry. Don't you dare leave without trying their incredible baked ham, carved in thick slices right off the bone.

THE GREATEST: Original Architecture

Casey's Diner $
36 South Ave., Natick, Mass., (508) 655-3761
Slide back the door to Casey's Diner, and you'll find yourself back at the turn of the century. Everything including the floor and (arguably) the prices are from the original diner. Casey's is housed in a 1922 Worcester diner car, which is like a tiny torpedo of a lunch cart that barely squeezes ten swivel stools along the counter. The all-oak interior is well worn; the take-out window gets a good workout; and the gas stove still sports porcelain handles. Serving up chopped ham sandwiches and apple pie, the short-order cooks are best known for the All Around Hot Dog, which is piled with relish, onion, and mustard.

THE GREATEST: **Atypical Menu**

Rosebud Diner $

381 Summer Street, Somerville, Mass., (617) 666-6015,
www.rosebuddiner.com

The Rosebud Diner in Somerville is a genuine throwback to the '50s with a refreshingly atypical menu. Their wide-ranging beverage repertoire includes wine,
microbrews on tap, and stiff Bloody Marys. The kitchen turns out comfort food
with Phantom favorites like the Cajun char-burger smothered in jalapeño cheese,
Flamin' Wings, nachos, and mushrooms doused in spicy sauce and blue cheese.
The atmosphere in the 1941 Worcester dining car is quite handsome, complete with
seasoned waitresses, blue tiling, and an old-style counter.

THE GREATEST: **Reuben Sandwich**

Sunny Day Diner $

Route 3, Lincoln, N.H., (603) 745-4833

Tucked away up in the White Mountains, Sunny Day Diner is the ultimate blue-
plate experience, with cheery chrome-lined atmosphere and the world's best
Reuben sandwich. Two hefty layers of warm corned beef are topped with juicy
beer-baked sauerkraut, a thick slab of Swiss cheese, and tangy dressing on grilled
marbled rye. The in-house baker turns out breads, berry-popping muffins, cakes,
crumb-topped pies, and old-fashioned ice cream. Fresh-squeezed orange juice and
cobb-smoked bacon are perfect with any plate.

THE GREATEST: **Yankee Recipes**

Maine Diner $

2265 Post Road (Rte. 1), Wells, Maine, (207) 646-4441,
www.mainediner.com

The Maine Diner is bigger and a lot more modern than any others in its class, but
the menu sticks to tradition with huge plates of soulful Yankee fare. Phantom loves
the creamy seafood chowder, the lobster club sandwich, and the hearty baked beans
infused with bacon and onions. The breaded fried clams are fantastic, and the outrageous lobster pie packs an awful lot of claw and tail meat under a buttery cracker
crumb topping. This has to be one of the only diners in the country that grows its
own greens; there's a fresh herb and vegetable garden out back.

THE GREATEST: **Milkshake**

50s Diner $
5 Commercial Cir., 900R Providence Hwy., Dedham, Mass., (781) 326-1955
Hidden behind Route 1, the 50s Diner is dedicated to the decade of doo-wop and
bobby socks. They have posters of Marilyn Monroe and Elvis on the walls, as well
as a Coca-Cola cooler and other memorabilia. The cramped kitchen cranks out big
breakfasts like strawberry-smothered Belgian waffles and Texas French toast finished with bananas and powdered sugar. The Everything Omelet spills over with
broccoli, spinach, tomato, onion, pepper, mushroom, bacon, sausage, ham, and
cheese. Phantom loves their bacon cheeseburger, and the rich, creamy milkshakes
are so impossibly thick, you could probably bust a lung trying to suck one up the
straw.

THE GREATEST: **Retro Diner**

MaryAnn's Diner $
29 E. Broadway, Derry, N.H., (603) 434-5785,
www.maryannsdiner.com
Mary Ann's Diner is extraordinarily retro, complete with neon signs, an old-
fashioned jukebox, an antique Texaco gas pump, and waitresses in poodle skirts
and ponytails. Pictures of American icons from the '50s and '60s cover the walls
with characters like Elvis, James Dean, and Marilyn Monroe. The first-rate, old-
fashioned food comes in portions that test even Phantom's legendary appetite.
Home fries are crisp and crusty, the savory sausage and gravy comes on a toasted
biscuit, and the waffles are piled high with strawberries, blueberries, and vanilla ice
cream.

THE GREATEST: **Late-Night Diner**

Kenmore Diner $
250 Franklin St., Worcester, Mass., (508) 792-5125
Known as "Diner City," Worcester has a high concentration of delicious specimens
like the Kenmore. This establishment has recovered beautifully from a devastating
fire in 1999, but these days it's open only at night (from 11 p.m. on)! The location
is slightly spooky, hidden under exit 14 of Route 290, but it's the perfect greasy reward for a night out on the town. A massive renovation has turned the Kenmore
into a sparkling-clean, modern structure including a checkerboard floor. Shiny red
booths match the counter stools, which line up across from the sizzling open grill.
The menu is fairly streamlined with eggs, pancakes, burgers, cheesecake, and coffee, of course.

Ethnic Dining
GREAT ATE

Phantom believes that at least a quarter of your restaurant meals should be eaten at authentic ethnic eateries—and that doesn't include Chinese or Italian. One of the great pleasures of urban living is experiencing global restaurants inspired by African, Latin American, Asian, and Eastern European cultures. For the adventurous diner, they're usually an inexpensive trip to exciting, unanticipated flavors. The owners tend to be enthusiastic about introducing their native cuisine, and often they reward regulars with freebie tidbits. Phantom salutes the 8 GREATEST ethnic eateries.

TASTY TIP **Before you eat at a restaurant with an ethnic cuisine that you've never tried before, do your research. Learn the region's signature dish, make sure someone at your table orders it, and get experimental with the rest of your choices.**

THE GREATEST: Mediterranean Meal

Sabur $$
212 Holland St., Somerville, Mass., (617) 776-7890,
www.saburrestaurant.com

With handcrafted copper tables and the scent of 100-year-old recipes cooking away, Sabur transports you straight to Southeastern Europe. It's a two-room space where sheer curtains and woven pillows make you feel like you're miles away from Somerville's Teal Square. Many of the recipes on the exotic menu originate from the area around Bosnia, where the owner was born. There are also plenty of Mediterranean dishes, like Italian seafood stew packed with cod, clams, mussels, and shrimp. The house specialty is an unforgettable feast of lamb and vegetables, slow-roasted right in the dining room.

THE GREATEST: Indian Spice Bar

Masala Art $$$
990 Great Plain Ave., Needham, Mass., (781) 449-4050

If you're an Indian food newbie, Masala Art is the perfect place to start. The puffy tandoori breads (*naan*) are incredible, and chicken and lamb kebobs are a safe bet for anyone who can't take spiciness. For a truly memorable meal, you can sit at one of the nine seats at the curved Spice Bar and experience an interactive, pre-set menu. The chef explains each dish's spice in aromatic detail while cooking before your eyes. You can choose a course of vegetarian, non-vegetarian, or seafood dishes. Masala Art is also a feast for the eyes, full of silk cushions, a blue-lit bar, and images of mythical Indian characters that pop out of the wall.

THE GREATEST: Afghani Cuisine

The Helmand $$
143 First St., Cambridge, Mass., (617) 492-4646

Cambridge may be New England's best city for ethnic cuisine. Bolstering this case is The Helmand, located in the shadow of the CambridgeSide Galleria. A collection of knickknacks decorates the bright, colorful space that features oriental carpets and hand-painted plates. Country cupboards and a working fireplace add to the warm atmosphere, making it ideal for dinner on a cold winter night. The inexpensive menu is infused with turmeric, cinnamon, and cardamom, making dishes exceptionally spicy without any real heat. Vegetarians delight in eggplant and yogurt concoctions; carnivores should steer toward the incredible lamb dishes; and everyone enjoys the flatbread and aromatic baked rice.

THE GREATEST: Polish Restaurant

Café Polonia $$
611 Dorchester St., South Boston, Mass., (617) 269-0110,
www.cafepolonia.com

As Boston's only Polish restaurant, Café Polonia provides a respite from pretentious urban dining. The stone-walled interior is just six sturdy pine tables deep and pumping with polka music. The Polish menu stars robust traditional dishes of potatoes, cabbage, and meat, as well as Eastern European specialties and a great selection of Polish beer. Every table starts with sliced bread and a tasty spread of bacon-flecked lard. For rib-sticking entrées, try the potato pancakes and goulash topped with dill sour cream. Phantom also recommends the mashed-potato-stuffed pierogi dumplings and kielbasa sausage. Stock up on Polish pantry items, baked goods, newspapers, and frozen specialties at their sister market across the street.

THE GREATEST: Gourmet Greek

Meze Estiatorio $$$
100 City Square, Charlestown, Mass., (617) 242-MEZE,
www.mezeboston.com

At last, fine Greek dining has come to Boston! With a traditional thatched ceiling, live music from a bouzouki player, and a beautiful view of the Zakim Bridge, Meze is a sure recipe for a memorable evening out. A blue-tiled wood-burning stove cooks up scrumptious breads, meaty dishes of lamb and rabbit, and Mediterranean vegetables. Be sure to dip into the wine closet, stocked with Greek and southern

Italian vintages, along with domestic bottles produced by Greek Americans. The menu offers a huge selection of Greek tapas, along with olive oil-dressed salads, sweet desserts like honey baklava, and stone-ground Greek coffee heated over hot sand.

THE GREATEST: Turkish Takeout

Sultan's Kitchen $
116 State St., Boston, Mass., (617) 570-9009
Sultan's Kitchen is Boston's top Turkish restaurant and a healthy alternative to standard fast food. Since 1981, financial district workers have flocked in droves to the distinctive, affordable dishes that range from subtle to spicy. Grilled shish kebabs, exotic soups, and popular pita sandwiches are the reasons the lines stretch out the door at lunchtime. Salads and vegetable dishes are displayed at the registers, tempting taste buds with the fragrant aromas of herbs and Turkish spices. The menu is large and supplemented by even more choices on specials boards all over the walls. There are a few tables, but most customers take their food to go.

THE GREATEST: Persian Food & Art

Lala Rokh $$
97 Mount Vernon St., Boston, Mass., (617) 720-5511,
www.lalarokh.com
The cozy, intimate rooms at Lala Rokh are exotic and inviting. The soft lighting, beautiful Iranian art, and soothing music could relax the most frustrated lobbyist on The Hill. The brother-and-sister owners and their staff take great pride in explaining the Persian menu, which combines interesting selections of Mediterranean herbs, spices, fruits, and nuts. Meats and fragrant basmati rice are the emphasis, often accompanied by chutneys. Try the lamb and chicken kebobs or Mirza Ghasemi, a smoky dish of roasted eggplant, garlic, tomato, and saffron.

THE GREATEST: Cape Verdean Cuisine

Restaurante Cesaria $$
266 Bowdoin St., Dorchester, Mass., (617) 282-1998,
www.restaurantecesaria.com
Run by a staff that's brimming with ethnic pride, Cesaria salutes its colorful Cape Verdean roots with Portuguese-African fusion cuisine. Plates range from the exotic to the familiar, and there's plenty of sauced-up seafood, rice, and beans. Phantom likes to begin with garlicky linguica sausage and crispy, sweet-fried yucca paired with honey mustard dipping sauce. The house specialty *katchupada* is a stick-to-your-ribs porridge of hominy, fatty pork, rock beans, and kale. The baby grand piano adds to the spacious checkered dining room's party atmosphere.

Local Fast Food
GREAT ATE

McDonald's, Burger King, and Wendy's serve millions of customers around the globe, but some of Phantom's favorite quick stops can only be found in New England. Some meals are all about savoring the flavor, but these speedy joints are valued for their in-and-out mentality, so customers can re-fuel and get back to business. Still, a quick stop can still taste great. Phantom bellies up to the 8 GREATEST fast food registers around town.

TASTY TIP There's always a token local eatery in every mall food court. Give them a try, at least once. You never know which Fred's Pizza will be worthy of national acclaim.

THE GREATEST: Burritos

Anna's Taqueria $
1412 Beacon St., Brookline, Mass., (617) 739-7300
Anna's Taqueria in Brookline, Cambridge, and Somerville serves the best burritos in the area. The massive, affordable monsters are made to order with a choice of pulled chicken, grilled steak, veggies, or pork carnitas. As soon as the tortilla comes out of the steamer, it's a rapid-fire race to tell the line cook what you want: beans, rice, salsa, lettuce, guacamole, or hot sauce. The whole process takes 30 seconds, and it's handed off on a real plate with real silverware. Homey touches in the seating section include wooden furniture and chandeliers.

THE GREATEST: Donuts

Kane's Donuts $
120 Lincoln Avenue, Saugus, Mass., (781) 233-8499
Kane's Donuts is a mom & pop shop that makes the most delicious donuts. Every plump pastry ring is homemade and hand-cut, the same traditional way it's been done for five decades. You won't find oversugared, overmixed, cookie-cutter fare at Kane's. They make amazing jelly-filled donuts, plain donuts, sweet glazed donuts, and a wide-mouth, nine-by-four-inch coffee roll. It's also one of the few places left that still makes the bismarck, a donut filled with black raspberry jam and topped with fresh whipped cream.

THE GREATEST: **Pizza**

Papa Gino's $
www.papaginos.com

Papa Gino's serves up a great slice of pizza, making it Boston's most popular
pizzeria. Their secret recipe involves vine-ripened tomato sauce, a three-cheese
blend, and hand-stretched thin crust. Phantom usually gets one of the specialty
pies, like the chicken & roasted pepper, the spicy buffalo chicken, or the Paparoni,
which piles on twice the cheese and pepperoni. Papa Gino's goes way beyond
menu basics to offer salads, Barilla pasta dinners, cold subs, hot pockets, and
grilled panini. Plus, they throw kiddie birthday parties and hold Kids' Night every
Thursday, when children's meals start at just $3.

THE GREATEST: **Fast Food Deli**

Sam LaGrassa's $
44 Province St., Boston, Mass., (617) 357-6861,
www.samlagrassas.com

It's a bold statement to claim the world's number-one sandwiches, but Sam La-
Grassa's clearly knows a thing or two about running a deli. The lunch-only operation boasts "fresh from the pot" corned beef, honey-baked ham, and Black Angus
roast beef, which are all roasted, baked, and sliced in-house. Phantom recommends
the Famous Rumanian Pastrami Sandwich piled with sweet, ever-so-tender meat.
Grilled sandwiches are good too, with combos like turkey, honey-baked ham,
melted Swiss, and herb-infused coleslaw. Given the high quality, it's no surprise
that suits and students queue up out the door, cram into communal tables, and
smoosh along the stand-up counters. But the cafeteria-style line moves quickly, and
it's rather mesmerizing to watch the monster meat slicer going non-stop.

THE GREATEST: **Wraps**

Fresh City $
www.FreshCity.com

Coining the term "fresh fusion" to describe what they do, Fresh City blends a garden variety of meats, grains, and produce into wholesome tortilla bundles. It's not
your average sandwich shop that combines wild salmon, jasmine rice, and Dijon
mustard sauce or chicken, beans, salsa, and guacamole. The great Caesar wrap is
basically a one-handed salad, and the Peking duck includes Beijing slaw and hoisin
sauce. The wraps have hot and cold variety, and the menu also lists soups, noodles,
stir-fry, and smoothies. Locations include Logan Airport, Boston's Landmark Center, Framingham, and Newton.

THE GREATEST: Root Beer

Henry's Root Beer Stand $
232 Broadway, Taunton, Mass., (508) 824-6936
Henry's Root Beer Stand blows away the fizzy, mass-produced competition with an old-fashioned soda that's just like Phantom's favorite uncle: smooth and rich. It's made with equipment that's almost impossible to find these days, resulting in conservative carbonation that allows the vanilla undertones to finish strong. Phantom loves the root beer straight up, but it's even better as a brown cow, a frappe, or a float. Henry's does classic carhop cuisine like burgers, dogs, and onion rings. It looks like a drive-in, but customers have to hoof it inside to order before staking out a picnic table. South Shore fast foodies can get their sassafras fix at Henry's second location in Cohasset.

THE GREATEST: Grilled Panini

Pressed Sandwiches $
2 Oliver St., Boston, Mass., (617) 482-9700,
www.pressedsandwiches.com
Stock is up at Pressed Sandwiches, a hot little Financial District storefront. The artichoke-themed atmosphere is as toasty as the sandwiches themselves, which are grilled panini-style until they gush gooey cheese from their crust. For breakfast, there's egg and cheddar on brioche. Afternoon creations include prosciutto and fig, bresaola and fontina, or tuna and artichoke. The two-counter operation is super-quick, but neighborhood suits feel right at home in the classy setting dressed up with blackboard walls and raised stools. The espresso bar steams up high-octane bevvies. There's a second location with an outdoor patio and free Wi-Fi access in Central Square, Cambridge.

THE GREATEST: Steak & Cheese

Carl's Steak Subs $
55 Prospect St., Waltham, Mass., (781) 893-9313,
www.thecheesesteakguys.com
Forget about Philly; the best cheese steaks in the country come from Carl's, where there's barely enough room for the take-out counter. Their steak bombs pack in over a pound of meat made from a secret two-beef blend. There are 30 variations on the original, and many have never before been on the steak and cheese circuit. The Firecracker adds in pepperoni and tomato sauce, while the Kamikaze includes sausage, ham, bacon, and barbecue sauce. There's also the Misteak with meatballs, sausage, mushrooms, and onion, and the Mexican spiced up with hot jalapeños. If you can't make it to Carl's, you can score the same steak bombs at their sister restaurants: Tory's in Leominster and T. C. Lando's in Acton and Hudson.

National Fast Food
GREAT ATE

Phantom defines fast food by the number five. It should be served in five minutes or less, cost $5 or less, and most of their sales should be five items or less. Let other, stuffy restaurant critics scoff! Phantom proclaims his love for fast food with the 8 GREATEST national chains.

At drive-thru windows, always over-order by at least 20 percent. Chances are they'll leave something out of the bag, so if you want 4 burgers and 9 chicken nuggets, ask for 5 burgers and 12 nuggets. And don't forget to ask for sauce and ketchup!

THE GREATEST: Fast Food Burger

Wendy's $
www.wendys.com

Wendy's remains the classiest of the Big Three (topping McDonald's and Burger King). Since founder Dave Thomas went to that great drive-thru in the sky, this chain hasn't missed a beat. The trademark square burgers are so delicious that Phantom once ate for what he calls "the cycle": a single, double, triple, and Big Bacon Classic in one sitting. The salads are a more interactive experience than Phantom would like (at last count there were three separate packets he had to open and add to the bowl), but they're fresh and filling. The baked potato is a great option at a fast food place, and Phantom is also a "Phan" of the cheddar-topped chili and the impossibly thick Frosty.

THE GREATEST: Quick, Classy Sandwiches

Cosí $
www.xandocosi.com

Cosí is an East Coast legend with an imaginative menu and trendy atmosphere to match. The decor of wooden tables and warm yellow walls wraps around the sandwich bar, where selections are made on the spot. Their excellent crusty flatbread is baked throughout the day in hearth-fired ovens. Splendid sandwich stuffings include spinach artichoke spread, caramelized onions, and tandoori grilled chicken. The State Street Cosí gets a lot of Financial District business, and anyone with Wi-Fi capabilities can "surf and sip" at the Milk Street and Federal Street locations.

THE GREATEST: French Fries

McDonald's $
www.mcdonalds.com
There's no question about it. McDonald's fries are the king of the category, with their sublime saltiness and crunchy, tapered ends. These days, new Golden Arches locations are dressed up with some nice accessories like flatscreen TVs, chandeliers, and Wi-Fi access. Even after years of new product introductions, the Quarter Pounder remains a fast food classic. The chicken nuggets are now all white meat, and they're pretty darn tasty. Phantom hates to admit it, but the addition of salads and fruit has helped revive this American icon. Kids Meals now come with apple dippers and milk or juice.

THE GREATEST: Pizza Delivery

Papa John's $
www.papajohns.com
Call Phantom a hometown loyalist if you will, but he prefers local pizza chain Papa Gino's to the national Papa John's. What really sets PJ's apart is the garlic butter that's served on the side. It's so potent that it could make cardboard taste irresistible. A lot of fast food places add so many items that the counter menu looks like a Las Vegas sports book. To its credit, Papa John's has stayed focused on a streamlined pizza selection, along with eight dipping sauces. Papa John's locations aren't real pretty, so Phantom recommends takeout or delivery. It couldn't be easier thanks to online ordering.

THE GREATEST: Fried Chicken

Popeye's Chicken 'N Biscuits $
www.popeyes.com
Phantom is a huge KFC fan, and he's gone on record saying they still make the single best coleslaw into which he's ever dug a spork (that genius combination of fork and spoon). However, Popeye still out-muscles the Colonel. The Louisiana-based chain serves New Orleans–style chicken that's crispy and crunchy on the outside, but underneath the coating the chicken is hot and juicy. The delectable birds come in two styles: mild-seasoned and spicy hot. Skip the fries and onion rings, which can be found at any standard burger joint. Instead, get crazy and try the savory Cajun rice and some flaky buttermilk biscuits. In the Bay State, there's just one location at the Westgate Mall in Brockton.

THE GREATEST: **Toasted Sandwiches**

Quizno's $
www.quiznos.com

To get ahead in the brutally competitive sandwich wars, Quizno's toasted bread strategy has turned up the heat on national competitors like Panera Bread and D'Angelo. The extra effort results in superior 'wiches with crisp, warm edges. Sitting in the red-and-green-colored dining room, Phantom enjoys the mesquite chicken with melted cheddar, ranch dressing, and moist slices of white meat. Slightly better is the Bistro Beef featuring roast beef and herb mayo on tasty cheddar onion cibatta bread.

THE GREATEST: **Mexican Munchies**

Baja Fresh $
www.bajafresh.com

A mere baby compared to these other fast food behemoths, Baja Fresh may expand faster than Phantom's purple waistline. The design is sleek with black-and-white-checkered floors and raised tables. Defying fast food tradition, Baja sports an open kitchen with no shortcuts like can openers or microwaves. The Tex-Mex grill bangs out everything on site as ordered, with only a 10-minute wait. Phantom enjoys the crunchy, toasted nachos stacked generously with chunky salsa, melted jack and cheddar cheese, and awesome guacamole. If you like a little spice, there's a self-service salsa bar.

THE GREATEST: **Rapid Roast Beef**

Arby's $
www.arbys.com

Kelly's Roast Beef owns the local market for roast beef, but Arby's does this sandwich delicacy best on a national level. It's what Phantom would call a "highway chain," meaning he only visits when he's one) ravenously hungry and two) doesn't want to stray off the driving route. The King Beef 'n Cheddar sandwich is the star offering, featuring Arby's lean roast beef, hot cheddar cheese sauce, and a special dressing served on a grilled onion bun. The Big Montana is a half-pound mountain of roast beef jacked up on a toasted sesame seed bun.

Fine Dining
GREAT ATE

Phantom doesn't don his purple tux very often. But when it's time to dress up and splurge on a memorable meal, there are plenty of places that fit the (enormous) bill. These days, an opulent display isn't always the case; some of Boston's finest restaurants allow a more casual atmosphere, pouring every extra cent into extravagant flavors on the plate. Phantom gets out the platinum card for the 8 GREATEST fine dining rooms.

TASTY TIP The record for the fastest running of the Boston Marathon is 2:07:15. If your meal in any of these restaurants takes less time than that, you have failed.

THE GREATEST: Wine & Dine Destination

Aujourd'hui $$$
200 Boylston St., Boston, Mass., (617) 338-4400,
www.fourseasons.com/boston/dining
Aujourd'hui is worth its weight in caviar, especially for the million-dollar view of the Boston Public Garden. The luxurious dining room rolls out the red carpet in a contemporary formal setting where high society is alive and eating well. The decor features pretty floral chairs, Italian linens, and Bernaudeau china. On the seasonal menu, fantastic French cuisine pairs with an impressive wine list from around the world. In between the amuse bouche and petits fours, save room for dishes like butternut squash & lobster bisque, presented in a pot and poured into the bowl at the table. Another standout is the cured foie gras with rhubarb and Szechuan pepper gelée.

THE GREATEST: Rare Cuisine

Clio $$$
370 Commonwealth Ave., Boston, Mass., (617) 536-7200,
www.cliorestaurant.com
Clio's understated elegance and extreme cuisine make for an unpredictably special splurge. Blanched walls, a lattice ceiling, and leopard skin carpets create an uptown setting for a downtown clientele. Chef/owner Ken Oringer crafts a wildly artistic menu, where European and Asian influences are shaken up with incredibly rare ingredients and food lab experiments like foams and infusions. The ingenious results are palate-challenging, like lacquered foie gras with sweet and sour lemon and bee

pollen. Phantom also loves the salmon tartare with avocado, gold beets, and red ginger. Oringer can often be seen at Uni, the annexed sashimi bar downstairs.

THE GREATEST: New England Classic

Locke-Ober $$$
3 Winter Pl., Boston, Mass., (617) 542-1340,
www.locke-ober.com
Generations of Bostonians have grown up with downtown Boston's timeless Locke-Ober. The famed JFK lobster stew is part of the tradition, renamed for its biggest fan. The rich concoction yields a hint of sherry and cayenne pepper, finished with a pat of butter. An exquisite American menu includes New England seafood, a fine oyster bar, and some newer creative fare from chef/owner Lydia Shire. Her bold cooking style results in dishes like halibut and grilled oysters with a nage of lemongrass and lime. The superb, old world setting is refined, detailed with dark mahogany and luxury leather. While the first and second floors are rich with history, the third floor is divided into six private chambers (the JFK room is the most prestigious) for intimate private parties and business meetings.

THE GREATEST: Proposal Restaurant

L'Espalier $$$
30 Gloucester St., Boston, Mass., (617) 262-3023,
www.lespalier.com
If you're looking to pop the question, L'Espalier is perfectly romantic, intimate, and formal. The elegant townhouse features marble fireplaces in each room, and the classical French cuisine is both unpronounceable and fabulous. Chef/owner Frank McClelland uses farm-fresh, regional ingredients in his elaborate tasting menus, with themes like "caviar and truffles," "vegetarian," or straight-up "seasonal." Dinners begin with an amuse bouche and conclude with a guided tour of the 30-selection artisanal cheese tray. They also do Wine Mondays (themed four-course tasting menus paired with wine) and Fantasy Tea Parties (full tea with small bites) every Saturday and Sunday at 2 p.m.

THE GREATEST: Splurge with a View

Spiced Pear $$$
The Chanler at Cliff Walk, 117 Memorial Blvd., Newport, R.I.,
(401) 847-2244,
www.spicedpear.com
The Spiced Pear offers a magical experience of original, high-fashion cuisine in a luxurious boutique hotel. Several cliffside rooms swim in glittery ocean views that

spill onto a gorgeous veranda. Inside, the decor affects a regal manor setting of fireplaces and framed portraits. Dinner is a global fusion affair of tasting menus delivered in four to 12 flights of fancy. The chef's love of Southern cooking comes through in dishes like Atlantic cod over bacon-infused beans crowned with creamy, crunchy carrot slaw.

THE GREATEST: Understated Elegance

Seasons   **$$$**
Millennium Bostonian Hotel, 26 North St., Boston, Mass., (617) 523-4119,
www.millenniumhotels.com/boston
With understated elegance, Seasons in the Millennium Bostonian Hotel is a natural celebration venue. A draped cloth ceiling and well-spaced, handsome tables produce an impeccable setting with plenty of privacy. All eyes are on the elevated view of the Faneuil Hall Marketplace and the city's skyline. Both the extensive American wine list and the intriguing New American cuisine stand out on the menu, with dishes like molasses duck breast and shiitake dusted cod. Visual presentation is impressive, with many dishes towering vertically, multilayered, or blazing with color.

THE GREATEST: Chef's Tasting Menu

No. 9 Park   **$$$**
9 Park St., Boston, Mass., (617) 742-9991,
www.no9park.com
No. 9 Park is the ultimate Beacon Hill destination, overlooking the Boston Common from a nineteenth-century mansion. Chef/owner Barbara Lynch's country European cuisine includes masterful creations like roasted lamb chops with preserved lemon or tempura cod cheeks. The gnocchi, made from Idaho potatoes, is by far her best dish, dressed in luxury accents like prunes and seared foie gras, pumpkin, lobster, or truffle oil. For an over-the-top adventure, order the seven- or nine-course tasting menu paired with rare wines from boutique vintners. The retro-elegant dining area has tan walls with an olive trim, and silk-shirted servers work the Italian marble bar tables.

THE GREATEST: Fine French

Salts   **$$$**
798 Main St., Cambridge, Mass., (617) 876-8444
www.saltsrestaurant.com
Salts achieves a rare level of sophistication, appointed with velvety wine-colored curtains and candlelit chandeliers. The intimate room is homey and inviting, too,

without any pretense at the elegant linen-dressed tables. The French kitchen will jolt your senses to the way extraordinary food is meant to be enjoyed, in perfect step with the seasons. The ballotine of chicken is the most succulent slow-roasted bird Phantom has ever eaten, and the lemon soufflé tart is like eating warm citrus clouds on a sugar cookie crust. For a special treat, order the whole roasted duck for two, which is carved tableside and served with truffled peaches.

French Fries
GREAT ATE

Hot dogs and hamburgers (and Phantom) would be lonely without their culinary counterpart, the celebrated French fry. Much like a good set of pearls, you can dress them up or down depending on the venue. Few other eats double as standard pub grub and à la carte sides at fine French restaurants. Phantom gets out the ketchup for the 8 GREATEST golden sticks from heaven.

TASTY TIP The "French" in French fries refers to the method of cutting the potatoes into thin strips. The finger-lickin' classic was actually born in Belgium.

THE GREATEST: Gravy Fries

Deluxe Town Diner $
627 Mount Auburn St., Watertown, Mass., (617) 926-8400,
www.deluxetowndiner.com
Deluxe Town Diner is an expanded 1930s Worcester dining car, completely restored with porcelain blue tiles, vinyl booths, and neon lights. Their upscale diner food includes Phantom's favorite gravy fries, better known as Wets. Hand-cut spuds are cooked to a sink-your-teeth-in state that's somewhere between crunchy and tender, all slathered with meaty gravy concocted from the pan juices. Other gourmet blue-plate specials include the all-natural Kobe beef burger, apple crumb pie with vanilla bean ice cream, and sweet potato pancakes.

THE GREATEST: Old-Fashioned Fries

Al's French Frys $
1251 Williston Rd., Burlington, Vt., (802) 862-9203,
www.alsfrenchfrys.com
Al's French Frys is a '50s classic with checkered floors, red booths, and neon lights. The crispy, crunchy, greasy golden twigs take the main stage, as customers watch mounds of whole russets go through the entire process of being peeled, cut, and fried. Salt, ketchup, and vinegar are stationed at every table, but the two most popular add-ons are turkey gravy and cheddar cheese sauce. Other tummy-tempting items include beefy burgers, hearty hot dogs, and old-fashioned milk shakes.

THE GREATEST: **Sweet Potato Fries**

Bison County $$
275 Moody St., Waltham, Mass., (781) 642-9720,
www.bisoncounty.com
Bison County makes Phantom's favorite sweet potato fries. Thin structure and
well-done crunchiness give them a familiar texture, but the natural sugars of the
sweet potato add a sweet, irresistible flavor that the common spud can't match.
Texas and Southern-style barbeque are cooked up on an eight-foot open grill in the
dining room. Bison County specializes in low-fat, low-cholesterol meat like bison
burgers and grilled buffalo tips. Phantom also enjoys the South Carolina wings,
which are slow-smoked and slathered with spicy mustard barbecue sauce.

THE GREATEST: **Steak Frites**

Aquitaine $$$
569 Tremont St., Boston, Mass., (617) 424-8577,
www.aquitaineboston.com
Building a case as Boston's best bistro, Aquitaine serves up a fine plate of steak
frites, the classic French recipe for meat and potatoes. Aquitaine's steak drips in
Perigord black truffle vinaigrette with crunchy, bronzed fries and a lovely water-
cress side salad. The kitchen also serves outstanding mussels from a copper pot full
of lemony shallots and thyme. For dessert, try any of their fresh fruit tarts finished
off with honey crème fraîche. The tall, industrial space is boisterous and romantic,
decked out in leather booths and oversized mirrors. Their Chestnut Hill sister,
Aquitaine Bis, has the same full-figured wine list and beloved steak frites.

THE GREATEST: **Flavored Fries**

Sunset Grill & Tap $$
130 Brighton Ave., Allston, Mass., (617) 254-1331,
www.allstonsfinest.com
Any place that serves over 500 different beers MUST serve good pub grub, includ-
ing crispy fries. Sunset's half pound burgers are cooked on a steam grill to seal in
the flavors and juices. And as for the fries, the quality Curly-Qs come to the table in
a gigantic basket that easily serves 10 voracious appetites. The fries are deliciously
addictive by themselves but even better topped with sour cream and chives or Cajun
fire. For the ultimate indulgent spud spree, check out the Green Monster potato
skins with pesto chicken strips, roasted red peppers, and mozzarella.

THE GREATEST: **Suzie Q Potato**

Skip's Snack Bar $
92 East Main St., Merrimac, Mass., (978) 346-8686
There are thousands of ways to slice a spud, but no one does it quite like Skip's Snack Bar. Since 1947, this Merrimac mainstay has cranked out millions of pounds of their signature Suzie Q Potato. Shaped like a spiral phone cord, the curly Suzie Q has been made the same way, on the same hand-powered slicers, for 60 years. While most of the curls are 8 inches long, the record is a whopping 16 feet, made from one giant spud. The '50s-themed quick stop makes other fast food, too. Grilled hot dogs, turkey clubs, and chicken fingers are pretty popular. But Phantom's favorite is the double cheeseburger made from Angus beef patties.

THE GREATEST: **Pommes Frites**

Brasserie Jo $$$
Colonnade Hotel, 120 Huntington Ave., Boston, Mass., (617) 425-3240,
www.colonnadehotel.com
Brasserie Jo masters old-world atmosphere and caters to a lively, social crowd. The casual cuisine is authentic French brasserie, which means it's perfectly okay to stop by for snacks instead of an entire meal. Whether your main selection is the hanger steak, the coq au vin, or a cheesy Croque Monsieur, a side of the pommes frites is an absolute must. Executed to a perfect golden hue and served vertically in an overflowing cup, they have excellent stick structure and are best eaten the way the French do: with Dijon mustard. The 1940s decor includes vintage French posters, comfortable banquettes, handsome cherrywood, and butcher paper spread over the tables.

THE GREATEST: **Curly Fries**

Coolidge Corner Clubhouse $$
307 Harvard Street, Brookline, Mass., (617) 566-4948
Affectionately known as the "CCC" to neighborhood sports fans, the Coolidge Corner Clubhouse is a fun place to watch a game and sip some suds. Athlete-named dishes, like the Cam Neely burger, come with a side of curly fries so absurdly gigantic, it's almost impossible to find the entrée underneath. In fact, it's one of the only restaurants where Phantom has to ask for a doggy bag to take the extras home (or at least to the car). Every day there's a sports trivia question up on the menu board, and anyone who answers correctly (no cell phones or Internet access allowed!) gets a free slice of chocolate mud pie.

Fried Clams
GREAT ATE

Fried clams are the ultimate shoreline finger food, with their juicy-sweet brine sealed into chubby, piping-hot packages. Unlike West Coast clams, East Coast varieties are available year-round. Still, some shacks open seasonally from about March to November. Call ahead before making the trek. Phantom rocks his cholesterol level to uncover the 8 GREATEST clam shacks.

TASTY TIP **Don't be upset when you find a random French fry, onion ring, or fried scallop hidden in your box of clams. Rejoice, celebrate, and ask for extra tartar sauce!**

THE GREATEST: Original Fried Clam

Woodman's of Essex $$
121 Main St. (Rt. 133), Essex, Mass., (978) 768-6057,
www.woodmans.com
Woodman's of Essex is the Mecca of the fried clam world, and it's also the alleged inventor of the fried mollusk. In 1916, Lawrence "Chubby" Woodman took the meat out of the steamers, tossed it in the fryer, and never looked back. Whether the restaurant's lore is myth or bivalve history, no other clam shack comes close to Woodman's tender, plump clam in a light batter fry. Woodman's also has steamed lobster to round out a proper New England clambake. The paper plate feasts are served to eat-in-the-rough diehards vying for spots at spare wooden booths.

THE GREATEST: Essex Soft Shells

Village Restaurant $$
55 Main St., Essex, Mass., (978) 768-6400,
www.wedigclams.com
At Village Restaurant, the bronzed Essex clams practically take flight with a light, airy batter and flawless sea flavor. Unlike most fried seafood hot spots, this Cape Ann eatery is a sit-down joint with full service and real silverware. There's lots of local history displayed on the walls, in a room that holds a whopping 200 seats. The fresh catches come in generous portions, and the house desserts are divine. There's deep-molasses-baked Indian pudding, a pumpkin spice pilgrim sundae, and cinnamon Grapenut custard.

THE GREATEST: Ipswich Clams

J.T. Farnham's $$
88 Eastern Ave. (Rt. 133), Essex, Mass., (978) 768-6643
J.T. Farnham's makes a righteous case for using sweet, superior Ipswich clams. The rich soft shells practically jump out of the muddy flats and into the tiny clam shack. With lots of down-home charm, it's a scenic setting of picnic tables positioned over the Essex Salt Marsh. Inside, the full-bellied critters take a dip in egg wash and corn flour and emerge from the friolator with a delicate, crunchy coating. The hot, golden garb dissolves instantaneously on the tongue, releasing a straightforward flavor.

THE GREATEST: Clam Cakes

Harraseeket Lunch $$
Town Landing, 36 Main Street, South Freeport, Maine, (207) 865-4888
At Harraseeket Lunch, the dive bombing seagulls are a testament to the wickedly delicious clam cakes. The tasty, soft patties are constituted from briny bivalve niblets fried into texture-rich cakes. Other house specialties include the hot boiled lobster, breaded fried seafood baskets, and golden onion middles with a light crumb coating. Located right on the town wharf, the seafood shanty even does a darn good dessert course including roly-poly whoopie pies. The BYOB policy contributes to a shockingly inexpensive meal.

THE GREATEST: Clam Strips

Kream 'N Kone $
961 Main St. (Rt. 28), West Dennis, Mass., (508) 394-0808,
www.kreamnkone.com
Kream 'N Kone is a Cape Cod favorite with legendary fried seafood like Phantom's favorite clam strips. Without the messy whole bellies (which some people might not like), all that's left is the neck. They're wonderfully tender, cooked up to a gorgeous 14-karat color with just enough chew. Kream 'N Kone also offers seven kinds of seafood rolls, outstanding onion rings, and 24 flavors of soft serve. Their newly remodeled, air-conditioned location sits right on Swan River.

THE GREATEST: Clam Shack Style

The Clam Box $$
246 High St., Ipswich, Mass., (978) 356-9707,
www.ipswichma.com/clambox
The Clam Box is a counter service shack shaped just like the well-known container used for takeout. Since 1935, they've built a loyal following that guarantees long

lines on hot summer days. But it's worth the wait for a heaping portion of caramel-colored native fried clams that are crispy and crunchy, without any heavy grease. Boxes and plates overflow with fabulous portions of fried seafood and sides of coleslaw, onion rings, and French fries.

THE GREATEST: **Breaded Fried Clams**

Hingham Lobster Pound $$

4 Broad Cove Rd. (Rt. 3A), Hingham, Mass., (781) 749-1984

Once a bait shop, Hingham Lobster Pound is now a take-out clam shack that has Nantasket Beach goers swerving off 3A for their breaded fried clams. Many seafood specialists find flour to be a cheaper, lighter alternative, but the Pound spares no expense to create a second skin of blistering crunch over each briny burst of full-bellied clams. The onion rings crackle with the same fried sensation, and the delicious banana fritters melt in your mouth. Nostalgic pictures of Hingham and Nantasket cover every inch of the ordering galley, and customers can quiz themselves with Trivial Pursuit cards while they wait. Call ahead two hours for steamed lobster.

THE GREATEST: **Upscale Fried Clams**

Red Rock Bistro $$

141 Humphrey St., Swampscott, Mass., (781) 595-1414,
www.redrockbistro.com

Who says fried clams and martinis don't mix?! Red Rock puts an upscale, not-so-greasy twist on the favorite finger food, using sweet Maine bellies. Red Rock still keeps it real, though, serving the piping-hot finger food in a brown paper bag with tartar sauce. The elegant bistro's windows open onto a breathtaking view of the ocean and the Boston skyline across the bay. Live jazz heats things up on the weekends and for Sunday brunch, when challah French toast and Vermont maple syrup take the stage, too.

Healthy
GREAT ATE

When Phantom wants to trim a few feet from his ever-expanding waistline, he refuses to cut out the flavor, too. The truth is eating healthy can be tasty, exciting, and fulfilling. Certain restaurants around town are especially gifted in low-cal cooking. Phantom finds full-flavored nourishment at the 8 GREATEST healthy eateries.

 TASTY TIP If you want to eat healthy in a restaurant, that's fine. Just make like a pot and keep a lid on it; Phantom says that it's unwise to lecture dining companions on the latest fad diet.

THE GREATEST: Bodybuilder's Paradise

KnowFat! Lifestyle Grille $
222 Arsenal St., Watertown, Mass., (617) 923-7676, www.knowfat.com

KnowFat! Lifestyle Grille makes healthy living as simple as (low-carb) pie with fast, affordable food that's grilled, steamed, and wrapped. The owner is a former bodybuilder who understands that you are what you eat, and the dishes here bear out his philosophy. Fat-free marinades give lots of flavor to high-protein dishes like steak tips and chicken meatballs. Plus, the cool juice bar pumps protein into fruit-bursting smoothies. Nutritional info is listed under every menu item and on customer receipts. Other heart-healthy locations include Boston's Downtown Crossing, Shrewsbury, and Woburn.

THE GREATEST: Fruit Bouquet

Edible Arrangements $$
www.ediblearrangements.com

Cross a bouquet of flowers with a bowl of fruit, and you get the hottest new concept in gift-giving. Edible Arrangements improves on the traditional fruit basket by sculpting skewered fruit into intricate floral arrangements. The unique results make tasty gifts for any occasion. Phantom loves the bouquet of chocolate-dipped strawberries. And the signature Delicious Fruit Design incorporates pineapple "daisies," cantaloupe, honeydew, strawberries, and grapes. Customers can add fudge dipping sauce, balloons, or a teddy bear, and every order is made the same day it's needed. Launched in East Haven, Connecticut, Edible Arrangements has quickly expanded to other cities like Brockton, Natick, and Cambridge. Walk-in customers are welcome, but most orders are taken in advance and delivered by refrigerated van.

THE GREATEST: No-Fry Fries

b.good $

131 Dartmouth St., Boston, Mass., (617) 424-5252,
www.bgood.com

This local fast food joint serves surprisingly delicious no-fry fries. Their healthy version of the spud is crisped in the oven rather than dunked in the friolator. The bodacious baked result is a mere 140 calories and four grams of unsaturated fat. In fact, the entire menu sticks to fast food classics everyone loves, while cutting calories by grilling or using other dry heat methods. Burgers, steak bombs, and frozen yogurt shakes are served counter-style in a bright eatery decorated with café tables and paintings by local artists. "Phans" of b.good can also check out their second location on Dunster Street in Harvard Square.

THE GREATEST: Nutritious Fast Food

O'Naturals $

187 Elm Street, Somerville, Mass., (617) 666-2233,
www.onaturals.com

O'Naturals is pioneering a fast food revolution with quick-stop snacks and meals made from all natural, organic ingredients They're also environmentally friendly, with on-site recycling and real silverware rather than the plastic stuff. The earthy atmosphere, leather chairs, and newspapers are inviting, but hurried customers can bank on fast service from the cafeteria-style kitchen. Healthful dishes of the freshest ingredients include flatbread sandwiches and pizzas, spicy peanut salad, five spice noodles, carrot ginger soup, and even dessert. O'Naturals also brings its act to Acton, Massachusetts; Falmouth, Maine; and Portland, Maine.

THE GREATEST: Wholesome Pizza

Veggie Planet $

Club Passim, 47 Palmer St., Cambridge, Mass., (617) 661-1513,
www.veggieplanet.net

Veggie Planet turns out eclectic vegetarian and vegan cooking from a super-fast oven. Meat-free pizza and coconut rice win over the most carnivorous customers with soulful toppings like roasted butternut squash, caramelized onions, goat cheese, and fried sage. The brightly colored, underground café is tiny, attached to the legendary folk music forum, Club Passim. Veggie Planet donates a percentage of sales to nonprofit organizations working for environmental change. For something a little heartier, check out chef/owner Didi's more elaborate dinners held the first Monday of every other month.

The Other Side Cosmic Café $

407 Newbury St., Boston, Mass., (617) 536-9477

The Other Side Cosmic Café has a West Coast feel, with two floors of eclectic art and mismatched furniture. Their ultra-fresh sandwiches are superbly stacked with healthful style. The Buffalo Tom combines fresh mozzarella, basil, prosciutto, and tomato-basil vinaigrette. The Brie sandwich matches imported cheese with sliced apples and pears. Soups and salads are also available, along with fresh fruit and veggie beverages. Phantom feels like such a health nut after sipping the pineapple mint wheatgrass smoothie; it's almost enough to inspire a workout.

THE GREATEST: Juice Bar

Blue Shirt Café $

424 Highland Ave., Somerville, Mass., (617) 629-7641

Blue Shirt Café is the best juice bar around. Their smoothies and juices feature wild combinations from ingredients like red peppers, limes, celery, ginger, pears, mint, guava, and raspberries. They're jolted with boosters like Echinacea, Spirulina, and Vitamin C. Phantom loves the Peaches & Cream and the Peanut Butter Delight. The vegetarian menu also offers whopping sandwiches, wraps, soups, and salads at fair prices. And the colorful, if cramped space has lots of funky personality and artsy tabletops.

THE GREATEST: Healthy To-Go

Whole Foods Market $$

www.wholefoodsmarket.com

When Phantom's in the mood for fast food, but he's looking for farm-fresh quality, there's only one place to go. Whole Foods Market stocks their aisles with gorgeous produce, organic goods, and all-natural groceries. They also have a stunning salad bar, and the in-house kitchen whips up a huge variety of prepared dishes like sushi, seafood, grilled meats, veggies, and sugary desserts. The assortment comes with plenty of hot and cold options, and most locations have a seating area for enjoying it all on the spot.

Hidden Jewels
GREAT ATE

Whether they're tucked away on a discreet corner or they just haven't received proper acclaim in the mainstream food media, Hidden Jewels are waiting to be discovered. The all-knowing Phantom goes super-sleuth to uncover the 8 GREATEST Hidden Jewels.

 TASTY TIP So how does Phantom find all those incredible, edible Hidden Jewels? Most of the time, it's Phantom "Phans" that tip him off! If you have a delicious lead, tell the Caped Critic about it in the FEEDback Forum on www.PhantomGourmet.com.

THE GREATEST: Back-Door Italian

Vinny's at Night $$
76 Broadway, Somerville, Mass., (617) 628-1921
Truly hidden in back of a convenience store (Vinny's Superette), Vinny's at Night is an unadvertised, genuine Italian eatery. The curtained-off space is cozily small with mismatched Tiffany lamps and more Italian customers than you could shake a meatball at. Lots of red sauce and seafood favorites rule the Sicilian menu. The Grand Marnier shrimp are lick-the-plate delicious, just like the double-thick pork chops with sweet peppers. You can also expect a complimentary plate of fruit and a joke from the owner, both of which contribute to the fun, family feel of this unique spot.

THE GREATEST: Mexican Munchies

El Pelón $
92 Peterborough St., Boston, Mass., (617) 262-9090,
www.elpelon.com
El Pelón is a cramped, super-cheap storefront decorated with miniature Mexican dolls and picnic-table seating. Most recipes reflect the northern Mexican style of cooking. While the majority of the food isn't spicy, seven hot sauces and salsas give heat seekers plenty of options. Belly-busting burritos come as a choice of steak, chicken, or pork, and the tortilla is completely stuffed with rice, beans, cheese, lettuce, and fire-roasted salsa. The grilled chicken enchiladas are even better with sassy sides like golden fried plantains, pickled cabbage, or limed onions. If you need to cool off from all the chile peppers, the homemade horchata beverage tastes like liquid rice pudding.

THE GREATEST: Quirky Muffins

Gingerbread Construction Co $

52 Main St., Wakefield, Mass., (781) 246-2200,
www.gingerbreadusa.com

The Gingerbread Construction Co. builds ornamented gingerbread houses for any occasion, but they're best known for baking deliciously decadent muffins. Their 19 innovative flavors include chocolate chip, gingerbread with cream cheese icing, and chocolate raspberry topped with chocolate flakes and chocolate icing. The strawberry shortcake muffin is a summer specialty, enveloping ripe fruit and whipped cream. But Phantom's absolute favorite is the Chocolate Dreme, made by injecting a moist chocolate muffin with luscious chocolate cream. There's a second sugary location in Winchester.

THE GREATEST: Takeout Pizza

Sweet Tomatoes $

47 Langley Rd., Newton Center, Mass., (617) 558-0222,
www.sweettomatoespizza.com

Cooking up a new recipe for pizza, Sweet Tomatoes is THE go-to takeout for discerning diners in Newton Center. Like the funky, nine-seat space, the Neapolitan pies are fun and fresh, served in 14- and 18-inch sizes. Rolled ultra-thin, they're not topped with regular sauce, but a lighter, healthier concoction with a base of uncooked, chopped tomatoes. Regular pies are the norm, but you can also order them "red" (without mozzarella) or "white" (without sauce). A great selection of two dozen toppings includes the usual pepperoni and sausage, plus jalapeño peppers, fresh garlic, artichoke hearts, bacon, and eggplant. Phantom recommends the white shrimp pizza or the Pesto Splash. There's a second suburban location in West Newton.

THE GREATEST: Buffalo Wings

Wendell's Pub $

30 West Main St., Norton, Mass., (508) 285-3829

For almost 20 years, heat-seekers have flocked to unassuming Wendell's Pub for their legendary Buffalo wings. It's a down-and-dirty spot featuring fresh (not frozen!) wings. The skilled kitchen uses a longer deep-fry process than most restaurants, giving an extra-crispy result. The cooks have also perfected the "Wendell Flip," ensuring a proper sauce slather and even distribution over every wing. Heat levels include Sissy, Regular, Half-and-Half, 3.5, Spicy, and Suicidal. "Double Dare" is so hot, it's not even listed on the menu. One-pound orders are so cheap and delicious, this place is a must visit for any wing fanatic.

THE GREATEST: Crazy Cannoli

Wholly Cannoli $

488 Grafton St., Worcester, Mass., (508) 753-0224

With more than 20 flavors, Wholly Cannoli claims to have the largest cannoli assortment on the entire East Coast. The traditional recipe of this Italian pastry has a crispy shell and heavenly sweet ricotta filling. But Wholly Cannoli's true talent comes through in crazy flavors like citrus, peanut butter, pumpkin, and mint chocolate chip. The chocolate amaretto cannoli has a Florentine shell and piña colada filling, and the banana split cannoli is bursting with ripe fruit flavor. Their most explosive offering is the Dynamite Stick, a crunchy chocolate shell fluffed full of rich ricotta infused with gooey caramel.

THE GREATEST: Giant Subs

Dino's $

141 Salem St., Boston, Mass., (617) 227-1991,
www.dinosboston.com

Dino's is THE speedy spot for no-frills feasts in the North End. The 18-seat corner sub shop concentrates on quality and quantity instead of fancy trimmings. Belly-busting 16-inch subs come in hot and cold variations. The Sicilian Steak is topped with mushrooms and tomatoes, and the Chicken Parm sub wears a gooey blend of sauce and melted cheese. The Italian sub is a fat, packed classic of provolone, salami, mortadella, capicola ham, oil, vinegar, and hot peppers. Phantom strongly advises NOT to ask for a half sandwich, and DEFINITELY have your cash ready and in hand. For food this abundant and cheap, you gotta play by their rules.

THE GREATEST: Dining Cart Dogs

Gilley's $

175 Fleet St., Portsmouth, N.H., (603) 431-6343,
www.gilleyspmlunch.com

For deliciously cheap burgers and dogs, Phantom heads to Gilley's. Named after a dedicated employee who stayed on for five decades, this classic Worcester diner car tops the charts with all-American variations like hot dogs, kraut dogs, chili dogs, cheese dogs, cheeseburgers, chiliburgers, hamburgers, and beans and burgers. Seasoned customers know the lingo when ordering. "The Works" means mustard, relish and onion. "Loaded" means "The Works" plus ketchup. Pickles and mayo are also in Gilley's condiment arsenal, and fresh-baked brownies are Phantom's favorite dessert option.

Hot Dog
GREAT ATE

From foot-long franks to cocktail weenies, hot dogs are the official link of American life. Phantom unleashes the mustard and relish at the 8 GREATEST hot dog havens.

TASTY TIP **The best way to "top" a hot dog is to "bottom" it. Place your ketchup, mustard, onions, and relish on the bun, under the link. This technique is a lot neater and provides a truer frank flavor.**

THE GREATEST: Hot Sauce

Flo's Steamed Hot Dogs $
Route 1, Cape Neddick, Maine, no phone

Flo's ranks among the best roadside wieneries in the entire country, serving delectable dogs that can be downed in three bites. Most people should anticipate putting down a minimum of four, as only a "Flo virgin" would order less. Despite the cramped quarters, the low sloping ceiling, and just six wooden stools, the sassy owner can boast of quite a lunch counter community. There's not much to eat here except outstanding hot dogs on silky, steamed buns. Made in-house, the incredible hot sauce is a top-secret blend of barbecue sauce and caramelized onions with a spicy, salty bite that goes well with mayo. Flo's is open for lunch only, every day except Wednesday.

THE GREATEST: Quirky Dogs

Popo's Hot Dogs $
168 Humphrey St., Swampscott, Mass., (781) 592-9992

Popo's has a magical menu of eccentric hot dogs. The tube steaks can be grilled or steamed with a choice of kosher or natural casing, and the rolls are buttered and grilled. Their quirky recipes include the Texas Dog with chili, cheese sauce, sautéed onions, bacon, and jalapeño peppers. The adventurous Thai Dog is a surprisingly successful blend of peanut sauce and sautéed onions, and the Reuben Dog packs in sauerkraut, shredded Swiss cheese, and Russian dressing. Phantom likes to finish it all off with ice cream scooped into an old-fashioned float. The sunny, mustard-colored storefront is framed in North Shore postcards and sailboats trapped in bottles, with a dozen seats lining the counter.

THE GREATEST: Link Variety

Code 10 $
1638 Washington St., Boston, Mass., (617) 375-6333
In a neighborhood where trendy, upscale dining is the norm, Code 10 offers a quick
bite at a cheap price. The name comes from the police lingo for "lunch break," and
the colorful café puts a gourmet spin on the all-American dog. Their vast hot dog
variety includes all-beef Pearl Kountry Klubs, kosher Hebrew National, Rhode Island Reds, turkey dogs, and veggie dogs. The menu heats up with hot pepper Buffalo sausage and chicken-jalapeño sausage. Plus, they offer a large variety of
hard-to-find ketchups and mustards. To top it all off, Code 10 dishes out Ron's
Gourmet Ice Cream and old-fashioned soda fountain drinks.

THE GREATEST: All-Beef Wiener

Spike's Junk Yard Dogs $
108 Brighton Ave., Allston, Mass., (617) 254-7700,
www.spikesjunkyarddogs.com
A junkyard may not be your first stop for culinary creations, but this Allston storefront is a haven for hot dogs. The 100 percent all-beef wieners are a special recipe
made exclusively for Spike's by a fourth-generation German Wurst company. The
quality continues with oversized French rolls baked in-house and seriously inventive toppings. Phantom likes the Texas Ranger, which is loaded with barbecue
sauce, cheddar, and bacon. The Buffalo is slathered with hot sauce, blue cheese,
and scallions, and the German Shepherd piles on sauerkraut and mustard. The top
dog, though, is Spike's original Junkyard Dog, wearing sliced tomato, pickle, mustard, scallions and pepperoncini. The local chain has eight other locations in Rhode
Island.

THE GREATEST: Fenway Frank

Fenway Park $$
4 Yawkey Way, Boston, Mass., (617) 267-8661,
www.redsox.com
Nothing beats a Fenway Frank . . . or the Sox, now that we've won the World Se-
ries. Sure, Fenway Park sells the most overpriced hot dog around, but what other
Boston restaurant can hold 33,000 of your closest friends? The flavorful steamed
links come on a New England–style bun, and they're slathered in mustard and rel-
ish. This winning combination is so scrumptious, it's enough to make the park's
famed Monster turn green with envy. Improving on the Fenway Frank isn't easy,
but a seat on the Budweiser right field roof (complete with tableside service) is like
a celery salt bonus on top—if you can swing it.

THE GREATEST: Dog with "The Works"

George's Coney Island Hot Dogs $
158 Southbridge St., Worcester, Mass., (508) 753-4362,
www.coneyislandlunch.com
From the 60-foot neon hot dog sign to the graffiti walls carved with customer
names, George's Coney Island is a historic hot dog landmark. The art deco design
features wooden booths, tile floors, and a stool-lined counter. Since 1918, they've
been grilling pork-and-beef wieners, served in steamed buns. The links are small
and tasty, with the perfect blend of sweet and spicy. The most popular Coney Island
"Up" is a hot dog with "the works," including mustard, secret recipe chili sauce,
and chopped onions.

THE GREATEST: Gourmet Toppings

Top Dog of Rockport $
2 Doyles Cove Rd., Rockport, Mass., (978) 546-0006,
www.topdogrockport.com
Top Dog, in the seacoast village of Rockport, is a tasty little shack that serves
plump, juicy wieners with condiment pizzazz. The comfy wood-lined joint is cozy
and rustic with a great view of the water. The menu lists more than a dozen hot dog
creations that come grilled or steamed, but always loaded with sloppy toppings like
coleslaw, Vidalia onion and carrot relish, bacon, jalapeño peppers, and Boston
baked beans. On the side, the Onion Brick is a condensed loaf of scrumptious fried
onion strings that makes for a fun peel-away treat.

THE GREATEST: Dessert Dog

Papa Jim's Exotic Hot Dogs $
344 School St., Winchendon, Mass., (978) 297-1751
Papa Jim's Exotic Hot Dogs is a roadside shanty sporting candy cane stripes and
mini hot dog plaques depicting the menu. The eye-catching name is well deserved,
given the 40 wild wiener selections in outlandish combinations. For example, the
Ranch Dog is stuffed with a squirt of creamy dressing, along with carrots, celery,
peppers, and onions, while the Love Dog is an intoxicating assembly of horseradish, mustard, red peppers, and Cheese Whiz. The Skunk Dog goes boldly
where no dog has gone before, combining peanut butter, chocolate, and marshmallow Fluff; once you get over the initial shock, the sweet-salty contrast is rather
tasty. If you're into spicy challenges, try to top the latest record in Volcano Dog
consumption.

Hotel
GREAT ATE

Hotel restaurants get a bad rap as overpriced tourist traps, but many of Boston's hottest dining destinations are just a bellhop away. Phantom checks in at the 8 GREATEST hotel dining rooms.

TASTY TIP **Want that chic hotel dining experience without the monster bill? You can enjoy the same stylish atmosphere for the mere price of a cocktail at the bar. Bar menus also offer less expensive dishes from the same haute cuisine kitchen.**

THE GREATEST: Stylish Seafood

Great Bay $$$
Hotel Commonwealth, 500 Commonwealth Ave., Boston, Mass.,
(617) 532-5300, www.greatbayrestaurant.com
At the very hip Great Bay in Hotel Commonwealth, well-heeled diners are surrounded by a rusty-colored décor like the belly of a salmon. The citrus backlit bar, blue scale lighting, and colorful sea anemone above add to the underwater theme. Spilling the ocean's bounty, the ceviche island offers tuna tartare and spicy halibut tacos. The modern seafood menu also features lemongrass lobster poached in tarragon butter. Phantom suggests finishing with ultra smooth butterscotch pudding and caramelized pecans.

THE GREATEST: Luxury Menu

Azure $$$
Lenox Hotel, 61 Exeter St., Boston, Mass., (617) 933-4800,
www.azureboston.com
Azure in the Lenox Hotel is a high-society scene with a clubby atmosphere and a mixed clientele of young revelers and distinguished older patrons. Lounge music and velvet chairs fill the tall space, in addition to glowing curtains and handblown glass chandeliers. The boldly different menu balances seafood and fine meats with exotic ingredients. If you're ready to walk on Chef Robert Fathman's wild side, open your mind and your mouth to Oysters in Potato Bondage or flat iron steak with avocado mousse and orange-chipotle sauce.

THE GREATEST: Modern Extravagance

Spire   **$$$**
Nine Zero Hotel, 90 Tremont St., Boston, Mass., (617) 772-0202,
www.spirerestaurant.com
Spire is an intoxicatingly beautiful space in the plush and polished Nine Zero Ho-
tel. The dashing dining room makes a material statement with bamboo, black gran-
ite floors, and lustrous curtains hanging from the ceiling. The elite atmosphere
extends to the glass bar, which is almost visible from the dining room through a
hazy panel of glass. The fine European cuisine makes use of lots of New England
seafood, which is plated in modern, provocative poses. Phantom loves the kobe
beef shooters and the halibut beet tartare with caviar and dashi broth.

THE GREATEST: Mediterranean Fare

Rialto   **$$$**
Charles Hotel, 1 Bennett Street, Cambridge, Mass., (617) 661-5050,
www.rialto-restaurant.com
As the famed chef/owner of Rialto in the Charles Hotel, Jodie Adams turns to
France, Italy, Spain, and even North Africa for inspiration in creating her seasonal
menus. The upscale homey ambiance of oversized floor lamps and dark shutters
spills into a beautifully tiled open kitchen. Phantom likes to sink into a plush, burnt-
orange banquette, sip a big Californian cabernet, and savor complex dishes like
buckwheat polenta fondue with leeks, caramelized pears, and fried sage leaves.
This is low-key dining at its delicious best.

THE GREATEST: Daring Design

Bambara   **$$**
Hotel Marlowe, 25 Edwin H. Land Blvd., Cambridge, Mass., (617) 868-4444,
www.bambara-cambridge.com
Bambara in the bold Hotel Marlowe is a modern, wraparound space with striking
geometric shapes. The red backlit bar is surrounded by two levels of banquette
seating. Eclectic American cuisine dominates the menu, which particularly show-
cases New England ingredients. Phantom loves the Atlantic bouillabaisse and the
braised veal shank with Vermont mascarpone ravioli. Pairing wines has never been
less intimidating, thanks to the easy-to-navigate list organized by light and heavy
selections. Bambara's Wine Rewards Program includes a wine card for keeping
track of your selections and offers a $10 discount on a bottle of wine on a subse-
quent visit.

THE GREATEST: Cutting-Edge Cuisine

Clio $$$
Eliot Suite Hotel, 370 Commonwealth Ave., Boston, Mass., (617) 536-7200,
www.cliorestaurant.com

In the Eliot Suite Hotel, Clio's understated elegance and extreme cuisine make for
a special dining occasion. Blanched walls, a lattice ceiling, and leopard-skin carpets create a romantic, uptown setting for a downtown clientele. The bold creations
of chef/owner Ken Oringer flaunt Asian and European influence with palate-
challenging ingenuity. There's lemon lacquered foie gras with bee pollen, sea
urchin cassolette, and muscovy duck with black radish confit. Dessert includes
chicory ice cream with salted caramel. Downstairs, Uni is a den-like sashimi bar
that pairs exclusive selections with a dozen fine sakes.

THE GREATEST: Dessert Cart

Beacon Hill Bistro $$$
Beacon Hill Hotel, 25 Charles St., Boston, Mass., (617) 723-7575,
www.beaconhillhotel.com

The Beacon Hill Bistro is a true neighborhood eatery with reasonable prices, good
food, and a comfortable atmosphere. Paned glass allows Charles Street passersby
to steal a look inside the handsome space, which features tuxedo-tiled floors and
dark wood trim. Blackboards announce the daily specials of seasonal French fare
and fish entrées. Escargot, roast quail, and steak frites all make their presence felt.
Phantom always saves room for the dessert cart, tiered with delicate berry tarts,
crème brûlée, and fallen chocolate cake.

THE GREATEST: Cocktail Lounge

Cuffs $$
Jurys Boston Hotel, 350 Stuart St., Boston, Mass., (617) 532-3828

It's hard to imagine a jail as a hot spot for socializing, but Cuffs in the Jurys Boston
Hotel is just that. As the city's former police headquarters, the renovated hotel
fashions its Irish roots into a popular destination where night owls come just for
cocktails. They work the "behind bars" theme by displaying billy clubs and vintage
riot gear throughout the beautiful bar, which revolves around a toasty fireplace and
flatscreen TVs. The space is highly social with quiet, shadowy nooks and twin pa-
tios for sky-lit imbibing. Cuffs is always good for a proper pint, and the upscale bar
food includes pesto chicken flatbread and blackened angus burgers.

Ice Cream
GREAT ATE

Ice cream has a worldwide following, but nowhere are frappes, mix-ins, and cones quite as good as they are in New England. Not even a brain freeze could deter Phantom from the 8 GREATEST ice cream parlors.

TASTY TIP Vanilla is a flavor, just like chocolate or strawberry. "Plain" ice cream is actually "sweet cream," and purists sample it to determine the underlying quality and craft.

THE GREATEST: Ice Cream Playground

Kimball Farm $
400 Littleton Rd., Westford, Mass., (978) 486-3891,
www.kimballfarm.com

Families flock to Kimball Farm for outstanding ice cream and an entire day of entertainment. Their massive property includes farm animals, a driving range, and a country store. There's minigolf with full-sized working waterfalls and a 6,000-square-foot bumper boat pond. Ice cream lovers line up at the barn windows and choose from 40 intriguing flavors like gingersnap molasses, Grapenut, Kahlúa crunch, and moo tracks. Check out other locations in Carlisle, Massachusetts; Saco, Maine; and Jaffrey, New Hampshire.

THE GREATEST: Farm-Fresh Ice Cream

Richardson's Ice Cream $
156 South Main St. (Rt. 114), Middleton, Mass., (978) 774-5450,
www.richardsonsicecream.com

At Richardson's the secret to the premium ice cream is the freshness of the milk and cream, which come straight from the cows out back. Smooth, scrumptious flavors range from caramel flan to chocolate cheesecake. Customers can lick away at their cones while visiting the sheep, ducks, and 300 cows on the farm. Plus, there's a recreation complex with batting cages, miniature golf, and a heated driving range. If you can't make it to the dairy bar, check out the Richardson's counter at Jordan's Furniture in Reading.

THE GREATEST: Exotic Flavors

Christina's Ice Cream $
1255 Cambridge St., Cambridge, Mass., (617) 492-7021
Christina's caters to the adventurous, sophisticated ice cream palate with more than 40 insanely inventive flavors, inspired by their sister spice shop next door. Basics like Mexican chocolate and garden fresh mint are utterly amazing, but Phantom goes for the exotic cardamom, Japanese adzuki bean, lemon thyme, burnt sugar, white chocolate lavender, saffron, and carrot cake. The creamy texture comes from an outstanding 14 percent butterfat content. Sorbets step into uncharted territory like lemon hibiscus or champagne. The charming décor includes antique church pews and local art. Christina's also concocts exclusive flavors for area restaurants, like goat cheese ice cream for Hamersley's Bistro and black sesame for Ginza.

THE GREATEST: Ice Cream and Bowling

Ron's Gourmet Ice Cream and 20th Century Bowling $
1231 Hyde Park Ave., Hyde Park, Mass., (617) 364-5274
www.ronsicecream.com
Ron's Gourmet Ice Cream and 20th Century Bowling is one of the few places where bowlers can recover from a 7-10 split with a banana split. The most unusual marriage of freezer treats and candlepins makes for a family-friendly outing. The snack bar serves ice cream and sundaes with high-quality ingredients. Freshly baked brownies are mixed into the famous brownie nut ice cream, and coffee madness is jammed with bits of Oreo, chocolate chips, and almonds. Peanut sunrise is made with real peanut butter swirled into a vanilla base.

THE GREATEST: Ice Cream Pyramid

Cabot's $
743 Washington St., Newton, Mass., (617) 964-9200,
www.cabots.com
Cabot's mind-boggling menu compiles a massive 70-plus flavor list (using Richardson's ice cream) along with frozen yogurt and 30 different toppings. Custom creations can be piped inside a puff pastry shell, served over Belgian waffles, or packed into a banana split. The magical malt shop practically overflows with ice cream sodas, frappes, freezes, floats, and parfaits. Their biggest belly-buster is the 60-pint Great Pyramid Sundae made with 12 quarts of toppings, marshmallow, nuts, and cherries. Served like a buffet, it feeds nearly 200 people.

THE GREATEST: Oversized Scoops

Hodgie's $
71 Haverhill Rd, Amesbury, Mass., (978) 388-1211
When it comes to humungous helpings, Hodgie's knows how to pile on the monstrous scoops. Their version of the kiddie cone challenges even Phantom's insatiable appetite. The flavors are tried and true, like chunky peanut butter cup and refreshingly peppermint. Other ice cream options include fresh fruit frappes, seductive sundaes, and fresh strawberry shortcake. Helpful local students shuffle steadily behind the counter, and picnic tables in a woodsy area out back allow for lingering while you lick. In addition to ice cream, Hodgie's serves hot dogs, hamburgers, and sandwiches.

THE GREATEST: Ice Cream for Ice Cream Snobs

PICCO $$
513 Tremont St., Boston, Mass., (617) 927-0066
PICCO (Pizza & Ice Cream COmpany) churns out handmade ice cream in small batches with expensive, gourmet ingredients. Exquisite flavors include Scharffen Berger chocolate, Kona coffee, and Madagascar vanilla bean. Sundaes sink into classic parfait dishes with extra-tall spoons and just-whipped cream. You can even order an old-fashioned float from the soda fountain. The retro décor evokes an old-school ice cream parlor and includes cherry-colored chairs and trailing votives. If you're looking for savory (not sweet), try an upscale pizza finessed with toppings like bacon, onion, sour cream, and Gruyère.

THE GREATEST: Mix-Ins

Cold Stone Creamery $
www.coldstonecreamery.com
At Cold Stone Creamery customers choose their flavor and mix-ins and watch on as the staff smooshes it all together on a slab of frozen granite. The super-premium ice cream is made every day, along with chocolatey brownies and crunchy waffle cones. On the menu, they offer a dozen smooth, creamy ice creams, plus 40 mix-ins like Kit Kat, Snickers, Heath Bar, and Butterfinger. Or, opt for a Cold Stone original like birthday cake remix made with cake batter ice cream, brownies, rainbow sprinkles, and fudge. Locations include Boston's Theater District and the Landmark Center.

 # Italian
GREAT ATE

When Phantom craves a no-fuss Italian feast with rustic pasta and red wine, it's all about the classics. Phantom fills up on meatballs and marinara at the 8 GREATEST old-school Italian eateries.

 TASTY TIP **To eat like a true Italian, order a pasta course (primi) between the antipasti and the entrée (secondi). Restaurants are usually happy to halve their pasta portions, so this three-course tradition won't weigh you down.**

THE GREATEST: Panini

Domenic's Italian Bakery And Deli $$
987 Main St., Waltham, Mass., (781) 899-3817

Domenic's Italian Bakery and Deli sells the best freshly baked Italian bread, transformed into fabulous panini sandwiches, like the Parma ham stuffed with mozzarella, tomato, and basil. The bread is lightly misted with olive oil and grilled so that the cheese melts and the insides are warm. Domenic's also features hearty soups, homemade pasta, calzones, Sicilian-style pizza, and crackly cannoli. The hopping take-out operation has a few tables, but most action happens across the counter.

THE GREATEST: Mix & Match Menu

Giacomo's $$
355 Hanover St., Boston, Mass., (617) 523-9026

Giacomo's is a tiny trattoria with wonderfully simple, straightforward Italian food. Lines form outside early in the evening, and customers are rushed in and out of the charming, crowded little eatery. A huge chalkboard menu covers one brick wall, with daily specials on the other side of the room. The concept is refreshingly basic; customers mix and match a dish of fresh seafood, pasta, and a choice of five flavorful sauces. Phantom recommends sticking to classics, like huge plates of linguine marinara laced with succulent shellfish. There's a second, more spacious Giacomo's in the South End.

THE GREATEST: Veal Selection

Carlo's Cucina Italiana $$
131 Brighton Ave., Allston, Mass., (617) 254-9759
At Carlo's Cucina Italiana, white meat is their strong suit. Most preparations come
with a choice of veal or chicken, served in heaping helpings that Phantom finds per-
fect for sharing. The minimalist décor is far from glamorous, but the lengthy red
sauce menu is reason enough to put up with sitting elbow-to-elbow. House special-
ties include stuffed eggplant, fusilli with sausage and broccoli raab, and veal rolled
with prosciutto, spinach, and Fontina cheese.

THE GREATEST: Wood Oven Italian

Campania $$$
504 Main St., Waltham, Mass., (781) 894-4280
Campania has entrancing romantic appeal and heartwarming, country atmosphere
with antique cupboards, buttery walls, and a copper pot kitchen. Old-world, wood-
oven cuisine includes crusty peasant bread, seafood, tender braised meats, and fish
that's deboned and filleted tableside. Phantom especially swoons for the hearty potato gnocchi with white truffle oil and a treasure trove of woodsy wild mushrooms.
For dessert, the hot chocolate soufflé harbors a steamy, gooey interior, and it's
served with vanilla bean gelato.

THE GREATEST: Eggplant Parm

Angelo's Civita Farnese $$
141 Atwells Ave., Providence, R.I., (401) 621-8171
For three quarters of a century, Angelo's Civita Farnese has served homestyle Ital-
ian classics at incredibly low prices. Their eggplant parm is out of this world, but
Phantom also goes for yummy Southern Italian fare like spaghetti and meatballs,
tripe, or veal Parmigiana. Communal seating at formica tables is less than sexy, but
service is quick and portions are huge. Where else can customers wet their whistle
with respectable wine by the jug?

THE GREATEST: Southern Italian

Paolo's Trattoria $$
251 Main St., Charlestown, Mass., (617) 242-7229,
www.paolosboston.com
Paolo's Trattoria serves southern Italian cuisine in a charming neighborhood eatery.
A large blue-tiled wood-burning stove adds to the rustic atmosphere. The Mediterranean menu draws from regions in France, Greece, and Italy. Gorgeous locally

grown produce teams with imported ingredients to achieve crowd-pleasing success. Phantom loves the stuffed roasted red bell pepper filled with goat cheese, eggplant, and basil. The uniquely topped Rosa Pizza is wood-grilled and topped with herbs and crushed pistachios.

THE GREATEST: Italian Hideaway

Saporito's Florence Club Café $$

11 Rockland Circle, Hull, Mass., (781) 925-3023,
www.saporitoscafe.com

Stowed away on a South Shore peninsula, Saporito's is Phantom's idea of a secret neighborhood joint. The unremarkable cottage exterior hides a charming little restaurant with creative Italian cooking. Intimate tables and wooden pews give the homey space a romantic atmosphere, with a vine-entangled trellis running the length of the ceiling and a four-seat wine bar at the back. The upscale Italian menu lists homemade pasta, rustic hot pots, and elegant entrées sprinkled with just-picked herbs from the garden. Phantom usually opts for the pizzetta of the day, topped with combinations like caramelized onions and mozzarella. The spaghetti in plum tomato sauce is also quite tasty, infused with basil, rosemary, and oregano.

THE GREATEST: Sicilian Steal

Galleria Umberto $

289 Hanover St., Boston, Mass., (617) 227-5709

Galleria Umberto is hit hard during lunch hours (it's not open for dinner). The doors of the cafeteria-style eatery stay open until the Sicilian food runs out. So go early for the best selection of calzones. Rectangular slices of cheese pizza come on a thick, chewy crust, and deep-fried rice balls hide a cache of peas and gravy. The price is right, with every item costing less than $4, and tiny Dixie cups of table wine are perfect for the honest fare.

Late-Night
GREAT ATE

Boston restaurants are notorious for closing early, but a new crop of savvy chefs are stoking the fires for the after-hours crowd. Phantom gets his second wind at the 8 GREATEST late-night spots.

TASTY TIP When Phantom's burning the midnight oil, he likes a cup of coffee. Other "stimulating" foods to stay wide-eyed and as sharp as cheddar include bacon, cheese, chocolate, Chinese food, eggplant, sauerkraut, sausage, and tomatoes.

THE GREATEST: Round-the-Clock Diner

South Street Diner $
178 Kneeland St. Boston, Mass., (617) 350-0028,
www.southstreetdiner.com

South Street Diner is a 1950s greasy spoon with neon lights, an old-fashioned jukebox, and vintage photos of James Dean. A colorful, atypical diner crowd filters in 24 hours a day, 7 days a week, and the tattooed servers are spunky. Cheap diner dishes include burgers, banana-stuffed French toast, onion rings, and a solid selection of pie. Beer and coffee are also on the list, along with extra-thick frappes. In warm weather, they even put a few raised tables on the sidewalk for moonlit dining.

THE GREATEST: Wine Bar Open Late

Les Zygomates $$$
129 South St., Boston, Mass., (617) 542-5108,
www.winebar.com

Les Zygomates is a wonderfully inviting bistro and wine bar where customers unwind with live jazz and blues (there's never a cover!) until 1 a.m. There's a stylish zinc bar and a candlelit dining room. No matter where you sit, you'll be served French fare like steak frites topped with truffled foie gras butter. The affordable wine list highlights 75 selections by the glass, also available in two-ounce pours. The three-course prix fixe menu is a steal, and Wine Tasting Tuesdays are a great avenue for varietal exploration.

THE GREATEST: Full Menu Into the Morning

Franklin Café $$
278 Shawmut Ave., Boston, Mass., (617) 350-0010

Franklin Café is a cozy martini boite where hobnobbing scenesters and off-duty chefs order from a full menu until 1:30 a.m. The cranberry-colored room has just nine tables, and a boutique bar gives the space cosmopolitan flair. There's a no-reservations policy, but the wait will fly by as you contemplate a bling bling cocktail, like the pear-infused Franklin sidecar. On the menu, designer comfort food includes turkey meat loaf with fig gravy or seared scallops with coconut curry cauliflower puree.

THE GREATEST: After-Dark Delivery

News $$
150 Kneeland St., Boston, Mass., (617) 426-NEWS,
www.newsboston.com

News is a hot spot for clubbers, and late at night the wide-eyed party hoppers stop by to refuel. Delivery lasts until 5 a.m., but Phantom suggests making a cameo before the 4 a.m. closing; you can get nachos, smoothies, late-night breakfast standbys, and specialties from the sushi bar. Newspapers and magazines fill the front hall, but techno trance and fabulous martinis draw diners into a sit-down scene of comfy leather couches, free Web access, and flatscreen TVs.

THE GREATEST: Cocktail Cuisine

Pho Republique $$
1415 Washington St., Boston, Mass., (617) 262-0005,
www.phorepublique.net

So the service isn't exactly smooth and the food is not Chinatown cheap, but Pho Republique is a happening South End spot serving hot Asian fusion. The sultry after-dark chamber is primed for action, with bamboo chairs and rainbow lanterns contained in rouge walls. The kitchen keeps kicking until 1 a.m., and dishes of dim sum, pineapple kung pao chicken, Thai curry, and pho noodle soup get better with every cocktail. Phantom's favorite jazzed-up drinks are the coconut martinis, Indochine punch, and gigantic scorpion bowls.

THE GREATEST: 24/7 Bakery

Bova's Bakery $
134 Salem St., Boston, Mass., (617) 523-5601,
www.northendboston.com/bovabakery
Early risers and night owls alike can eat on the cheap at Bova's Bakery. Open 24
hours, 7 days a week, Bova's counters overflow with everything you'd ever want
from an Italian bakery: Italian loaves, ricotta cannoli, tiramisu, fruit tarts, Neopoli-
tans, cream puffs, whoopie pies, and sfogliatelle. They also make mean oversized
subs, Sicilian pizza, and calzones. Phantom's favorite is a foot-long baguette lined
with prosciutto, buffalo mozzarella, whole basil leaves, tomatoes, and balsamic
vinaigrette. Bova's is takeout only.

THE GREATEST: Breakfast All Day (and Night)

Friendly Toast $$
121 Congress St., Portsmouth, N.H., (603) 430-2154
Open 24 hours on weekends, Friendly Toast is an all-time breakfast favorite with
fresh vegetarian options, too. The eclectic eatery is full of flea market finds,'50s
kitsch, and the best collection of bad art north of Manhattan's East Village. It's a
funky feast for both the eyes and the stomach, serving greasy spoon goodies with a
sophisticated twist. Phantom is nuts about the Almond Joy Pancakes and the Green
Eggs & Ham on anadama toast. The huge menu also includes wildly delicious din-
ner fare like sweet potato Orleans fries topped with brown sugar, Tabasco, and sour
cream.

THE GREATEST: Midnight Munchies on Wheels

Haven Brothers Diner $
72 Spruce St. Providence, R.I., (401) 861-7777
Haven Brothers in Providence is a mobile stainless-steel diner on wheels. Every
evening it rolls into City Hall around 5 p.m. and plugs into an electric outlet that
fires up the grill until 4 a.m. Politicians and professionals stop by on their way
home, followed by partygoers looking for a late-night nosh. Phantom loves the All-
The-Way Dogs (mustard, onions, relish, and celery salt), bacon cheeseburgers, and
chili cheese fries. The outrageously messy Murder Burger is a double-decker piled
high with cheese, chili, bacon, mushrooms, onions, lettuce, tomatoes, and mayon-
naise.

Latin & Caribbean
GREAT ATE

The vibrant Latin countries from the Caribbean to Central and South America bring spice to our lives and our palates. When Phantom is on the hunt for exotic flavors and lively rhythms, he salsas over to one of the 8 GREATEST Latin & Caribbean eateries up North.

TASTY TIP If you can't stand the heat, get out of the Caribbean kitchen. Spicy foods cool the body down naturally, which is why most spicy cuisines come from hot countries like Mexico, India, and China.

THE GREATEST: Rodizio

Midwest Grill $$
1122 Cambridge St., Cambridge, Mass., (617) 354-7536,
www.midwestgrill.com
The Midwest Grill is a meat lover's protein paradise with a rodizio-style bottomless pit of Brazilian meats and sausages. The all-you-can-eat buffet of salads, rice, beans, and potatoes is supplemented by servers who skip from table to table with swords of just-grilled meat. Customers unload as much lamb, pork tenderloin, sirloin, and chicken hearts as they can stomach. The wood-on-brick décor is casually pleasant, and live music adds to the authentic festivity.

THE GREATEST: Venezuelan

La Casa de Pedro $$
51 Main St., Watertown, Mass., (617) 923-8025,
www.lacasadepedro.com
At La Casa de Pedro, the clay-colored walls and tropical paintings are complemented by Latin music and an open kitchen run by Venezuelan cooks. Native dishes mix European spices with exotic fruits, lots of cilantro, and Caribbean root vegetables like yucca. Snack-sized empanadas have a sweet corn crust, filled with chicken, beef, cheese, or black beans. Phantom's favorite is the paella with shellfish, chicken, chorizo, and tender fried squid atop saffron rice. Try the flan, which is a top-notch custard, jammed with coconut and finished with a perfect caramelized top.

THE GREATEST: **Dominican**

Merengue   **$$**
156-160 Blue Hill Ave., Boston, Mass., (617) 445-5403,
www.merenguerestaurant.com
Merengue serves up traditional Dominican cuisine, which consists of fried meat,
grilled seafood, rice, and beans. Phantom loves the fried cassava sticks, coconut red
snapper, and tres leches cake. He also recommends ordering a freshly squeezed
juice like orange, lemonade, or passion fruit. The crowd is largely Dominican (a
great indication of authenticity), and a swirl of island colors like watermelon pink
and eye-popping blue on the walls is set off with whirling propeller fans and slate-
tiled floors.

THE GREATEST: **Tropical Drinks**

Bomboa   **$$$**
35 Stanhope St., Boston, Mass., (617) 236-6363,
www.bomboa.com
The French-Brazilian Bomboa is known for its sexy salsa rhythms and flashy food.
The Latin theme pours over from behind the zinc bar, where cool tropical drinks include the white rum mojito, the lime caipirinha, paradise punch, and the pomegran-
ate martini poured over an edible orchid. When you start seeing colors, it's not
from one too many drinks; it's just the mood-lit bar, cycling through different hues
of the rainbow. Exotic entrées include mahimahi wrapped with plantains. On the
appetizer side, oxtail & peanut pot stickers and calamari tempura make a succulent
start. The room has an urban lounge vibe, decorated in vibrant color splashes, rich
fabrics, and even an aquarium.

THE GREATEST: **Peruvian-Italian Fusion**

Taranta   **$$$**
210 Hanover St., Boston, Mass., (617) 720-0052,
www.tarantarist.com
The North End is almost exclusively known for its pasta and pizza, but Taranta
takes a delicious detour by fusing Peruvian and Italian flavors into one exquisite
cuisine. It's a fascinating marriage of hot-sweet chili infusions and Mediterranean
fare, full of seafood, spice, pasta, and root vegetables. Phantom's favorite is the
brined pork chop with a sugarcane-rocoto red pepper glaze, caramelized onions,
and a yucca cake. The saffron butter basted trout is just as exotic, served with giant
Peruvian corn. There are rustic exposed brick walls and curved velour banquettes,
and terra cotta dishes come straight from the oven to the tiny linen-covered tables.

THE GREATEST: Cuban Fusion

Chez Henri $$$
One Shepard St., Cambridge, Mass., (617) 354-8980,
www.chezhenri.com

Chez Henri is a sultry bistro that's caught among four worlds: Harvard and Porter
Squares (physically) and France and Cuba (thematically). The fusion menu gives
familiar dishes a fresh identity. Grilled tuna teams with a lime-chile glaze; smoked
pork ribs wear guava BBQ sauce; and seared mahimahi is dressed in spicy citrus
ginger. The casual setting is relaxed but flirtatious, with low lighting, deep red col-
oring, and bright still lifes painted by Chef Paul O'Connell's wife. On the bar side,
the cubano sandwich with roasted veggies is one of Phantom's favorite plates.

THE GREATEST: Argentinean

Tango $$
464 Massachusetts Ave., Arlington, Mass., (781) 443-9000,
www.tangoarlington.com

Brightly decorated with sunshine yellow patches and exposed brick, Tango is a
cozy, intimate space with outstanding Argentinean food. The authentic menu favors beef, beef, and more beef, with lots of grilled cuts cooked up in Latin flavors.
Chimichurri sauce is as common in Argentina as ketchup is in the states, and
Tango's version is quite tasty and tangy. The thick herb mélange mixes olive oil,
vinegar, minced parsley, oregano, onion, and garlic. It's a perfectly light pair with
the flank steak or the fried fillet.

THE GREATEST: Brazilian

Café Brazil $$
421 Cambridge St., Allston, Mass., (617) 789-5980,
www.cafebrazilrestaurant.com

Covering the mural walls of Café Brazil, a beachy Rio scene has a transporting ef-
fect, along with bossa nova tunes and cheap, hearty food. The specialties of the
house are meat, meat, and more meat! After digging into links of linguica sausage,
continue your high-protein outing with grilled pork, sirloin steak, or chicken thighs.
For a balanced meal, add on some fried plantains, black beans, and rice. Café
Brazil also offers passion fruit mousse and coconut pudding with plum caramel. To
drink, try Brazil's national soda, Guarana.

Lobster
GREAT ATE

Seafood lovers from all over the world journey to New England for sweet, succulent lobster straight out of the Atlantic. The green stuff inside the lobster is called tomalley, and it's a delicacy that can be eaten alone or used to enrich and thicken sauces. Give it a try! Phantom ties on his purple bib and cracks through the 8 GREATEST lobster shacks.

 TASTY TIP If you like tail meat, ask for a female lobster. If you like the claws, order a male. And if you just don't care, order a lobster roll.

THE GREATEST: Lobster Picnic

Chauncey Creek Lobster Pier $$
16 Chauncey Creek Rd., Kittery Point, Maine, (207) 439-1030, www.chaunceycreek.com
Chauncey Creek Lobster Pier is a rare find that combines scenic outdoor picnicking with New England clambake cuisine. Customers can even supplement the meal by bringing extra sides, wine, or beer. Crayola-colored tables line the deck, which juts out over the glittering waters of Kittery Point, Maine. Chauncey Creek is worth the trouble for the ambiance alone, but the awesome food rounds out the experience. When you're ready to order, head to the seafood shack to choose from a classic menu of boiled lobster, lobster rolls, steamers, chowder, and even raw bar offerings.

THE GREATEST: Gigantic Lobster Roll

Raw Bar $$
252 Shore Dr., Mashpee, Mass., (508) 539-4858, www.therawbar.com
The Raw Bar serves a killer lobster roll that's so gigantic, it has to be eaten with a knife and fork. The no-frills sandwich forgoes lettuce and celery. Nothing but huge chunks of sweet lobster meat and mayonnaise are piled onto a roll with a big ice cream scoop. Other oversized offerings include the lobster feed bag of steamed lobster, chowder, steamers, kielbasa, and hot buttered corn on the cob. The modest bar setting can get rowdy, so Phantom likes to chill out with a frozen mudslide.

THE GREATEST: **Oversized Lobster**

Lobster Pot $$
3155 Cranberry Highway, East Wareham, Mass., (508) 759-3876

The Lobster Pot is a rustic Cape Cod favorite with a spacious dining room of big wooden booths and fun fisherman décor. They take special orders for fresh lobsters up to 20 whopping pounds, and the budget-friendly menu also includes fried, baked, and broiled fruits of the sea. Phantom suggests tacking on some golden fried onion rings, too. Home cooks can stop by the adjoining fish market for the fresh catch of the day.

THE GREATEST: **Surf & Turf**

Palm Restaurant $$$
200 Dartmouth St., the Westin Copley Plaza, Boston, Mass.,
(617) 867-9292,
www.thepalm.com

Uniting the best of both worlds, the Palm turns out Phantom's favorite surf & turf. Defying conventions, the Palm roasts its Nova Scotia beauties, which are a minimum of three gargantuan pounds. The special preparation makes the meat difficult to separate from the shell, but the resulting taste is a rare succulent sensation. This Italian seafood steakhouse also makes a mean filet mignon. Every location of this nationwide family chain embraces a local personality with cartoons and caricature paintings of the areas politicians and celebrities.

THE GREATEST: **Pan-Roasted Lobster**

Jasper White's Summer Shack $$
149 Alewife Brook Pkwy., Cambridge, Mass., (617) 520-9500,
www.summershackrestaurant.com

Jasper White's Summer Shack is a casual clam shack with Phantom's favorite pan-roasted lobster. Cooked in bourbon and doused in melted butter with chervil and chives, this is the most decadent dish in town! In other incredible renditions, the lobster is wood-grilled, shrimp-stuffed, and wok-seared with scallions and ginger. The vibe here is fun and playful, with Chinese lanterns and 300 seats. Don't worry about how they'll feed all those guests; the huge industrial kitchen works to capacity with a 1,200 gallon lobster tank. There's also a smaller Shack in Boston's Back Bay, a speedy Shack at Logan Airport, and a giant Shack at Mohegan Sun in Connecticut.

THE GREATEST: Lobster Plain & Simple

Roy Moore Lobster Co. $$
39 Bearskin Neck, Rockport, Mass., (978) 546-6696
Roy Moore Lobster Co. is Phantom's favorite place for wallet-friendly lobster
served simply. This place is actually not a restaurant at all, but a seafood market
that also boils lobsters on request, using ocean water to seal in a naturally briny fla-
vor. Customers can even sit out back on lobster traps while cracking open the
claws. For those leaving town, Roy Moore will package live lobsters with seaweed
and gel ice in an airplane-safe carton that keeps them fresh for 30 hours.

THE GREATEST: Boiled Lobster

Ogunquit Lobster Pound $$
Route 1, Ogunquit, Maine, (207) 646-2516
Ogunquit Lobster Pound has a 20-year following for the best boiled lobster on the
eastern seaboard. Their secret procedure involves boiling the speckled crustaceans
outside in a big pot of seawater. So many are prepared at once that the lobsters actually cook in their own juices, producing extra intensity of flavor. The Lobster
Pound also cuts and cracks the clawed kings for you, making the succulent meal a
snap to eat without the sticky, briny mess. Their fruit-filled pies are a great dessert
if you can save room for the extra course.

THE GREATEST: All-You-Can-Eat Lobster

Nordic Lodge $$$
178 East Pasquisset Trail, Charlestown, R.I., (401) 783-4515,
www.nordic-lodge.com
The Nordic Lodge is home of the legendary Giant Viking Buffet. For $65 per per-
son, the all-you-can-eat blowout features high-end foods like shrimp, scallops,
prime rib, and lobster, lobster, lobster! The average customer (amazingly) cracks
into a half-dozen hard bodies in a single sitting. There's also a fried food bar, a raw
bar, and for those who don't quit, a Häagen-Dazs ice cream bar. Every eater is al-
lotted two hours of uninterrupted mealtime, and the ban on doggy bags is strictly
enforced.

Mexican
GREAT ATE

Technically, New England is not south of the border. But several Mexican food masters up North put a potent hot pepper spell on the plate. Recently, Mexican food has been on the rise all over the food scene, and Greater Boston is embracing the exciting flavors. Phantom salutes the 8 GREAT-EST Mexican restaurants.

TASTY TIP Dairy (milk or yogurt) helps cut the spiciness if you overdose on mouth-burning chili peppers. Those without the hotter-than-heck spice tolerance of Phantom's palette should steer clear of the pepper's interior veins and seeds, where the heat is concentrated.

THE GREATEST: Flan

Tu Y Yo $$
858 Broadway, Somerville, Mass., (617) 623-5411,
www.tuyyomexicanfonda.com

Tu Y Yo near Tufts isn't terribly scenic, but it is authentic, which is why you won't find chips, burritos, and especially not nachos. The menu is filled with family recipes spanning 100-plus years, like stuffed jalapeños, sopes, flautas, tamales, and Phantom's favorite dessert flan. Prepared "a la Doris," by an 80-something-year-old family friend, the incredible caramel custard is decked out in tangy cinnamon cream. A cobalt-tiled bar adds a touch of personality, and prices are even afford-able enough for undergrads.

THE GREATEST: Mexican Seafood

Salsa's $$
118 Dorchester St., South Boston, Mass., (617) 269-7878,
www.salsas-mexicangrill.com

South Boston isn't exactly known for Mexican cuisine, but Salsa's is proving that it's not all corned beef and cabbage down there. The owner is Fenway's famed Sausage Guy, but the chef hails from Cuernavaca, not far from Mexico City. She's particularly skilled with seafood dishes like garlic shrimp with mango salsa, pineapple-grilled sea bass, and sizzling shrimp fajitas. Every meal kicks off with chips and salsa, which does the restaurant name proud with a spicy-hot garden recipe full of cumin and cilantro. The salsa-colored dining room is decked out in piñatas and sombreros. There's a second location in Hingham.

THE GREATEST: Mexican Takeout

Ándale! $
125 Summer St., Boston, Mass., (617) 737-2820

Ándale! is a busy take-out joint cranking out real Mexican food like chicken mole made from 27 spices. Phantom also likes the charbroiled beef with peppers and onions, the meaty portobello enchiladas, and the shredded chicken burrito that incorporates orange, tomato, and chile sauce. Open Monday through Friday for lunch only, the small eight-seat space is surprisingly big on atmosphere. Clay-colored walls, Mexican artifacts, and rhythmic Latin music all add up to a take-out shop you won't want to leave.

THE GREATEST: Sangria

Casa Romero $$
30 Gloucester St., Boston, Mass., (617) 536-4341,
www.casaromero.com

Casa Romero is a hidden gold mine of romantic atmosphere, traditional Mexican cooking, and cool margaritas. Accessible by an alleyway entrance, it's decked out with imported ceramic tiles from Puebla and tin lamps; there's also a secluded outdoor patio. Casa Romero's killer sangria is a sparkling red wine beverage that's steeped for a few days in brandy and fresh fruit, including lemons, peaches, and apples. On the menu, try specialties like lemony pozole stew or pork tenderloin with oranges and smoked chipotle peppers.

THE GREATEST: Salsa Selection

Picante Mexican Grill $
735 Massachusetts Ave., Cambridge, Mass., (617) 576-6394,
www.picantemex.com

Picante Mexican Grill is a tiny taqueria with Boston's best salsa selection. Customers stock up at the salsa bar on a half-dozen red and green concoctions that range in heat, smokiness, and spice. There's Yankee salsa with roasted tomatoes, smoky chipotle salsa, avocado salsa, mango salsa, super-hot picante salsa, and fresh grilled jalapeño peppers. Daily specials keep the selections unpredictably interesting, and extra efforts like grilling the burritos add additional flavor and texture. Picante prides itself on health-conscious cooking with secret spice blends instead of lard, and they're also vegan and vegetarian-friendly with options like portobello tacos and breakfast burritos..

THE GREATEST: **Margaritas & Munchies**

Jose's Mexican Restaurant $$

131 Sherman St., North Cambridge, Mass., (617) 354-0335,
www.josesmexicanrestaurant.com

Hidden in the less traveled streets of North Cambridge (near Fresh Pond), Jose's draws a rice and beans kind of crowd with free parking and fiesta flavor. They stock an amazing selection of 32 tequilas by the shot, plus 10 bottled beers from Mexico. You'll have no problem picking out the colorful three-story building from the street, and the sombreros and gem-toned walls give the energetic cantina a wide-awake atmosphere. On the menu, they offer big plates for small bills. You have to sort through Americanized salsa wings and "Mexican" pizzas, but if you skip to the crispy tacos, flattened tostadas, and stuffed chili relleno, you'll be in a mariachi mood in no time.

THE GREATEST: **Guacamole**

Olé Mexican Grill $$

11 Springfield St., Cambridge, Mass., (617) 492-4495,
www.olegrill.com

Olé Mexican Grill in Inman Square serves regional dishes from Veracruz, Oaxaca, and Mexico City. Phantom loves their oversized, premium tequila margaritas and the area's absolute best guacamole en molcajete. Prepared tableside, the awesome appetizer is mashed up in a lava rock mortar with sea salt, onion, tomato, lime, jalapeños, and even the seeds if you can stand the heat. Sunday brunch is equally festive, and the attention turns to enchiladas smothered in cheese, huevos rancheros (eggs over beans and tortillas), and Mexican steak & eggs. This spot is a cozy, casual space done in bright, blazing colors and beautiful tiles.

THE GREATEST: **Tortas**

Taqueria Mexico $

24 Charles St., Waltham, Mass., (781) 893-2205 or (781) 647-0166

The family-run Taqueria Mexico has modest digs brightened with sombreros, and all-Mexican tunes play on the jukebox. The winning combination of dirt-cheap and delicious food starts with chips and salsa or mountainous nachos piled high with cheese, refried beans, lettuce, tomato, onion, and jalapeños. Other favorites include chicken enchiladas and chorizo burritos. Taqueria Mexico's amazing Mexican sandwiches, or tortas, fill a sweet, delicious roll with any number of grilled meats and seafood. To ease the heat from the spicy dishes, they serve blended fruit drinks and horchada, a dairy-free rice drink spiced with cinnamon and almonds.

Outdoor Dining
GREAT ATE

Perfect weather might make you think of the beach, golfing, or gardening, but Phantom's idea of fun in the sun is al fresco eating. Phantom busts out his purple shades at the 8 GREATEST outdoor restaurants.

TASTY TIP Oftentimes there's a surcharge for dining outdoors, but it's worth the splurge if you coincide your meal with the sunset.

THE GREATEST: Snacks & Swimming

Roof Top Pool $$$
Colonnade Hotel, 120 Huntington Ave., Boston, Mass., (617) 424-7000, www.rooftoppool.com
There's nothing quite like sipping a frozen daiquiri in your bathing suit while taking in a sunset view of the Boston skyline. Twelve stories above the noise, hustle, and stress of the city, the Roof Top Pool on the Colonnade Hotel is a secret oasis of sun and fun. From Memorial Day to Labor Day, it's the ultimate office escape. The waiters double as lifeguards, serving up cocktails, frosty beers, and light lunches like coconut shrimp. There's also a lobster-crab martini and a tasty blue cheese burger. The utopian experience does come at a price. Admission is free for hotel guests but $40 per person for the visiting public.

THE GREATEST: Island Dining

Rockmore $$
94 Wharf St., Salem, Mass., (978) 740-1001, www.rockmore.us
The Rockmore offers the unusual experience of eating on the water. The restaurant is snuggled amongst the boats in beautiful Salem Harbor, completely surrounded by water—the Rockmore is buoyed by a system of floating tanks; there's an on-board kitchen and a full bar. It's only accessible by water, so customers can motor up and tie off or take the shuttle over from the mainland. The seafood-rich menu includes a tasty lobster roll and a fisherman's platter piled high with fried morsels. Landlubbers can chow down on bacon burgers and turkey rollups.

THE GREATEST: Rooftop Dining

Fiore $$
250 Hanover St., Boston, Mass., (617) 371-1176,
www.ristorantefiore.com

Dining in the North End is always special; dining on a North End rooftop is paradise. Fiore is one of the biggest restaurants in Boston's Little Italy, and it's one of the only restaurants in the city with rooftop dining. Take advantage of the full liquor license for a cocktail before ordering an Italian Pinot Grigio to complement a light and airy pizza. The strength of the menu is in the seafood, like the swordfish with garlic and white wine or the homemade pasta with lobster and shrimp in vodka sauce. After dinner, head across Hanover Street to Modern Pastry for the best cannoli in the neighborhood.

THE GREATEST: Moonlight, Waterfront Dining

Intrigue Café $$
Boston Harbor Hotel, 70 Rowes Wharf, Boston, Mass., (617) 439-7000,
www.bhh.com/intrigue.cfm

Intrigue Café has premium harbor-front seating, with tables that spill onto the sidewalk. Tucked away behind the Boston Harbor Hotel, the lounge eatery is just 20 feet from the bobbing yachts tied off at Rowes Wharf. Inside the glass doors, the café is a comfy setting of straight-backed chairs, mismatched fabrics, and relaxing couches. The global menu disregards conventional mealtimes, serving breakfast at sundown and dinner all day. Every bargain-priced dish comes out of the same kitchen as Meritage, the posh restaurant upstairs. Elegant entrées include the Regal Meatloaf, roasted lobster with corn pudding, and butternut squash sage ravioli.

THE GREATEST: Harbor-Side Seafood

Barking Crab $$
88 Sleeper St., Boston, Mass., (617) 426-2722,
www.barkingcrab.com

If you're looking for top-notch seafood, head to Great Bay, Legal Sea Foods, or Neptune Oyster. But if it's waterside dining and imbibing you want, The Barking Crab is perfect. The tent-covered, open-air deck is lined with picnic tables and draws a rambunctious crowd. The Fort Point channel view of the Financial District is grand, and it's perfectly relaxed for winding down after work. Stick to basics like peel & eat shrimp or fish & chips. The Barking Crab does a decent job with the traditional New England clambake.

THE GREATEST: **Pasta on the Patio**

Via Matta   **$$$**
79 Park Plaza, Boston, Mass., (617) 422-0008,
www.viamattarestaurant.com
Star chef Michael Schlow gets crazily experimental at Radius, but Via Matta is his
venue for whipping up Italian food he'd serve you at his house (although eating
here is a lot more expensive). The outdoor patio is ideal for al fresco noshing, but
there's also a wine bar, a late-night café, and an elegant dining room done in mo-
saic tiles and antique iron gates. The menu covers the regional cuisines from Pied-
mont to Tuscany with standouts like seared sea bass and fettuccine with sweet and
sour peppers. For an extra treat, diners can sit at the chef's table in the kitchen and
watch Schlow at work.

THE GREATEST: **People Watching**

Plaza III   **$$$**
101 South Market, Boston, Mass., (617) 720-5570
Plaza III has tasty Prime grade beef flown in from Kansas City, but the real reason
to eat here is the corner seat outside. As the crossroads of the North End, the Financial District, and Government Center, it's THE Faneuil Hall hot spot for people
watching. Inside, the fun Western atmosphere includes mounted trophies, a massive plastic steer, and cowboy art. The "menu" is wheeled to the table so customers
can choose from a visual presentation of corn-fed beef, thick chops, and seafood.
The meaty steak soup is their signature starter, and steaks are aged in their
temperature-controlled beef locker for extreme tenderness and exceptional flavor.

THE GREATEST: **Sidewalk Seating**

Armani Café   **$$$**
214 Newbury St., Boston, Mass., (617) 437-0909
Newbury Street is home to Boston's most beautiful people. If they're not eating at
Armani Café, then they're sure to walk by on the way to Stephanie's, Sonsie, or a
dozen other eateries nearby. Next to the Armani clothing store, the café's interior
lighting is so dim that it's tough to read the designer labels worn by the young, Eu-
ropean crowd. On the Italian menu, you'll find hardy pastas, fish, and mostly white
meat. The diet-sized crowd seems to pass on dessert, but Phantom can't resist their
tiramisu soaked with rum and espresso. This kind of choice sidewalk seating is just
where you want to be on a beautiful summer night.

Pasta
GREAT ATE

The Mysterious Critic has four good reasons for curbing the low-carb diet: spaghetti, macaroni, gnocchi, and rigatoni. Phantom gets his fill at the 8 GREATEST pasta joints.

TASTY TIP Fresh pasta is made with eggs instead of water, so it's much richer and more flavorful than the dried variety. It also cooks a heck of a lot faster, which means you'll be eating soon after you place your order.

THE GREATEST: Red Sauce Pasta

Bambino's $$
7 Highland Ave., Malden, Mass., (781) 322-9160,
www.bambinosrestaurante.com

Bambino's is a Phantom favorite for red sauce pasta, loaded with plum tomatoes and whole basil leaves. The two room restaurant is family friendly, dominated by a 17-foot mural of a Venice canal. Classic old-school dishes include baked stuffed shells, tortellini Alfredo, gnocchi Bolognese, and fettuccine carbonara. For an extra-special entrée, try the lobster fra diavolo with tender sea scallops in spicy marinara sauce. Bambino's signature dish is the robust Tuscan salad. It comes in three sizes, as a hardy ensemble of romaine lettuce, Italian meats, cheese, roasted potatoes, garlic, and peppers, dressed in balsamic vinaigrette.

THE GREATEST: Ravioli

Costantino's Venda Ravioli $
265 Atwells Ave., Providence, R.I., (401) 421-9105,
www.vendaravioli.com

Costantino's Venda Ravioli is an Italian food emporium that's a deli, a café, and a specialty store all under one roof. Their homemade pasta selection includes 250 varieties in fresh and frozen assortments. Ravioli are the specialty of the kitchen, stuffed with gourmet ingredients like lobster, spinach, basil, and ricotta. Phantom also flips for their tri-color cheese tortellini and the agnolotti with pine nuts, basil, and cheese. A huge four-sided deli case dominates the room, packed with cold cuts, butchered meats, an astounding assortment of olives, and 100 different cheeses. Venda serves lunch every afternoon at tables spread out around the store.

THE GREATEST: Northern-Style Pasta

La Morra $$
48 Boylston St., Brookline Village, Mass., 617-739-0007,
www.lamorra.com

La Morra takes the (risotto) cake as one of the area's best northern Italian kitchens with Tuscan-style wood grilled fare. Rice, polenta, and beans are the staples, but tagliatelle is the scrumptious, signature pasta. Wide noodle ribbons weave into savory ensembles like veal ragu, tomatoes, and vermouth. Before arriving at antipasti, the menu kicks off with tiny Venetian-style snacks like fried sage leaves and anchovy, stuffed olives, or salt cod. The two-level trattoria is completely cozy and rustic with an inviting bar downstairs and a wood-beamed ceiling.

THE GREATEST: Pasta to Go

Bottega Fiorentina $
313B Harvard St., Brookline, Mass., (617) 232-2661,
www.bottegabrookline.com

Bottega Fiorentina serves Florentine cuisine, using more cream than tomatoes. Pasta selections change daily, but sautéed penne Fedora always tops the list. It's a sumptuous pink sauce made with rosemary, garlic, tomato, and a touch of cream. For a more portable meal, there's grilled focaccia or awesome sandwiches stuffed with prosciutto, soppressata, mozzarella, roasted peppers, and olive oil. A lone communal picnic table is the only seating option, so customers can share the space and make new friends or get it to go. In addition to the Coolidge Corner location, there's a second Bottega Fiorentina in Brookline Village.

THE GREATEST: Lunchtime Pasta

Sorriso $$
107 South St., Boston, Mass., (617) 259-1560,
www.sorrisoboston.com

With an effervescent bar scene, Sorriso is an after-work magnet for the Downtown crowd. True to all the press, their brick-oven thin-crust pizzas are awesome. Cooked right in the dining room, they're available for home delivery, too. But the lunch and dinner pastas are equally incredible. Peas and porcini mushrooms enrich the lobster risotto, and the ear-shaped orrechiette gets a garlicky, green topping of pesto, tomatoes, and yummy rock shrimp. The arresting atmosphere includes a slate bar, burlap curtains, and masterpiece murals painted on the brick walls. If you're more in the mood for all things French, head next door to their sister wine bar, Les Zygomates.

THE GREATEST: Family-Style Pasta

Maggiano's Little Italy $$
4 Columbus Avenue, Boston, Mass., (617) 542-3456,
www.maggianos.com

Maggiano's Little Italy is an enthusiastic Italian chain with red checkered table-cloths and family portraits all over the walls. It's contagiously fun and friendly with endless seating and lots of old-world charm. Classic Italian-American dishes make up the menu, and there's a family-style banquet for groups of four or more. Half portions are available, too, but Phantom likes to rally the troops for family-style plates of gnocchi in vodka sauce, linguini with clams, and spaghetti with meatballs. Other house specialties include fried calamari, veal Parmesan, and chicken piccata. The gigantic portions are so monstrous, you'll be singing Sinatra all the way home (doggy bag in hand).

THE GREATEST: Linguine Selections

Delfino $$
754 South St., Roslindale, Mass., (617) 327-8359,
www.delfinorestaurant.com

Delfino is a neighborhood eatery with fragrant garlic wafting from the open kitchen. The Italian menu has the familiar chicken and veal Parm, plus unexpected dishes like open-faced lobster ravioli. Phantom is particularly impressed with their dress-up options for the house specialty, linguine. Customers choose their seafood component from a list of calamari, mussels, shrimp, scallops, or all of the above plus an entire lobster. Then there's a selection of sauce: red, pesto, spicy fra diablo, garlicky white, or pink (marinara and béchamel). If you can't decide, go with the linguine Puttanesca (capers, anchovies, olives, and plum tomato sauce). Phantom also adores their exceptional fried calamari, tossed with potato strings, greens, and Champagne vinaigrette.

THE GREATEST: Pasta Portions

Tomasso Trattoria & Enoteca $$
154 Turnpike Rd./Rte. 9, Southborough, Mass., (508) 481-8484,
www.tomassotrattoria.com

Most Italian restaurants in America serve gigantic mounds of starchy pasta, but Tomasso plates their homemade noodles the traditional way, as a manageable second course before the entrée. This way you can order more plates without erupting like Mount Vesuvius. Phantom's pick is the orechietti with sausage and broccoli rabe. Tomasso is also outstanding for its small antipasti plates like chickpea fries and ricotta meatballs. The hand-picked wine list and quick, professional service are just the parmigiano on top. Plus, you'll still have room for dolci desserts like free-form tiramisu and rustic fruit tarts. All of the above is served in a stylish space with a huge bar and counter seats along the open kitchen.

Pizza
GREAT ATE

Italy (the motherland) has authentic ingredients; Chicago invented deep-dish; and New York perfects the flop and fold. But in Boston, you can find all these styles in one city. Phantom cuts into superior slices at the 8 GREATEST pizzerias.

TASTY TIP **The best way to reheat leftover pizza is on a pizza stone in a 500-degree oven, but when Phantom is in a hurry, he skips the microwave, which results in a soggy crust, and pops it in the toaster oven or a dry skillet, stovetop. And when he's really hungry, he just eats it cold.**

THE GREATEST: Cheese Pizza

Pizzeria Regina $
11½ Thacher St., Boston, Mass., (617) 227-0765,
www.pizzeriaregina.com

Pizzeria Regina is THE North End destination to get thin-crust Neapolitan pizza cooked in a piping-hot, 103-year-old brick oven. A special blend of high-butterfat cheese results in glimmering oil across the top, just the way Italians like it. Phantom is particularly fond of the Quatro Formaggio blend of whole-milk mozzarella, ricotta, Pecorino Romano, and Parmesan, which also boasts a hefty dose of garlic. Marinara-colored floor tiles, wooden booths, and mustard-colored walls jive with the old school atmosphere. There are additional locations at Faneuil Hall, the Pru, South Station, and the Burlington Mall, but none compares to the original.

THE GREATEST: Slice & Salad Combo

Upper Crust $
20 Charles St., Boston, Mass., (617) 723-9600,
www.theuppercrustpizzeria.com

The Upper Crust turns out fantastic thin-crust pizza in imaginative combinations. Communal dining and counter service make this pizzeria perfect for grabbing a slice, and the metal wave ceiling gives the space a hip industrial atmosphere. The menu focuses on Neapolitan-style pies with 30 topping choices and inspiring pre-conceived pies. Phantom digs the vegetarian MGH pie with broccoli, spinach, and feta and the Beacon Hill pizza topped with sundried tomatoes and eggplant. Phantom likes to swing in for lunch and get their $5 combo, which includes one slice of the day and a Greek salad. There's a second location in Coolidge Corner, Brookline.

THE GREATEST: Old School Pies

Santarpio's Pizza $
111 Chelsea St., East Boston, Mass., (617) 567-9871
Santarpio's is a grimy pizza shop with feisty waiters who don't mind yelling at anyone in their way. It's a dive, and that's exactly the charm of the place. Plus, they make the most classic, old-school pies around. The crust is a perfect balance of chewy crispness, and traditional toppings don't stray far from pepperoni, mushrooms, and onions. The only appetizer on the menu is barbecued lamb and sausage, served piping hot with Italian bread and cherry peppers. If you can take your eyes off the pizza pies, there's quite a collection of autographed boxing pictures hanging above the ripped vinyl benches and Formica tables.

THE GREATEST: Grilled Pizza

Cambridge, 1 $$
27 Church St, Cambridge, Mass., (617) 576-1111
Transformed from a former Harvard Square firehouse, Cambridge, 1, is a raw, urban space with elevated slate booths and exposed pipes. The limited menu concentrates on gourmet salads and sensational chargrilled, ultra-thin-crust pies. High-end toppings include roasted red peppers, Gorgonzola, rosemary, portobello mushrooms, fontina, and caramelized onions. Microbrews and flatscreen TVs occupy everyone's attention at the bar, and the only dessert on the menu is Toscanini's tiramisu ice cream.

THE GREATEST: Cheeseburger Pizza

Big City $$
138 Brighton Avenue, Allston, Mass., (617) 782-2020,
www.allstonsfinest.com
Big City is a restaurant, bar, and pool hall that serves outrageous beer-infused pizzas to accompany 83 beers on tap. The paper-thin, free-form pies come in three color categories: Red, White, and Green. The Red use tomato-based sauces; the White stick to cheese or creamy sauces; and the Green are made from pesto or finished off with field greens. The most popular choice is the cheeseburger pizza with pickles, lettuce, American cheese and shoestring fries! Big City also makes dessert pizzas like the sweet 3 Berry Cherry Cheesecake Pie. The atmosphere incorporates city-themed décor and 20 championship-sized pool tables upstairs.

THE GREATEST: Gourmet Toppings

Emma's Pizza $
40 Hampshire St., Cambridge, Mass., (617) 864-8534,
www.emmaspizza.com
Emma's serves up a double threat of great (if unusual) toppings and brittle, crispy-as-a-cracker crust. The experimental menu lists three dozen toppings comprised of the basics (garlic, green peppers), the gourmet (thyme-roasted mushrooms, rosemary sauce), and the absolutely bizarre (sweet potato, dried cranberries). After starting with the Famous Fling Salad (Gorgonzola, Granny Smith apples), you can move on to the main course of layered pizzas with hot smoked sausage, calamata olives, and caramelized onions. The charming space is packed with pastel chairs tucked into wooden tables. Phantom likes to make a night of it by catching a flick at the nearby Kendall Square Cinema.

THE GREATEST: Exotic Pizza

Pizza Oggi $
131 Broad St., Boston, Mass., (617) 345-0022,
www.pizzaoggi.com
Pizza Oggi's off-the-hook pizza pies start with light, fluffy dough that's brushed with oil, sesame seeds, and onion flakes. The sauce is homemade, the crust is crispy, and all of the toppings receive extra attention through marinating, roasting, or smoking. Even the plain cheese goes above and beyond with the addition of roasted garlic. If that's too simple, just add wild mushrooms, truffle oil, and fresh lobster. Phantom savors the goat cheese pizza with toasted almonds and cherry tomatoes, but the most popular pie is the Hawaiian with roasted pineapple, smoked ham, and scallions. For a truly unique combination, sink into a sweet-savory pizza topped with roasted peaches and prosciutto.

THE GREATEST: Bar Pie

Lynwood Café $
320 Center Street, Randolph, Mass., (781) 963-9894
If you're looking for gourmet cuisine and a romantic dining room, DON'T go to the Lynwood Café. If you want a simple slice of heavenly pizza with old-school atmosphere, this IS your place! The high energy watering hole has a serious collection of Budweiser décor and antique arcade games. The pizza menu is far from fancy, focusing on single-serving 10-inch bar pies that have a stiff, greasy crunch of a buttery crust. Pepperoni is a tasty classic, but for something unusually delicious, try the salty-sweet Bean Pie topped with diced salami and Boston baked beans.

Romantic Dining
GREAT ATE

Whether you're sparking a new romance or rekindling an old flame, all relationships should start with a great meal. Phantom salutes 8 GREATEST romantic restaurants.

Valentine's Day is the restaurant industry's busiest night of the year. The dining rooms have to be reconfigured to accommodate tables for two, and the kitchen offers simplified versions of the regular menu so they can crank out food more efficiently. To avoid the hubbub Phantom recommends making dinner reservations the day before or after Valentine's Day.

THE GREATEST: Gypsy Lair

Dali $$
415 Washington St., Somerville, Mass., (617) 661-3254,
www.dalirestaurant.com
Dali has an exotic, eclectic atmosphere of seduction. The dimly lit space is set with copper ceilings, sexy Latin music, recessed alcoves with beaded curtains, and a happening bar decked out in flea market finds. Fruit-infused sangria pairs magically with Spanish tapas like roast duckling in berry sauce or fried cheese over caramelized onions and honey. Phantom swoons for the signature striped bass baked in a blanket of coarse salt.

THE GREATEST: Quiet Escape

Marco Cucina Romana $$
253 Hanover St., 2nd floor, Boston, Mass., (617) 742-1276,
www.marcoboston.com
Making a quiet escape on the North End's main drag seems as likely as Phantom scoring a date in the first place, but this second-floor hideaway is well above the street hustle. The rustic interior features wood beams, brick walls, and hardwood floors. Chef Marc Orfally has shown us fierce French fare at Pigalle, but this latest venture crosses the border into homestyle Italian. Big bowls of unfussy pasta and house-cured salumi reflect authentic regional roots with occasional Orfally flair. Menu highlights include gnocchi with brown butter and sage, veal osso buco, and fried polenta. Most couples slink off to a candlelit corner, but singles can look for love at the stool-lined food bar along the open kitchen.

THE GREATEST: **Exclusive Dining**

Newburyport Lighthouse $$$
61½ Water St., Newburyport, Mass., (800) 727-BEAM
For the ultimate romantic dinner, the Newburyport Lighthouse provides a unique private dining experience. Guests ascend 55 steps and settle in for a BYOB night of panoramic scenery and a spectacular multi-course meal. Five of the town's top restaurants offer their cooking services, including the Black Cow and Blue Water Café. Reservations are required months in advance for the season (April to December). A worthy splurge of $350 per couple covers the food with tip and secures the lighthouse for the entire evening.

THE GREATEST: **Italian Amore**

Il Capriccio $$$
888 Main St., Waltham, Mass., (781) 894-2234
Il Capriccio serves contemporary Northern Italian cuisine, which translates to polenta, beans, sausage, and rice dishes like lobster risotto. The food is superbly rich and hearty, with Phantom favorites like the Parmesan porcini soufflé and spiced shrimp with roasted tomatoes. The knockout 20-page wine list runs deep with full-bodied reds from Tuscany and Piedmont, which the owners handpick on their many trips to Italy. Earth tones dominate the restaurant's color scheme, and desserts like the lemon blueberry trifle and the chocolate hazelnut torte are perfectly paired with a flute of sweet, sparkling Asti.

THE GREATEST: **Skyline Dining**

Top of the Hub $$$
Prudential Center, Boston, Mass., (617) 536-1775,
www.prudentialcenter.com/dine/topofthehub.html
The Top of the Hub greets diners on the 52nd floor of the Prudential Center, where sophistication, live jazz, and the Boston skyline make for a spectacular, memorable meal. The mouthwatering menu of exciting New American dishes is just as moving as the setting sun in the distance. Culinary standouts include the spicy lobster soup in lemongrass, ginger coconut broth. And for dessert, there's the fantastic cookie plate of piping-hot, baked-to-order medallions, served with cinnamon whipped cream and fresh berries.

THE GREATEST: Rustic Escape

Red Lion Inn $$$
71 South Main St., Cohasset, Mass., (781) 383-1704,
www.redlioninn1704.com
The Red Lion Inn rekindles romance in its country French setting of low, wood-beamed ceilings, candelabras, and crackling brick fireplaces in each of their four dimly lit rooms. A glass-encased European kitchen is framed in stacks of copper pots, and the New England menu offers a great variety of native seafood. Favorites include the steamed Prince Edward Island mussels in luscious lemon cream sauce and the classic clam chowder jammed with hearty potatoes, celery, onions, and meaty shellfish.

THE GREATEST: Wine & Dine

Icarus $$$
3 Appleton St., Boston, Mass., (617) 426-1790,
www.icarusrestaurant.com
Icarus is a bi-level restaurant with exquisitely dim lighting and the finest of fine dining. The distinguished atmosphere includes eclectic art featuring a statue of Icarus himself, making the illustrious venue perfect for a milestone celebration. The contemporary menu emphasizes locally grown produce, which finds its way into dishes like the signature grilled shrimp with mango jalapeño sorbet. Couples fall in love all over again with the $18 chocolate molten soufflé cake with raspberry sauce and vanilla bean ice cream.

THE GREATEST: Exotic Atmosphere

Tangierino $$$
83 Main St., Charlestown, Mass., (617) 242-6009,
www.tangierino.com
Tangierino is a lavish date place with exotic North African flavor. The dark, luxurious space is a sensual feast for the eyes with velvet seating and ornate hanging lamps. And every evening there's belly dancing, in and around the tables. Red draperies give some of the low couches a little privacy, and the annexed Casbah Lounge is a plush hookah den. The Moroccan menu favors olive oil, grains, and fruit, which result in sweet-savory dishes. Phantom recommends any of the traditional tagines; presented in a cone-shaped clay dish that gently cooks the contents, they're often propped up on a bed of feathery couscous. The falling-off-the-bone Tagine of Mrouzia features succulent braised lamb shank with honey, dried plums, and toasted almonds.

Sandwiches
GREAT ATE

Boston is a city on the go, and no meal is more portable than one that's stuffed between two slices of bread. Whether you prefer your crust intact or removed, quality and quantity of ingredients are equally important. Pre-made sandwiches can be delicious, but watch out for tomatoes, which can make it soggy. Phantom slathers on the mayo at the 8 GREATEST sandwich shops.

TASTY TIP Try ordering your next sandwich "Phantom Style." That means piled up with double meat, double cheese, and potato chips stacked inside the bread for a little extra crunch.

THE GREATEST: Roast Beef Sandwich

Kelly's Roast Beef $
410 Revere Beach Blvd., Revere, Mass., (781) 284-9129,
www.kellysroastbeef.com
Kelly's Roast Beef has Revere beachgoers lining up at a dozen take-out windows for the "original roast beef sandwich." Rosy choice beef gets sliced thin and piled into a grilled poppy seed roll with super-sloppy condiments like mayo and barbecue sauce. Somewhere between the sun, the sand, and the fearless seagulls, this local legend finds its fast food niche. The rest of the menu builds around a New England repertoire of burgers, fried seafood, and quarter-pound lobster rolls. Additional locations include Danvers, Saugus, and Natick.

THE GREATEST: Italian Sandwich

Tutto Italiano $$
1893 River St., Hyde Park, Mass., (617) 361-4700
Tutto Italiano is an authentic Italian delicatessen selling pasta, fragrant olive oils, sundried tomatoes, and all things Italian. Customers head to this "salute of the Boot" for wine tastings on Saturdays and custom-made sandwiches. While there's no set menu, any cold cut combination with freshly baked bread is available on request. Classic toppings include oil, vinegar, oregano, hot peppers, tomato, and basil, and they even make the mozzarella in-house. Additional outposts are located in Wellesley, Lakeville, Hingham, and Boston's North End.

THE GREATEST: **Cheese Steak**

Moogy's $
154 Chestnut Hill Ave., Brighton, Mass., (617) 254-8114,
www.moogys.com
Moogy's is a funky storefront where college kids grab some grub, challenge each
other to board games, and relax with a beer. It's no place for health nuts, but Phantom loves their extensive menu of authentic Philly cheese steaks. The basic version
consists of two kinds of beef with provolone and American cheese. But the Caped
Critic's favorite is undoubtedly the Phantom Royal with Cheese, packed with onion
rings and BBQ sauce. If it's variety you crave, order up one of their dozen chicken
steaks or try their all-day breakfast.

THE GREATEST: **Celebrity Chef Sandwiches**

Parish Café $$
361 Boylston St., Boston, Mass., (617) 247-4777,
www.parishcafe.com
At the Parish Café, sandwiches are named after the city's hottest chefs. All the
recipes are submitted by the stars themselves so it's possible to eat their top-notch
cuisine at a fraction of the price. The most popular is the Cottonwood Café zuni
roll with turkey, bacon, and dill havarti cheese rolled into a flour tortilla. Chris
Schlesinger of East Coast Grill designed a banana nut bread standout piled with
smoked ham and mango chutney. Parish is artsy with sidewalk seating and a
snaking bar serving more than 60 different beers.

THE GREATEST: **Chilean Sandwich**

Chacarero $
426 Washington St., Boston, Mass., (617) 542-0392,
www.chacarero.com
Chacarero is not only the name of this tiny take-out counter in Downtown Cross-
ing, but it's also the only item on the menu: a cheap Chilean sandwich. The con-
tents are deliciously simple, including grilled chicken or beef, plush round bread,
Muenster cheese, tomato, roasted red peppers, avocado spread, hot sauce, and
steamed green beans. The homemade hot sauce comes in two grades of intensity,
and while the green beans are an unexpected addition, they add garden crunch and
color. There's usually a very long line, but some sandwiches are worth the wait.
Just a couple blocks away, the Province Street location opens for breakfast, too, and
the spacious digs allow for sit-down enjoyment.

THE GREATEST: Quirky Sandwiches

Darwin's Limited $

148 Mt. Auburn St., Cambridge, Mass., (617) 354-5233

Darwin's Limited is a word-of-mouth find with quirky general store atmosphere, artsy sandwiches, and the fastest sandwich makers this side of the Charles. The adjoining room is painted in sunset colors with endearing coffee shop character. A chalkboard menu uses Harvard Square street names to identify the tantalizing creations, which are packed with imported meats and cheeses. Phantom loves the delectably messy Mount Auburn with smoked turkey, Swiss, avocado, mayo, vinaigrette, and tomato. And the Ash piles on roast beef, sprouts, and decadent triple cream Boursin cheese on olive bread. A second location on the other side of Harvard's campus (Cambridge Street) also offers free wireless Internet access.

THE GREATEST: Corned Beef

Michael's Deli $

256 Harvard St., Brookline, Mass., (617) 738-3354

Michael's Deli is a hole-in-the-wall sandwich king serving superior cold cuts and unbelievable corned beef. The menu may not be kosher, but Jewish deli items are imported daily from the Big Apple. If you can stray from the potato knishes and genuine New York bagels, dig into gargantuan sandwiches that cost next to nothing. Try the prime rib and beef brisket with horseradish sauce or the Thanksgiving sandwich of warm turkey breast, tangy cranberry, and super-soft stuffing between plush whole wheat slices.

THE GREATEST: Fresh Baked Breads

G.H. Bent Co $

7 Pleasant St., Milton, Mass, (617) 698-5945,
www.bentscookiefactory.com

The G.H. Bent Company is well known for hardtack crackers, which they've made since the Civil War. But it's their sandwiches that'll go down in Phantom's history book. The Wildcat Club is a triple decker of turkey breast, ham, Muenster, bacon, honey Dijon, and mayo on toasted sourdough. The Blue Hills sandwich is a vegetarian feast of Jack cheese, avocado, sprouts, tomato salad, and buttermilk dressing on cornmeal and molasses bread. Those who like to tinker can mix and match several meats, cheeses, garnishes, and breads.

Seafood
GREAT ATE

Most New England restaurants just drop anchor out back for seafood that's "off the hook" fresh. Phantom goes fishing for the 8 GREATEST seafood eateries.

TASTY TIP Phantom recommends trying seafood specials on Friday and Saturday night, when the chef probably found "Phan-tastic" specimens at the fish market. But skip them on Sunday and Monday, when the restaurant might be trying to move weekend leftovers.

THE GREATEST: Seafood Chain

Legal Sea Foods $$$
www.legalseafoods.com

Legal Sea Foods started as a modest fish market 50 years ago, and today it's the best seafood chain around. Their fish is the freshest, and their buttery, creamy New England clam chowder is the perfect balance of clams, potatoes, and thick richness. Sleek restaurant design and a humongous selection of 40 types of fresh fish make Legal Sea Foods THE seafood authority. Whether you're slurping chowder solo at the bar or showing out-of-towners what New England is all about, it's a fun, happening place to be. Guest chefs from around the world have generated exciting recipe additions to the menu, including authentic influences from China, the Caribbean, and India. Their 14 Massachusetts locations include the Prudential Center, Long Wharf, Chestnut Hill, and Framingham.

THE GREATEST: Raw Bar

Neptune Oyster $$
63 Salem St., Boston, Mass., (617) 742-3474,
www.neptuneoyster.com

Shucking its way to the top, Neptune Oyster is the freshest raw bar around. The attractive clam-shack-sized room has all the luster of a South Pacific pearl. Three dozen seats hug the long, marble bar, trimmed in vintage mirrors and set off by a textured tin ceiling. Their spread of iced scallops, a dozen different oysters, and littleneck clams awaits the slip of the blade, and they serve up gorgeous wines to match. Giving a nod to the neighborhood, the kitchen also turns out Italian seafood like lobster cioppino, fried calamari, and shellfish stew with saffron rice.

THE GREATEST: Cuban Flair

Naked Fish $$
www.nakedfish.com

Naked Fish takes a fresh perspective on maximizing true fish flavor without heavy sauces. All six locations (including Faneuil Hall, Framingham, and Waltham) flaunt Cuban flair with cocktails, cuisine, and samba tunes. Many dishes are simply brushed with olive oil, grilled, and served with lemon. But you can also order "dressed" entrées flavored with orange rum cream, citrus butter, or mango salsa. Phantom's favorites are the Mojo Jumbo Shrimp and the coconut calamari. The bar shakes things up, too, with jazzy cocktails like the mango mai tai and the pineapple rum Latin Love.

THE GREATEST: Lobster Fra Diablo

Out of the Blue $$
215 Elm St., Somerville, Mass., (617) 776-5020,
www.outofthebluerestaurant.com

Out of the Blue boasts imaginative seafaring atmosphere and Phantom's favorite lobster fra diablo. It's a sensational dish brimming with shellfish, calamari, scallops, and linguini, all dressed in spicy marinara. Now in a larger location in Davis Square, the neighborhood restaurant makes waves with a big menu of Italian seafood specialties. Large portions are quite a catch, and Phantom recommends ordering dessert just for the espresso-soaked tiramisu fluffed up on heavenly mascarpone. The sea-green walls make the room seem like it's below sea level, while miniature ships and lighthouse knickknacks complete the underwater theme.

THE GREATEST: Hip Seafood

Finz $$
76 Wharf St., Salem, Mass., (978) 744-8485,
www.hipfinz.com

Finz is parked right on the water, so you can practically spot the fresh catch of the day before it hits your plate. Glass walls give a crystal-clear view of the ocean, but the fireside lounge draws you back inside. The dining room is stylish with cobalt blue accents and crisp white walls. However, the copper raw bar is their chief asset, for unconventional items like oysters with wasabi caviar and raspberry Stoli or mango avocado salsa. The Oyster Flight includes eight assorted varieties, and for a doubly hot snack, Phantom dives into their crispy buffalo calamari.

THE GREATEST: Asian Seafood

Blue Ginger $$$
583 Washington St., Wellesley, Mass., (781) 283-5790,
www.ming.com
Blue Ginger is the kind of suburban restaurant that city dwellers are happy to re-verse commute for . . . if they can get a reservation. Famous for his "East meets West" approach, celebrity chef Ming Tsai cooks up his signature French-influenced Asian cuisine. The spicy garlic-black pepper lobster retains serious seafood flavor, served beside a lobster shell full of lemongrass fried rice. Mastering Feng Shui at-mosphere, the dining room displays Vietnamese waterscapes, rice paper screens, a trickling stone fountain, and a 40-foot open kitchen.

THE GREATEST: Barbecued Seafood

East Coast Grill & Raw Bar $$
1271 Cambridge St., Cambridge, Mass., (617) 491-6568,
www.eastcoastgrill.net
East Coast Grill is the rare barbecue joint that specializes in grilled seafood. Chef/owner Chris Schlesinger prepares amazing white pepper tuna with house pickled ginger, aged soy sauce, and fresh wasabi. Phantom also loves the mahimahi with pineapple salsa, the buttermilk fried oysters, and the chile-glazed shrimp and scallops. The fun, funky atmosphere involves a blackboard menu for the clams of-the-day, handblown glass lamps, and a "live" volcano that randomly erupts. For true heat seekers, East Coast creates one heck of a tongue-torching menu twice a year for their Hotter Than Hell Night.

THE GREATEST: Fisherman Recommended

No Name Restaurant $$
15½ Fish Pier, Boston, MA 02210, (617) 338-7539
No Name Restaurant isn't marked by a sign or even a name, but the nautical-themed double-decker is a seaside standout. It's completely old school, serving tra-ditional New England seafood the way a fisherman would want it. The beautiful harborside location on the Boston Fish Pier explains the incredibly fresh catches, and the semi-open kitchen cranks out great entrées by broiling, frying, and boiling. Their fried clams taste deliciously briny, with a crispy exterior and moist, juicy in-sides. The seafood chowder is filled with hunks of fish instead of potato fillers, and Phantom loves the sautéed lobster, shrimp, and scallops in a white wine butter sauce. Stick around for tasty desserts like strawberry rhubarb pie and Grape-Nuts custard.

Soup
GREAT ATE

When the weather starts to chill, Phantom warms up with a big bowl of steaming sustenance. Phantom ladles out the 8 GREATEST soup selections.

TASTY TIP

Phantom prefers his soup "lawsuit" hot. Ask servers to ladle from the bottom of the pot, where the ingredients are closer to the flame and all the good stuff sits.

THE GREATEST: Chicken Soup

New England Soup Factory $
2-4 Brookline Place, Brookline, Mass., (617) 739-1695,
www.nesoupfactory.com
With only a half dozen tables, New England Soup Factory is ideal for takeout. The rotating menu changes daily, featuring 10 of their 150 total made-from-scratch soups. The triple-strength chicken vegetable stocks a robust broth full of white meat chunks and tender carrots. Other slurpable standouts include sweet potato with caramelized onions or African chicken and peanut. Iced soups are served in warmer months, but you can always order overstuffed sandwiches, salads, brownies, blondies, and cookies. There's a second location in Newton.

THE GREATEST: Clam Chowder

Legal Sea Foods $$$
www.legalseafoods.com
At Legal Sea Foods, you can count on two things: serious seafood and the best "chowdah" on the coast. Their New England–style clam chowder is creamy but not too rich, thick but not heavy, and perfectly balanced with briny bivalves and potatoes. Sleek restaurant design and 40 varieties of fish make it a fun, happening place to dine. Guest chefs from abroad generate exciting menu influences from China, the Caribbean, and India.

THE GREATEST: Pho

Pho Pasteur $
300 Boylston St. (Atrium Mall), Chestnut Hill, Mass., (617) 928-0900
Pho Pasteur's Vietnamese specialty is pho, a steaming noodle soup brimming with clear broth, plus beef, tripe, chicken, or seafood. Garnished with crunchy bean

sprouts, fragrant basil, and lime, it has serious restorative powers. Most menu items are intrinsically healthy and low-fat, consisting of noodles, veggies, and a little meat or fish. The brightly colored, budget-friendly chain has locations in Harvard Square, Newbury Street, and Allston. But only the Chestnut Hill branch serves their silky taro tapioca pudding baked inside a coconut shell.

THE GREATEST: Lobster Stew

Locke-Ober $$$
3 Winter Pl., Boston, Mass., (617) 542-1340,
www.locke-ober.com

Generations of Bostonians have grown up with downtown Boston's timeless Locke-Ober. Their famed JFK lobster stew is part of the tradition, renamed for its biggest fan. The impossibly rich concoction yields a hint of sherry and cayenne pepper, finished with a pat of butter. The exquisite American menu includes New England seafood, a fine oyster bar, and distinguished wines from the cellar. The setting is perfectly refined, detailed with dark mahogany and luxury leather.

THE GREATEST: Oxtail Soup

Matt Murphy's Pub $$
14 Harvard St., Brookline Village, Mass., (617) 232-0188,
www.mattmurphyspub.com

Matt Murphy's is unmistakably Irish, with newspaper-wrapped food, thick accents, a stand-up bar, and chummy atmosphere. The authentic pub serves up superior ales from the brass tap and the most memorable Irish fare this side of the pond. Phantom likes to settle in for a night of live music and some hearty oxtail soup, featuring terrifically fatty meat simmered with root vegetables. Other rustic recipes include shepherd's pie, with mashed potatoes baked on top of chunky lamb stew.

THE GREATEST: French Onion Soup

Sandrine's $$$
8 Holyoke St., Cambridge, Mass., (617) 497-5300,
www.sandrines.com

Tucked down a side street of Harvard Square, Sandrine's is a transporting French bistro with Phantom's onion soupe gratinee, lavished with Riesling wine and baguette croutons, then covered in Swiss cheese and oven-broiled until bubbling. The rest of the large menu emphasizes the flavors of German-influenced Alsace, France. There's the specialty *flammekueche* pizza spread with fromage blanc and onions and the uberdelicious choucroute garnie, brimming with sauerkraut, sausage, hickory smoked bacon, and new potatoes. Warm colors permeate the elegant restaurant, which features an entrance that resembles a 1930s Paris Metro gate.

THE GREATEST: **Soup Chain**

Souper Salad $
www.soupersaladboston.com
Souper Salad specializes in steaming soups and fully stocked salad bars for professionals on the go. Each morning their local culinary center prepares 200 gallons of their soups and disperses them to each of their 10 locations. Reliable standbys include triple boost veggie, clam chowder, and country chicken stew, but Phantom goes for wild cards like pumpkin apple soup and Long Island duck with vegetables. To round out the meal, there are à la carte options like Asian noodles, sandwiches, wraps, and muffins.

THE GREATEST: **Liquid Lunch**

Stone Soup Café $$
0 Central St., Ipswich, Mass., (978) 356-4222
The homey Stone Soup Café is a fabulous find where local fishermen and foodies enjoy the farm-fresh fare atop white linens and flickering candles. Up to 10 soups are made daily in small batches for lunch. The clam chowder is a perennial award winner, but other soul-warming soups include tomato bisque, curried butternut squash, Cuban black bean, Italian wedding, and pasta e fagioli. Breakfast and lunch are walk-in, come-as-you-are affairs, but the mind-blowing dinners (Thursday, Friday, Saturday) require reservations weeks in advance.

Steak
GREAT ATE

Phantom is a meat-and-potatoes kind of critic who loves juicy sirloins and rib eyes that require a big honkin' steak knife. Armed with a tremendous appetite, Phantom slices into the 8 GREATEST steakhouses.

TASTY TIP Choosing the right cut of steak can be confounding. Each one has its merits, but generally it's a tradeoff of tenderness or flavor. Looking for buttery texture? Filet mignon is for you. Something with more heft and succulence? Order up a strip steak. Best of both worlds? Go with Phantom's favorite: the porterhouse.

THE GREATEST: Bone-In Filet

Abe & Louie's $$$
793 Boylston St., Boston, Mass., (617) 536-6300,
www.abeandlouies.com

Abe & Louie's serves the best steak in the Back Bay. Their exquisite Prime-quality meats come from corn-fed midwestern beef that's been aged four to five weeks. The house specialty is the mouthwatering bone-in filet served with a portobello demi-glace. Phantom recommends topping it off with aged cheddar cheese or Great Hill blue cheese. The open space has all the character of a refined steakhouse, but with louder, livelier energy. Investment bankers sink into oversized leather booths, surrounded by gold vaulted ceilings. It's great for fair weather dining, too, as the scene spills onto the outdoor patio. The wine list runs deep, but the classic martini is the accessory of choice at the mahogany bar.

THE GREATEST: Steak & Seafood

Grill 23 & Bar $$$
161 Berkeley St., Boston, Mass., (617) 542-2255,
www.grill23.com

Grill 23 & Bar perfects the Prime steakhouse concept and steps it up with awesome seafood. The à la carte menu is beefed up on big, fat steaks like the Kobe beef Delmonico and the 24-ounce porterhouse, which should never be ordered without the upscale mac & cheese, which is infused with slab bacon. On the surf side, they make a mean salmon fillet with ginger oil over asparagus. Phantom always starts with oysters on the half shell, served with minted cucumber and carrot mignonette. The loud, vibrant lounge fills with business mergers and stiff drinks, and the elegant dining room displays massive marble columns and an entourage of chefs' whites in the open kitchen.

THE GREATEST: Châteaubriand

Oak Room $$$
Fairmont Copley Plaza, 138 St. James Ave., Boston, Mass., (617) 267-5300,
www.theoakroom.com

The Oak Room in the Fairmont Copley Plaza is a striking, old-world shrine of refinement with elaborate woodwork, magnificent burgundy draperies, dripping crystal chandeliers, and animal trophies. The luxury steakhouse spares no expense with butter-rich seafood like crab stuffed mushrooms. For an especially extravagant entrée, get the tuxedo-dressed waiter to roll the Châteaubriand for two right to your table. The thick center-cut tenderloin is sliced right before your eyes, served with béarnaise and potatoes. Post-meal, it's best to digest in the swank martini lounge next door, where every martini comes with a second pour on ice.

THE GREATEST: Steakhouse Service

Morton's $$$
One Exeter Plaza, Boston, Mass., (617) 266-5858,
www.mortons.com

Vegetarians beware! At Morton's, waiters wheel a physical menu right to the table. Every party gets a visit from the rolling cart, piled with raw steaks, chops, and live lobsters. Each dish is explained in saucy detail before guests make their selections. In addition to the Prime aged beef, they have an outrageously delicious Godiva hot chocolate cake for dessert. A nationwide chain, Morton's feels like an underground boys' club with wall-to-wall celebrity photos, white linens, and built-in wine racks in the loud, masculine room.

THE GREATEST: Sizzling Steak

Frank's Steakhouse $$
2310 Massachusetts Ave., Cambridge, Mass., (617) 661-0666,
www.frankssteakhouse.com

Established in 1938, Frank's Steakhouse is the oldest in all of Greater Boston. It's also THE place to go for good old-fashioned meat and potatoes. Frank's Famous NY Sizzler Sirloin is practically on fire when it comes out of the kitchen on a cast-iron skillet. The boneless cut is particularly delicious with the deep-fried onion loaf, which was inspired by Norm on Cheers. He repeatedly waxed poetic about the culinary creation on the show. Otherwise, the menu delves into seafood, burgers, pasta, and affordable pub grub. The casual atmosphere is just right for families and wearing jeans, and the piano bar fills with regulars who've been coming since birth.

THE GREATEST: Italian Steakhouse

Davio's $$$
75 Arlington St., Boston, Mass., (617) 357-4810,
www.davios.com
With locations in Boston's Back Bay and Cambridge, Davio's is Phantom's favorite Italian steakhouse. The huge open kitchen puts out chops, aged Prime beef, and rich sides like mac & cheese with white truffle oil, along with antipasti and red sauce pasta. The grilled porterhouse veal is an impressive cut of meat, but Phantom's hands-down favorite is the Prime Kobe beef rib eye. There's also a pizza bar and an in-house bakery whipping up desserts, pastries, and oven-fresh breads. Thick interior columns and wide windows mark the spacious, elegant setting, and the open wine room displays 300 selections.

THE GREATEST: Steak Tips

New Bridge Café $
650 Washington Ave., Chelsea, Mass., (617) 884-0134
The New Bridge Café is no high-end steakhouse, but they've got the best steak tips in New England. In fact, 75 percent of their business comes from the juicy, sweet, sought-after tips. The menu also offers lamb tips, pork tips, and turkey tips, plus a fantastic rack of baby back ribs. Whether you settle into a vinyl booth or opt for a seat at the bar, nothing on the TV will distract your attention from the secret sauce covering those succulent cubes of meat. No wonder they won't spill the secret ingredients in the marinade or in the house salad dressing, which is sweet and so delicious.

THE GREATEST: Modern Steakhouse

Metropolitan Club $$$
1210 Boylston St., Chestnut Hill, Mass., (617) 731-0600,
www.metclubandbar.com
Putting a hip steakhouse in the fast lane (Route 9) is possibly the tastiest trend Chestnut Hill has ever seen. It's so stylish, you might think you've stumbled off the Prime beef path and into a party scene. The menu is a stellar formula of seafood and bone-in rib eyes, but additions like tri-colored fries and pan-seared "watermelon steak" give it just the modern update that young beef-eaters applaud. The striking atmosphere takes walnut paneling and gives it eye-catching allure in copper accents and bright blue glass behind the bar. Brunch makes an equally bold statement with the Egg MetMuffin sandwich, which incorporates a poached egg, hollandaise, and Serrano ham (black truffle shavings and Sevruga caviar are optional).

Sushi
GREAT ATE

With the Atlantic coast just a fishing line away, New England slices and rolls some of the best sushi in the world. Phantom gets a lethal dose of wasabi while uncovering the 8 GREATEST sushi bars.

SUSHI ETIQUETTE: Once you've mastered the chopsticks, the rest is a piece of tamago, er, cake. Pick up the sushi, flip, and dip the fish (not the rice) in the soy sauce mixed with wasabi. Put the whole thing in your mouth, fish side down, so the distinct flavor connects with your tastebuds. To taste the true flavor of each fish, be sure to cleanse the palate with pickled ginger between bites.

THE GREATEST: Toro

Oishii $$
612 Hammond St., Chestnut Hill, Mass., (617) 277-7888

Oishii is a snug sushi bar with 10 coveted counter seats where customers can watch the sushi experts slice and roll. It's a bare-basics closet of a room, but there's no better-dressed fish in town (or out of town)! Chef Ting crafts generous portions of extremely tasty, fresh fish. Phantom goes for the toro, which is the most fantastically fatty part of the tuna. At Oishii, the salmon shimmers, the red clam comes paper-thin, and the spicy scallop hand rolls are sublime. Hot entrées are equally outstanding, with udon noodles and stone-grilled selections. Additional locations include Sudbury and Boston's South End.

THE GREATEST: Upscale Sushi

Fugakyu $$$
1280 Beacon St., Brookline, Mass., (617) 738-1268,
www.fugakyujapanese.com

Fugakyu is a beautiful Japanese restaurant staffed by kimono-dressed waitresses. Customers can watch the chefs in action at the circulating sushi bar or settle into the maze of the dining room, full of private tatami rooms hidden by sliding rice paper doors. Lively fish tanks show off future dinners of mackerel, sea urchin, lobster, and abalone. The chef's choice omakase prix fixe is a feast of appetizers, sushi, makimono, sashimi, soup, and salad.

THE GREATEST: Rare Sashimi

Uni $$$
370 Commonwealth Ave, Boston, Mass., (617) 536-7200,
www.cliorestaurant.com
Located down the faux leopard print stairs from the exquisite Clio dining room,
Uni is a den-like sashimi bar pairing extremely rare selections with nearly a dozen
fine sakes. Area foodies jockey for a seat at the black marble bar to witness chef
Ken Oringer in action. Exotic offerings include sea urchin with quail eggs, ku-
mamoto oysters with Japanese fruit, and lightly battered freshwater eel. Jaw-
dropping garnishes like caviar, wasabi foam, or green tea salt make each wickedly
expensive bite a sheer indulgence.

THE GREATEST: Sexy Sushi

10 Steak & Sushi $$$
55 Pine St., Providence, R.I. (401) 453-2333,
www.tenprimesteak.com
10 Steak & Sushi is a wildly untamed eatery where USDA Prime beef meets sexy
sushi. All of the nigiri, sashimi, and rolls are provocatively dressed to the nines and
given twenty-first-century names. The screaming salmon maki is quite spicy; the
Malibu maki combines crab, mango, tuna, snapper, and jalapeño; and the smokehouse maki includes portobellos and mozzarella. The exotic dining room is a blue
underwater world with glowing martinis, erotic art, and a 3-D dessert menu. It's not
just dining; it's eating entertainment.

THE GREATEST: Sushi Buffet

Minado $$
1282 Worcester Rd., Natick, Mass., (508) 647-0495,
www.minado.com
Phantom was skeptical, too. But the sushi buffet at Minado is expansive without
compromising quality. The cavernous 360-seat dining room invites seafood lovers
to sink their teeth into 100 selections, including maki, sashimi, and hand rolls.
Along with tuna, eel, and yellow tail, there's crab with avocado, fried salmon, and
shrimp tempura. Freshness is guaranteed, with no piece sitting out for more than 15
minutes. Other luxury items include oysters on the half-shell, lobster tails, and gi-
ant snow crab legs.

THE GREATEST: **Stylish Sushi**

Osushi $$
10 Huntington Ave., Boston, Mass., (617) 266-2788,
www.osushirestaurant.com
Osushi is Boston's hippest sushi boite, flooded by scenesters who slink into high-
backed booths to sip flowery, sake-tinis infused with Asian pear. The sleek décor
of red-on-black is trimmed in ruby votives and beaded curtains. The menu is more
conservative, offering cooked rolls for the squeamish and an amazing 20-selection
sake list. Miso soup and a sesame-dressed salad come with each combination meal,
like lustrous cuts of suzuki (sea bass), chutoro (tuna), and crystal rainbow rolls of
eel, avocado, and cucumber swirled into a ring of rice and capped with tuna, white-
fish, sake, and tobiko.

THE GREATEST: **Spider Maki**

Ginza $$$
16 Hudson St., Boston, Mass., (617) 338-2261
Ginza is a stark setting of blond wood latticework, with elbow-to-elbow seating
and a sushi bar toward the back. There's great late-night people watching when
clubbers gather until 4 a.m. The house specialty spider maki is artfully dramatic
with textural contrast. Deep-fried soft-shelled crab, creamy avocado, crisp cucumber, rice, and salty flying fish roe are wound into giant seaweed slices. The second
location in Brookline boasts the same perfect sticky rice and tempura green tea ice
cream.

THE GREATEST: **Blackened Sashimi**

Skipjack's $$
199 Clarendon St., Boston, Mass., (617) 536-3500,
www.skipjacks.com
Phantom's idea of a successful fishing trip is dinner at Skipjack's, where the
seafood selection comes in waves. They have one of the most comprehensive fish
menus (local and global) in town, and aside from raw bar shuckings, fried fish,
fresh fish, shellfish, and crustaceans, there's also a creative selection of sushi. The
house signature, blackened tuna "sashimi," is perfect for first-time sushi eaters who
prefer cooked fish. But Phantom also enjoys the rainbow rolls and Cape Cod maki
made of lobster salad, lettuce, and cucumber. Sand and sea colors team up for an
ocean-inspired, cruise ship theme. The Newton and Framingham locations serve
sushi, too.

Tiny Treasures
GREAT ATE

Sometimes the smallest restaurants offer the biggest portions, the best value, and the friendliest service. Phantom scours the neighborhood nooks and crannies for the 8 GREATEST tiny treasures.

TASTY TIP Cell phones in small spaces are as hypnotizing as a tableside flambé, only way more annoying. Turn it to silent, switch into text mode, or prepare for a food fight.

THE GREATEST: Cozy Creperie

Paris Creperie $
278 Harvard St., Brookline, Mass., (617) 232-1770
Paris Creperie is a cozy, skinny storefront cooking up Parisian street snacks, better known as crepes. The flat, steaming pancakes come in savory and sweet versions. Phantom's favorites include the Brie with apple, the buffalo chicken, and any of the Provençal-style, herb-infused crepes with tarragon, thyme, or cilantro blended right into the batter. Just be sure to save room for a gooey dessert crepe crammed full of Nutella and bananas. There's a second, not-so-tiny location in Beacon Hill.

THE GREATEST: Itty-Bitty Brunch Spot

Metropolis Café $
584 Tremont St., Boston, Mass., (617) 247-2931
If this tiny neighborhood eatery doesn't hook you with its bistro charm, it will with the fancy farm-fresh eggs. Converted from an ice cream parlor, the artsy decor includes a stool-lined, wraparound bar and a tin ceiling. Floating star lamps and jazz add to the appealing atmosphere, but once you're settled in, the real show starts with the food. Metropolis does dinner all week, but Phantom likes to hold out for the Saturday-Sunday brunch. Fancy translations of omelets and mimosas team up with grilled blueberry muffins, apple chicken sausage, and spectacular banana pancakes. Their huevos rancheros are especially delicious, balanced over cumin-spiced black bean hash.

THE GREATEST: Sandwich Nook

Strip T's $
93-95 School St., Watertown, Mass., (617) 923-4330,
www.stripts.com

Drawing their seemingly scandalous name from their original specialty sirloin sandwich, Strip T's is a colorful hangout with inventive meals. Customers settle into the cozy, 30-seat room and order up stellar stackings like the chicken cutlet stuffed with prosciutto, artichoke, and provolone on French bread. The ever-evolving menu includes fresh seafood like blackened sea scallops or ginger-scallion salmon. Value is Strip T's strongest suit, with bargain-priced wines, along with homemade sides and cookies.

THE GREATEST: Neighborhood Nest

Ten Tables $$$
597 Centre St., Jamaica Plain, Mass., (617) 524-8810,
www.tentables.net

Ten Tables is a tiny little one-room restaurant with no more seats than its name implies. The warm, brick-walled space spills into a wide-open kitchen framed in copper pots. It's French and Italian on the menu, loaded with local produce, house-cured meats, and homemade pasta. The meal begins with the chef's complimentary *amuse bouche* and progresses to dishes like the beet soufflé with chèvre, eggplant flatbread, and seared scallops with fennel and saffron. The $35, four-course wine dinner on Tuesdays is one of Boston's best bargains.

THE GREATEST: Spice Pantry

Christina's Spice & Specialty Foods $
1261 Cambridge St., Cambridge, Mass., (617) 492-7021

Christina's Spice only occupies a couple hundred square feet, but every inch is jammed with imported spices. Forty kinds of chiles are packed in with 20 varieties of rice and 15 different dried mushrooms. A selection of 15 salts includes Hawaiian pink, black smoked Mexican, and French fleur de sel. They even stock 50 botanicals, as well as many teas, heirloom beans, avocado leaves, cubeb, and grains of paradise. Compared to supermarkets, Christina's has a much broader, less expensive assortment. The spice store is an offshoot of Christina's Homemade Ice Cream next door, with spice-inspired flavors like banana cinnamon, coriander, fennel pollen, and cardamom.

THE GREATEST: **Pint-Sized Raw Bar**

B&G Oysters Ltd $$
550 Tremont St., Boston, Mass., (617) 423-0550,
www.bandgoysters.com

Chef/owner Barbara Lynch is shucking up a storm at B&G Oysters Ltd. It's the city's hottest nook of a raw bar, filled with just a few small black tables and a friendly bar. The cozy hideout is perfect for intimate conversation over impressively fresh seafood. The oyster selection changes daily, and it's supplemented by salads, New England clam chowder, fried shellfish, and heaping lobster rolls from an open kitchen. Beautiful sea-colored tiles brighten the mood as the lights dim for late-night jazz.

THE GREATEST: **Tiny Trattoria**

Daily Catch $$
323 Hanover St., Boston, Mass., (617) 523-8567,
www.dailycatch.com

Daily Catch in the North End is a teeny, tiny trattoria serving up all kinds of sensational seafood. The 20-seat dining room shares the same space as the kitchen, so customers get quite a show. Nicknamed the calamari café, Daily Catch serves multiple renditions of the Italian delicacy. They're fried, sautéed, steamed, marinated, stuffed, and even rolled into balls. The blackboard menu lists other Sicilian seafood like linguine with clams or monkfish Marsala with mushrooms. Wine and Moretti Beer are served in plastic cups. Additional locations include Brookline and Boston's waterfront.

THE GREATEST: **Intimate Date Place**

Delux Café $$
100 Chandler St., Boston, Mass., (617) 338-5258

Delux Café is one of those rare bar/restaurants with kitschy digs, a diverse crowd, cheap drinks, and yummy bargain food. The intimate atmosphere is attractive to couples, and it's certainly provocative enough to stir up some conversation. With the Elvis shrine, the TV cartoons, Schlitz advertisements, and permanent Christmas lights, something wacky seems to happen every time Phantom goes. The eclectic menu is totally affordable, with playful dishes like southwest chicken chili or pumpkin ravioli in sage brown butter.

Trendy
GREAT ATE

Combining big-city style with cutting-edge cuisine, Boston's hottest restaurants generate quite a buzz. Drop your dinner plans and reserve now at the 8 GREATEST, most trendy restaurants.

THE GREATEST: Updated Italian

Stella $$$
1525 Washington St., Boston, Mass., (617) 247-7747,
www.bostonstella.com

Bringing a fresh new look to the Italian table, Stella is heating up Boston's SoWa neighborhood, one plate of homemade pasta at a time. The stylish decor may be entirely white, but Chef Evan Deluty is no virgin to the restaurant scene. Torch in Beacon Hill is his romantic, eclectic sister restaurant, and it's nothing at all like this latest people-watching scene. The huge, open space seats nearly 200 people and spills onto a wraparound sidewalk patio. Inside, it's a snowy white landscape where the late-night bar stays wide awake until 2 a.m. serving watermelon martinis. The kitchen turns out grilled pizza, spicy tuna "arrabiatta," and Tuscan crispy fries topped with Parmesan and hot peppers.

THE GREATEST: Sky-High Scene

blu $$$
The Sports Club/L.A., 4 Avery St., Boston, Mass., (617) 375-8550,
www.blurestaurant.com

True, blu is located in the exclusive Sports Club/L.A. at the Ritz-Carlton Boston Common. But breaking a sweat is optional as you take the elevator to the modern fourth-floor dining room with a glittery skyline view of the Theater District. Elevated 100 feet above urban life, the sky-high seats look out through huge two-story windows. Lunch and dinner stick to elegant dishes like lobster bisque with sorrel crème fraîche and seared striped bass with basil butter. Those who do book a personal trainer before the reservation can go guilt-free with desserts like the caramel baked peach. The bar is especially popular after work, and the adjacent blu Café turns out portable sandwiches, salads, and smoothies to go.

THE GREATEST: Organic Italian

Mare $$$
135 Richmond St., Boston, Mass., (617) 723-6273,
www.mareorganic.com
Started by the same dynamic team that's behind Bricco and Umbria, Mare caught
the North End's attention before it even opened. The seafood-centric menu is Ital-
ian with fierce devotion to all things organic. In a neighborhood where restaurant
rent is already high, Mare's insistence on top quality translates to premium cuisine
at premium prices. Crabmeat and truffles make a royal crown for wide tubes of
pasta, and the butter-poached lobster teams with smoked porcinis for an other-
worldly indulgence. If you're not into the trance of the color-lit wall and surreal
flatscreen designs, there's plenty of distraction on the plate.

THE GREATEST: Pizza & Wine Bar

Nebo $$
90 North Washington St., Boston, Mass., (617) 723-6326,
www.nebopizzeria.com
Combining two of Phantom's favorite food groups, Nebo is a classy pizzeria with
a commendable wine list too. This deliciously stylish addition to the North End is
the only restaurant in the neighborhood with a hip hop and dance soundtrack.
Celebrity chefs and rockers like Peter Wolf and Steven Tyler are regulars, so
there's the added possibility of superstar sightings while you're unwinding with a
nice Chianti. Celebrities aside, the upscale slices are reason enough to pop in.
Phantom's favorite pie is the Christina with sausage and corn, but he's also in love
with the arancini rice balls stuffed with mushrooms, cheese, and honey sauce.

THE GREATEST: DJs & Dining

Middlesex Lounge $$
315 Mass. Ave., Cambridge, Mass., (617) 868-MSEX,
www.middlesexlounge.com
Middlesex Lounge is a hot little boite of trendy food, urban energy, and an eclectic
crowd that changes with the spinmaster DJ du jour. The sleek, boxy room is neatly
bound by wood panels and a wall of frosted windows. Come with all your com-
rades; the servers will wheel around the sunken tables and slate-colored suede seats
to accommodate. Pressed sandwiches are de rigueur at lunch, and evening nibbles
include Kobe beef burgers and one plate of 10 tiny tacos. Don't wait until the line
out the door subsides, Middlesex Lounge is happening now!

THE GREATEST: **Experimental Eats**

Restaurant L $$$
234 Berkeley St., Boston, Mass., (617) 266-4680,
www.louisboston.com

Restaurant L is fashionable, fun, and full of unexpected flavor. Much like its sister clothing store, Louis Boston, the crafty kitchen goes about its business like no other. Every dish redefines what it means to eat, challenging conventional tastes with exotic flavor infusions. The pan-Asian influence shows its colors with the Thai beef salad in caramelized lemongrass sauce, and the artsy cocktail list is crazy, too. Phantom's favorite elixir is the blood orange martini blended from mango and four melons with a fennel pollen rim. Servers look like they flew non-stop from Paris, dressed in designer jeans and retro Pumas, and every meal ends with individual sticks of cotton candy.

THE GREATEST: **Post Work Party**

Houston's $$$
60 State St., Boston, Mass., (617) 573-9777,
www.houstons.com

The Houston's chain is a trendsetting suit scene with an always-packed four-sided bar and a tiered, funky dining room with clubby lighting. Guests sink into red-hot leather booths and delve into an American menu of salads, steaks, burgers, and sandwiches. Chicago-style spinach dip is a must-order appetizer, and the Evil Jungle Steak Salad is an Asian-inspired masterpiece built on spicy noodles, avocado, basil, mango, and peanuts. Even the rest rooms are an entertaining, happening place to be with flatscreen TVs built into the wall.

THE GREATEST: **Zen Dining**

Om Restaurant & Lounge $$$
57 JFK St., Cambridge, Mass., (617) 576-2800,
www.omrestaurant.com

Stepping into Om, you can bet your feng shui that yin and yang are behind the design. This palace of Eastern energy greets guests with a waterfall wall that leads to a happening lounge. Old World artifacts like Tibetan paintings anchor the super-trendy setup complete with a color-changing bar and beaded curtains. The kitchen is wildly unpredictable, with scrumptious results. Instead of a boring breadbasket, diners start with Parmesan popcorn. For entrées, try the surf 'n turf, pairing grilled yellowfin tuna with beef short rib dumplings. Wash it all down with an aromatherapy martini, which infuses essential oils to arouse the senses. Desserts are off-the-wall delicious, including the flourless chocolate "pâté" and the ice cream sandwich constructed from carrot cake, parsnip ice cream, and habanero caramel.

Wine List
GREAT ATE

Some wine lists are so comprehensive and captivating, Phantom could curl up in bed and read them like a novel. Phantom pops the cork on the 8 GREATEST wine lists.

TASTY TIP Half bottles are creating the biggest buzz in the wine world since the Pinot Noir explosion of the movie *Sideways*. These manageable pours make it easy and more affordable to have white with the appetizers and red with the entrées.

THE GREATEST: Wine Cave

Silks $$$
Stonehedge Inn, 160 Pawtucket Blvd., Tyngsboro, Mass., (978) 649-4400, www.stonehedgeinn.com/silks.html
Silks in the Stonehedge Inn racks an unparalleled wine collection of 100,000 bottles housed in Phantom's favorite wine cellar. Unlike traditional vino storage, it's an aboveground structure. They buy their wines young, age them in the cave, and serve them at their peak. The elegant dining room is decorated with cathedral ceilings, large stained-glass windows, and colorful art depicting horse races. Aside from the encyclopedic wine list, Silks features an exquisite French menu and monthly wine dinners.

THE GREATEST: Varietal Wine List

Meritage $$$
Boston Harbor Hotel, 70 Rowes Wharf, Boston, Mass., (617) 439-3995, www.meritagetherestaurant.com
Meritage in the Boston Harbor Hotel breaks the mold by organizing its impressive wine list by grape varietal. In fact, their 12,000 bottles of 850 different wine selections sit on display in enormous cases that flank the long room. The atmosphere is clubby-chic, with a cranberry-colored bar, exotic wood floors, and one of Boston's best views of the harbor. The menu gives wine pairing suggestions, and every dish can be ordered as an appetizer or an entrée. Seasonal produce mixes with rarities like Kobe beef, ostrich, foie gras, and pheasant.

THE GREATEST: Vintage Selection

Federalist $$$
XV Beacon Hotel, 15 Beacon St., Boston, Mass., (877) xvbeacon or
(617) 670-2515,
www.xvbeacon.com
The Federalist in the high-style XV Beacon Hotel has a phenomenal wine cellar.
Private parties can even dine in the cellar itself, which is an underground hideout
with a vaulted ceiling, wine racked along the walls, and the reserve list behind bul-
letproof glass. Their premiere collection of 30,000 bottles includes rare old-world
finds. The most expensive? $14,000. The oldest? A 1795 Madeira, which goes for
$325 a glass. The chef turns out unbelievable fare like beef Wellington and the
tuna tartar tower, and there's a weekly tasting menu paired with wines.

THE GREATEST: Glass Wine Tower

Excelsior $$$
272 Boylston Street, Boston, Mass., (617) 426-7878,
www.excelsiorrestaurant.com
Overlooking the Boston Public Garden, Excelsior whisks dinner guests up the glass
elevator, so they get a sweeping view of the huge wine collection. This impressive
wine "cave" is more like a tower, occupying three stories of a temperature- and
humidity-controlled space. The elevator doors then open into a stylish room ablaze
with earth and fire tones. Warm wood walls and leather seats set the mood for a lavish dinner. The cutting-edge kitchen crafts a visionary menu of sassy pleasure
foods with wood-roasted highlights. Wild creations have included the lobster
sausage or crisp roast duck with lemon jam.

THE GREATEST: Wines by the Glass

Troquet $$$
140 Boylston St., Boston, Mass., (617) 695-9463
Troquet is a smart setting of burgundy walls lined with mirrors to give the sleek, intimate room a more spacious feel. Phantom gives a standing ovation to their rotating selection of fine wines by the glass. Four dozen choices are listed down the
center of the menu, with matching dishes off to the sides. Wines can be sampled in
two- and four-ounce pours. As for bottles, there are 350 varieties. The open kitchen
prepares fabulous wine-friendly cuisine like foie gras and roasted venison.

THE GREATEST: California Wine List

Sonoma $$$
206 Worcester Rd., Princeton, Mass., (978) 464-5775,
www.sonoma-princeton.com

Sonoma is tucked away in the hills of Princeton, but it's worth seeking out for un-forgettable global fare and an amazing California wine list. Silver-vested servers are skilled at suggesting an oaky Chardonnay or a crisp Sauvignon Blanc, and at the end of the meal, they offer a tour of the decadent dessert tray. All of the original artwork is for sale, but Phantom suggests saving your pennies for the likes of the mushroom-dusted venison chop or pumpkin soup served in a hollowed-out gourd.

THE GREATEST: Wine Mark-Up Deals

Silvertone $$
69 Bromfield St., Boston, Mass., (617) 338-7887

Silvertone attracts a 20-something cocktail crowd to its below-ground retro digs. Their wine list is the best value around, since they refuse to mark up a bottle more than $10 from retail. They only carry about 30 selections, but the choices vary greatly. The menu includes homey comfort foods like mac & cheese, roasted pep-per quesadillas, and meat loaf. And the old school, collector's decor includes vin-tage radios, weathered photos, and high-backed booths.

THE GREATEST: Wine Education

Piattini $$
226 Newbury St., Boston, Mass., (617) 536-2020,
www.piattini.com

Piattini is a cramped but charming little underground wine bar done in warm yel-low tones. Pounded copper tables, brick supports, and framed mirrors make the space stylish, and the small tapas-style Italian plates make sharing ideal. The fo-cused wine list shows great Italian variety, and each glass comes with an index card of information about the wine. It's like a mini crash course on vino that leaves you relaxed AND educated. There's a bigger, newer location in the South End.

Worth a Drive
GREAT ATE

Phantom loves neighborhood eateries, but certain restaurants are so scrumptious, they're worth driving 100 miles for dinner alone! Phantom's traveling taste buds sample the 8 GREATEST destination dining rooms in New England.

TASTY TIP Fuel economy, horsepower, and air bags are important automobile features. However, Phantom buys his purple cars based on one factor alone: cupholders! He needs a lot of them, and they all have to be big enough to fit a Dunkin' Donuts "Big One" coffee.

THE GREATEST: Airport Dining

Nancy's Air Field Café $

302 Boxboro Rd., Stow, Mass., (978) 897-3934,
www.nancysairfieldcafe.com

Next to a tiny landing strip, Nancy's Air Field Café is no "fly-by-night" operation. The bustling spot is where pilots and the hungry public come to refuel and relax. Virtually everything is made from scratch, with a fierce devotion to local ingredients. Blueberries burst from the fluffy pancakes, and the Vermont Country Club will have you on cloud nine. Everything except the $100 hamburger is incredibly affordable. Actually, the restaurant charges less than $10 for the burger, but the pilots who fly in for a meal spend another $90 in fuel. Topped with maple BBQ sauce, cheddar, and applewood-smoked bacon, the charbroiled beauty is one delicious ride.

THE GREATEST: Wood-Fired Cooking

Fore Street $$$

288 Fore St., Portland, Maine, (207) 775-2717

Whether it's grilled, roasted, or simmered, every dish at Fore Street is an unparalleled success. Set in a former furniture factory with soaring ceilings, exposed brick walls, and an amazing open kitchen, there's a definite energy and theatrical feel. It's rustic and casual, yet white lights make it a romantic setting. From the huge wood-fired oven come crispy, cracker-thin pizzas topped with goat cheese, while juicy rotisserie chickens do laps on the spit, and the grill sizzles full of steaks, chops, and fish.

THE GREATEST: Rustic Fine Dining

White Barn Inn   **$$$**
37 Beach Ave., Kennebunk, Maine, (207) 967-2321,
www.whitebarninn.com
The dazzling White Barn Inn is the ultimate in rustic fine dining, blending col-
lectible antiques and candle lighting with crystal, sterling silver, and farmyard art.
The nineteenth-century setting is captivating with live piano music and tuxedoed
waiters who unveil everyone's dish in theatrical coordination. The menu guides
guests through a four-course prix fixe menu of designer New England cuisine, in-
cluding a palate cleanser of blood orange sorbet. Phantom's favorite entrée is
steamed Maine lobster tail with ginger, carrots, and snow peas over cognac butter
fettuccine.

THE GREATEST: BBQ Pit

Curtis Bar-B-Que   **$**
Route 5 (exit 4 off I-91), Putney, VT., (802) 387-5474
Some people raise pigs to roast; others raise them as pets. At Curtis Bar-B-Que,
they do both. Customers pay a visit to Isabel, the grill master's beloved pot-bellied
friend, before lining up for amazing BBQ. Most of the magic happens under a tin
roof hardwood pit, but you'll be equally amazed at the kitchen, which operates out
of old-school buses. The meaty menu lists chicken, ribs, and pork, which can all be
enjoyed at picnic tables scattered across the lawn. Phantom also recommends the
pork-stuffed baked potato spilling over with mild BBQ sauce and chunks of meat.
Don't fret over Isabel's fate; she's not called "the boss" for nothin'.

THE GREATEST: Road Food

Super Duper Weenie   **$**
306 Black Rock Turnpike, Fairfield, Conn., (203) 334-DOGS,
www.superduperweenie.com
Super Duper Weenie is a small shack selling split-open hot dogs, grilled to crispy
plumpness. Their shoestring, fresh-cut fries are the ideal accessory to a stupendous
fast food meal. The leggy, bronzed twigs are perfectly thin with a hefty dousing of
salt and pepper. All of the condiments are made from scratch, including sweet and
hot relish, sauerkraut, chili, and onion sauce. Also on the sizzling menu are ham-
burgers, sausage, cheese steak, and grilled chicken. There's a second Connecticut
location on Route 25 in Monroe.

THE GREATEST: Dinner, Hayride & Music

Golden Lamb Buttery $$$
499 Wolf Den Rd., Brooklyn, Conn., (860) 774-4423

Golden Lamb Buttery in the backcountry of Connecticut is an extraordinary country escape with great home cooking. The husband and wife who orchestrate the evening are the best hosts that Phantom has ever found. They put guests in high spirits throughout cocktail hour in the knickknack-filled barn. Then, owner Bob Booth fires up his tractor as everyone piles in the back for a singalong hayride. The live music continues inside with an intimate dinner prepared by his rosy-cheeked wife, Jimmie. The prix-fixe menu is money well spent for an entire evening of farm entertainment and a three-course meal. Reservations required, cash only, jacket and tie for gentlemen.

THE GREATEST: Steak & Seafood

22 Bowens Wine Bar & Grille $$
22 Bowens Wharf, Newport, R.I., (401) 841-8884,
www.22bowens.com

22 Bowens wraps up several of Phantom's great loves into one delicious restaurant: Prime steaks, serious seafood, single vineyard wines, and a waterfront location. Set smack on the wharf, it has all the energy of downtown Newport with endless ocean views from the other side. Premium steaks are flown in from Chicago, and the fish come from local waters. Phantom likes to start with a raw bar selection of littlenecks or oysters, unless he's in a lobster fritters kind-of-mood. Then it's on to a center-cut filet aged 21 days for intense flavor. Entrées come with a selection of sauces like green peppercorn mustard, horseradish cream, or the Napa red wine demi-glace.

THE GREATEST: Gourmet Getaway

The Crystal Quail $$$
202 Pitman Rd., Center Barnstead, N.H., (603) 269-4151,
www.crystalquail.com

Get out the map to Crystal Quail, where a husband-wife team invites you into their country home for exceptional dining. Customers walk through the quaint, copper pot kitchen into a cozy wooden room with just a handful of tables. The prix-fixe menu is wonderfully diverse with herbs from their organic garden, and the menu changes nightly according to what's ready to be picked. Phantom likes the veal medallions in red wine shallot sauce and pheasant ravioli. ("Beware of bullets. It was hunted this afternoon," warns the host.) The BYOB policy is perfect for uncorking that special bottle you've been saving. Reservations are required, and credit cards are not accepted.

"GREAT ATES"
by Location

Back Bay
GREAT ATE

Wedged among Boston's elite shops and galleries lies a gaggle of restaurants that promise as much culinary pleasure as people watching. Phantom salutes the 8 GREATEST Back Bay eateries.

TASTY TIP If you don't want to shell out $20 for valet in the Back Bay, try parking at the Prudential Center Garage. Spend just $5 in the mall (which Phantom usually does at the food court), and ask the sales associate to stamp your parking ticket. You'll save much more than $5 on the discounted validated parking.

THE GREATEST: Steak

Abe & Louie's $$$
793 Boylston St., Boston, Mass., (617) 536-6300,
www.abeandlouies.com

Abe & Louie's serves the best steak in the neighborhood. Their exquisite Prime beef comes from corn-fed Midwestern beef that's been aged four to five weeks. The house specialty is the mouthwatering bone-in filet served with a portobello demi-glace. Phantom recommends topping it off with aged cheddar cheese. The open space has all the character of a refined steakhouse, but with louder, lively energy than most. Investment bankers sink into oversized leather booths, surrounded by gold vaulted ceilings, wood floors, and bronze chandeliers.

THE GREATEST: Lunch Buffet

Kashmir $$
279 Newbury St., Boston, Mass., (617) 536-1695,
www.kashmirrestaurant.com

Kashmir is an elegant Indian eatery that serves traditional fare with a refreshing range of vegetarian selections, rice, and tandoori dishes baked in a clay oven. All three intimate rooms are decked out in ornate art and packed with closely spaced, white linen tables set with cobalt blue glassware. Phantom's favorites include crisp potato and green pea samosas, rich stewed okra, and spicy lamb vindaloo. Exceptional curries range from mild to fiery hot, and Kashmir's daily lunch buffet is the best bargain in the Back Bay.

THE GREATEST: Scholarly Luncheon

Novel $$

Boston Public Library, 700 Boylston St., Boston, Mass., (617) 385-5660,
www.bpl.org

Housed in the Boston Public Library, Novel offers midday dining amongst fine art
with a fantastic view of the historic courtyard. The gorgeous lunchtime buffet
changes daily, and Phantom always sticks around for the awesomely decadent
desserts. With choices like cheesecake, fruit tortes, and rich chocolate cake, the
only problem is deciding which one (or how many slices). For savory selections, go
ahead and try the clam chowder, pizza, carved pork loin, or baked cod.

THE GREATEST: Mexican Fiesta

Casa Romero $$

30 Gloucester St., Boston, Mass., (617) 536-4341,
www.casaromero.com

Casa Romero is a hidden gold mine of romantic atmosphere and authentic Mexican cooking. Accessible by an alleyway entrance, it's decked out with ceramic
tiles imported from Mexico, exposed brick, and a perfectly secluded outdoor patio. Casa Romero's killer sangria is a sparkling, fruity red wine beverage that's
marinated for a few days in brandy and fresh fruit including lemons, peaches, and
apples. On the menu, try specialties like pork tenderloin with oranges and smoked
chipotle peppers.

THE GREATEST: Clam Bake

Jasper White's Summer Shack $$

50 Dalton St., Boston, Mass., (617) 867-9955,
www.summershackrestaurant.com

Located upstairs from Kings bowling alley, Jasper White's Summer Shack in the
Back Bay is a scaled-back version of the Alewife and Mohegan Sun locations. The
casual clam shack has a seafood menu packed with fried fish, several chowders,
and pan-roasted lobster. It's also home of the city's largest raw bar. Choose from
nine kinds of oysters, plus littlenecks, cherrystones, ceviche, and crab claws. The
laid-back atmosphere and picnic tables add an element of fun, while happy hour
and late-night menus save Phantom from getting famished between meals.

THE GREATEST: **People Watching**

Stephanie's On Newbury $$

190 Newbury St., Boston, Mass., (617) 236-0990,
www.stephaniesonnewbury.com

Stephanie's On Newbury is a delicious oasis from a long day of shopping. If you can tear yourself from the crackling fireplace, you can soak up a cozy bistro setting and sink into a banquette. But when the weather heats up, there's nothing hotter than Stephanie's high-profile sidewalk seating. The kitchen cooks up stylish comfort food like meat loaf with caramelized onions or a gingerbread sundae with molasses ice cream. It's food for the people, but you won't mind slipping into your newly purchased threads for the occasion.

THE GREATEST: **Break the Bank Fine Dining**

L'Espalier $$$

30 Gloucester St., Boston, Mass., (617) 262-3023,
www.lespalier.com

L'Espalier is THE celebration venue when you're looking to break the bank. It's romantic and formal, and every table is perfectly intimate. The elegant townhouse features marble fireplaces in each room, and the classical French cuisine is both unpronounceable and fabulous. Chef/owner Frank McClelland uses farm-fresh, regional ingredients in his elaborate tasting menus, with themes of seasonal specialties, caviar, or vegetarian dishes. Dinners begin with an *amuse bouche* and conclude with a guided tour of the 30 selection artisanal cheese tray.

THE GREATEST: **Bold Kitchen**

Excelsior $$$

272 Boylston Street, Boston, Mass., (617) 426-7878,
www.excelsiorrestaurant.com

Overlooking the Boston Public Garden, Excelsior whisks dinner guests up the glass elevator, so they get a sweeping view of the huge wine collection. This impressive wine "cave" is more like a tower, occupying three stories of a temperature- and humidity-controlled space. The elevator doors then open into a stylish room ablaze with earth and fire tones. Warm wood walls and leather seats set the mood for a lavish dinner. The cutting-edge kitchen crafts a visionary menu of sassy pleasure foods with wood-roasted highlights. Wild creations include the lobster sausage or crisp roast duck with lemon jam.

Beacon Hill
GREAT ATE

In this hilly, centuries-old neighborhood, an eclectic array of restaurants gathers in the shadow of the State House. Phantom follows the cobblestone streets to the 8 GREATEST Beacon Hill restaurants.

TASTY TIP Beacon Hill may be a blue-blooded neighborhood, but it's a red-hot dining destination. This is one of the few Boston neighborhoods that offers top-notch options for breakfast, lunch, AND dinner.

THE GREATEST: Intimate Italian

Grotto $$
37 Bowdoin St., Boston, Mass., (617) 227-3434,
www.grottorestaurant.com

With artsy style, Grotto promises decadent cuisine at outstanding prices. The spunky space is perfect for a romantic meal or a fashionable lunch with your favorite politician. Out of the way and below street level, with few seats and no bar, this place survives because of its reputation for great food . . . and by Phantom spreading the word. The free-form Italian menu is hearty with excellent daily specials. The Caped Critic likes to start by bobbing grilled steak tips in a bubbling cheese fondue of rich fontina and truffle oil. The prosciutto-wrapped tenderloin of beef is notably thick and juicy.

THE GREATEST: Triple Threat

The Paramount $$
44 Charles St., Boston, Mass., (617) 720-1152,
www.paramountboston.com

According to Phantom, a "triple threat" restaurant serves excellent breakfast, lunch, and dinner. The famous Paramount meets those criteria. This somewhat cramped spot has an unusual service system. You order at the counter, but you're not allowed to sit down until your food is ready. At breakfast, the Paramount bangs out tasty omelets, ham, sausage, bacon, and French toast. Lunch lives up to expectations with burgers, fancy salads, and a continued breakfast menu. At night, the Paramount pulls a Cinderella, adding waitress service, dimming the lights, and turning up the jazz.

THE GREATEST: Exotic Eats

Lala Rokh $$
97 Mount Vernon St., Boston, Mass., (617) 720-5511,
www.lalarokh.com

The cozy, intimate rooms at Lala Rokh are exotic and inviting. The soft lighting, beautiful Iranian art, comfortable seating, and soothing music could relax the most frustrated lobbyist on The Hill. The brother-and-sister owners and their staff take great pride in explaining the Persian menu, which combines unusual complements of Mediterranean herbs, spices, fruits, and nuts. Meats and fragrant basmati rice are the emphasis, often accompanied by chutneys. Try the lamb and chicken kebobs or Mirza Ghasemi, a smoky dish of roasted eggplant, garlic, tomato, and saffron.

THE GREATEST: Thin-Crust Pizza

Upper Crust $
20 Charles St., Boston, Mass., (617) 723-9600,
www.theuppercrustpizzeria.com

The Upper Crust serves "Phan-tastic" thin-crust pizza using fresh toppings. Communal dining and counter service make this pizzeria the perfect place to grab a slice as you stroll the boutiques up and down Charles Street. The menu focuses on Neapolitan-style pies with 30 topping choices or preconceived pies. The thin, crispy MGH pizza features a collection of spinach and chopped broccoli with a sprinkling of feta and chopped tomatoes. Also outstanding, the Canadian bacon and pineapple calzone injects a sesame seed crust with mozzarella, ricotta, and Asiago cheese. There's a second location in Coolidge Corner, Brookline.

THE GREATEST: Fine Dining

No. 9 Park $$$
9 Park St., Boston, Mass., (617) 742-9991,
www.no9park.com

No. 9 Park overlooks the Boston Common from a nineteenth-century mansion. The dining area is elegant, with a powerful clientele enjoying the distinguished surroundings and marble-topped bar tables. The best way to experience the exquisite country European cuisine and sublime pasta is a tasting menu of seven or nine courses. Save room for the cheese tray, which is one of the best in the city. The sister of Congressman Steven Lynch, chef/owner Barbara Lynch has two other hot spots in the South End: B&G Oysters Ltd. and The Butcher Shop.

THE GREATEST: Exotic Butcher Shop

Savenor's Market $$
160 Charles St., Boston, Mass., (617) 723-6328,
www.savenorsmarket.com

Savenor's Market is a throwback to the grocery stores of generations past. The boutique shop sells fresh fish, produce, gourmet oils, specialty pantry items, and even meals to go from area restaurant No. 9 Park. They also have an incredible butcher section with some of the best cuts of beef around. The U.S.D.A. grade Prime tenderloin is Savenor's top seller, and the top round is a relatively tender piece of beef with great flavor. If you fancy London broil, Savenor's Prime rump steak is incredibly juicy. On the exotic end, they offer venison, buffalo, ostrich, emu, bear, rattlesnake, and alligator tail. The experienced staff is glad to explain how to prepare any purchase. Savenor's now has a second location at its original outpost in Harvard Square (on Kirkland Street).

THE GREATEST: Beacon Hill Breakfast

Panificio $
144 Charles St., Boston, Mass., (617) 227-4340,
www.panificioboston.com

With the Beatles and the Beach Boys overhead and huge windows facing Charles Street, Panificio is the kind of place that will make you late for work. Customers order at the counter, but servers bring the food to your table, guided by portable numbers assigned to each guest. A small but solid breakfast menu focuses on eggs and omelets, and the counter supports a tempting selection of baked breads and pastries. The lunch menu has a good selection of salads and sandwiches. At dinner, Panificio adds candles and more serious fare like steak au poivre and potatoes.

THE GREATEST: Cocktails & Cuisine

75 Chestnut $$$
75 Chestnut St., Boston, Mass., (617) 227-2175,
www.75chestnut.com

Because the residents love their quiet neighborhood, Beacon Hill has granted very few full liquor licenses. Good choices are Toscano's, Beacon Hill Bistro, and Phantom's favorite spot for a cocktail, 75 Chestnut. With all the regulars, this place will remind you more of Cheers than the tourist trap nearby. The separate bar area has a great wood bar, four small TVs, and fruit marinating in big liquor bottles. The neighborhood menu provides good cocktail food like the bucket of pommes frites, beer-boiled shrimp cocktail, and half-pound burgers. The dining room has a more serious, old-Boston atmosphere of vintage art, antique fixtures, and plush chairs.

Cambridge
GREAT ATE

On the other side of the Charles, Cambridge is a fascinating web of ethnic eateries, celebrity chefs, and artsy bistros. From Fresh Pond to the CambridgeSide Galleria, Phantom finds the 8 GREATEST Cambridge restaurants.

TASTY TIP Comprised of Harvard Square, Inman Square, Central Square, Kendall Square, and Porter Square, Cambridge makes it easy to eat three square meals a day. Each neighborhood has distinctive dining character; try Harvard for fine dining, Inman and Central for ethnic eats, Kendall for pub grub, and the Porter Exchange (1815 Massachusetts Avenue) for a hidden world of Asian restaurants and shops.

THE GREATEST: Fine Dining

Upstairs on the Square $$$
91 Winthrop St., Cambridge, Mass., (617) 864-1933,
www.upstairsonthesquare.com
Upstairs on the Square near Harvard has two floors of eye-catching decor with animal print carpeting, eclectic chandeliers, and '40s panache. The opulent Soirée Room is a peach vision of metallic brushstrokes and fireplaces, while the Monday Club Bar features mint-green walls, a purple-and-pink-checkered floor, and a fuchsia porch. The eclectic menu is just as bold, with dishes like rabbit ragout over mushrooms and gnocchi. They also do a fabulous Sunday brunch with specialties like duck confit hash, brioche French toast, and lobster omelets.

THE GREATEST: Bakery

Hi-Rise Bread Company $
208 Concord Ave., Cambridge, Mass., (617) 876-8766
Bargain hunters beware. Hi-Rise is not thrifty, but it's undeniably delicious. Stepping into the country cupboard café, your eyes look right past the antique booths and community table toward the gorgeous spread of pastries, pies, and scones piled up at the counter. Almond macaroons and pretty iced sugar cookies sit like pretty gems on tiered petit fours plates. A stylish bake staff works from an open kitchen, with fresh-baked bread highlights like walnut, olive, cheddar-pepper, and babka. They also make killer sandwiches (expensive, but sharable) like the Nat Queen

Cool, combining pulled pork, avocado, cilantro, and harissa or Andi's Loose-Knit Crew with portobellos, gorgonzola, bacon, and spinach. There's also a takeout-only Hi-Rise in Harvard Square.

THE GREATEST: Thai

Sugar & Spice $$
1933 Massachusetts Ave., Cambridge, Mass., (617) 868-4200
Sugar & Spice bolsters the Porter Square dining scene with bright, cheery digs and an expert Thai kitchen. The blue-tiled walls and orbital mood lighting give the atmosphere a retro look that's fun and playful. The eager-to-please staff offers a delectable range of coconut curries, pan-fried noodles, and spice-induced rice dishes. Phantom's favorites are the green papaya salad, drunken noodles in hot basil sauce, steamed ginger fish, and tamarind duck.

THE GREATEST: Cocktails

Cuchi Cuchi $$
795 Main St., Cambridge, Mass., (617) 864-2929,
www.cuchicuchi.net
Cuchi Cuchi near Central Square has stylishly eccentric atmosphere and the best bartenders this side of the Charles. Dressed in all black with flashy rhinestones, these expert drink mixers whip up vintage cocktails like the Old Fashioned and the sidecar, plus hand-muddled Cuchi cocktails like the strawberry basil martini and the blackberry cosmo. The gorgeous old-world bar is set with ornate stained glass (purchased on eBay), and the international menu is served tapas-style for sharing. Phantom's favorites are the tuna carpaccio and salmon tartar, sizzling garlic shrimp, and the French banana bread.

THE GREATEST: Splurge

Craigie Street Bistrot $$$
5 Craigie Circle, Cambridge, Mass., (617) 497-5511,
www.craigiestreetbistrot.com
Tucked between Harvard Square and Huron Village, Craigie Street Bistrot has no end of diners capable of finding the basement-level location. Hefty prices, difficult parking, and tough reservations . . . no obstacle could deter Phantom. Once you've arrived, the French quaintness of the room stretches all the way to the newspaper-covered WC. The wait staff could pass a pop quiz on micro greens, and the hearty French fare is Lyon-inspired, yet fresh-faced, even for Cambridge. Think rillettes, eggs en cocotte, pig belly with crispy sweetbreads, and rosemary poached pears. The best deal on the clipboard menu is the $30, three-course Neighborhood Menu served Wednesday, Thursday, Sunday, and Fridays and Saturdays after 9:00 p.m.

THE GREATEST: Specialty Imports

Cardullo's Gourmet Shoppe $$
6 Brattle St., Cambridge, Mass., (617) 491-8888,
www.cardullos.com
Cardullo's Gourmet Shoppe is a Harvard Square specialty store packed to the ceiling with imported foods, beverages, and deli selections. Along with European teas, chocolates, fruit-filled candies, vintage wine, oils, jam, and honey, customers can shop for high-end sandwiches "to go." Phantom loves the Bambino with Italian prosciutto and mozzarella. But if you really want to blow your cash, order the $65 beluga caviar sandwich with crème fraîche.

THE GREATEST: Wine Bar

Central Kitchen $
567 Massachusetts Ave., Cambridge, Mass., (617) 491-5599,
www.centralkitchen.tv
Central Kitchen goes its own classy way in an otherwise ethnic, eclectic, hard-edged neighborhood. Opting instead for a pretty bistro setting, the Central Square standout delivers rustic Mediterranean fare. Diners experience a slow-down kind of meal at the blue-tiled bar or the copper tables. The chalk-on-slate menu lists olives and oysters to start, followed by duck confit with spiced rhubarb, mussels from Brussels, or roasted spring lamb. The food is flavorful, but it's the wine list that makes this place memorable. Famous châteaux flood the cellar selection, with reserve bottles and many wines by the glass, too.

THE GREATEST: Bargain

River Gods $
125 River St., Cambridge, Mass., (617) 576-1881
A crossroads of eclectic customers, locals, and punks, River Gods near Central Square is a bargain find with a small, but solid beer list. The fun decor includes antique tables and chairs with gargoyles, armor, and other rare treasures. There's also a blended music scene, where Boston's best DJs set up on the raised platform and spin a serious range of tunes. River Gods's underground following is backed by a tasty bar menu with a wild range of food like Thai curry, Irish sausage, steak sandwiches, and shrimp in coconut sauce. Live tunes rock the cozy lounge, and there's never a cover.

Chinatown
GREAT ATE

Boston's Chinatown is a foodie's exotic paradise, offering authentic Asian cuisine at bargain basement prices. Phantom salutes the 8 GREATEST Chinatown eateries.

THE GREATEST: Dumplings

King Fung Garden $
74 Kneeland St., Boston, Mass., (617) 357-5262

King Fung Garden may be a closet-sized hole-in-the-wall, but their ridiculously cheap Chinese dishes include legendary Peking ravioli. The perfect little dumplings are pan-fried and steamed, served with soy and fiery chili sauce. The crispy wontons are just as delicious, with more doughy heft around a pork nugget. Mongolian fire pots are also a house specialty, along with rice cakes, pea pod stems, and the three-course Peking duck that requires a 24-hour notice to prepare. Just remember to bring cash; credit cards are not accepted.

THE GREATEST: Shabu Shabu

Shabu-Zen $$
16 Tyler St, Boston, Mass., (617) 292-8828,
www.shabuzen.com

Shabu-Zen specializes in the Japanese style of cooking called shabu shabu. Seated at a horseshoe-shaped counter, customers select a flavored broth for their own personal hot pot. Uncooked meats, seafood, and veggies are brought out to swirl through the simmering liquid, which you devour with vermicelli noodles or jasmine rice. You also get to mix your own dipping sauce with soy, garlic, scallions, red chilies, and BBQ sauce. Phantom's favorite is the spicy kimchee broth and paper-thin slices of Prime rib eye, along with an icy-cold mango smoothie.

THE GREATEST: Sushi

Ginza $$$
16 Hudson St., Boston, Mass., (617) 338-2261

Ginza is a stark setting of blond wood latticework, with elbow-to-elbow seating and a sushi bar toward the back. There's great late-night people watching when clubbers stop in until 4 a.m. The house specialty spider maki is artfully dramatic with textural contrast. Deep-fried soft-shelled crab, creamy avocado, crisp cucumber, rice, and flying fish roe are wound into giant seaweed slices. The second location in Brookline boasts the same perfectly vinegared sticky rice and tempura green tea ice cream.

THE GREATEST: Regional Chinese

Jumbo Seafood $$
7 Hudson St., Boston, Mass., (617) 542-2823

Jumbo Seafood is Phantom's favorite place for regional Chinese. Just inside the door, there's a huge fish tank where customers can pick out a fresh dinner of lobster, crab, eel, conch, jellyfish, or giant clams and send it straight to the wok. Most dishes are simply breaded and fried Hunan-style and served with light sauces like black bean or soy ginger scallion. They also have spicy Szechuan dishes, sweet and sour specialties, and Cantonese delicacies like shark's fin soup. As a bonus, the inexpensive eatery is open late, until 2 a.m.

THE GREATEST: Exotic Atmosphere

Penang $$
685 Washington St., Boston, Mass., (617) 451-6373

Not all Asian places in Chinatown are Chinese. Penang is one of the most attractive eateries, with its bamboo hut motif and rope walls. The rich decor is matched by an exotic menu of Malaysian cuisine, combining Chinese, Middle Eastern, Thai, and Indian influences. Main flavors include ginger, garlic, black pepper, and chili peppers to heat things up. Phantom likes to start with a watermelon drink and some roti telur, or crispy egg-filled onion pancake served with curry chicken dipping sauce.

THE GREATEST: Seafood

Peach Farm $$
4 Tyler St., Boston, Mass., (617) 482-1116

It's no looker, and the name is unusually fruity, but Peach Farm is wickedly delicious and packed with non-English-speaking aficionados who know their noodles. Dishes include the perfectly crisped egg roll and sumptuous hot and sour soup, but

PF's specialty is Hong Kong–style seafood and sizzling specialties like sesame jellyfish. If you can make it past the twin lobsters with ginger and scallions, order up the pan-seared flounder, walnut shrimp, or salted squid.

THE GREATEST: Chinese Bakery

Eldo Cake House $

36 Harrison Ave., Boston, Mass., (617) 350-7977

Eldo Cake House is Phantom's favorite stop for scrumptious Chinese cakes. These light, tasty sponge cake treats are not as sweet as the typical American version, and they're stuffed with fresh fruit like peach, strawberry, or coconut. Eldo has a great selection of pastries like the egg custard tart made of flaky crust. Other specialties include boba tea, iced walnut rolls, barbecue pork buns, and hardy breakfast congee that could fuel an entire day of Freedom Trail walking.

THE GREATEST: Vegetarian

Buddha's Delight $

3 Beach St., Boston, Mass., (617) 451-2395

If your soul is strictly vegetarian but your heart can't go cold turkey, feed both at Buddha's Delight. Their unique cuisine contains no animal products, but vegan items like "duck" stir-fry, and "beef" chow fun are made with wheat gluten and tofu that imitate the texture and taste of the real deal. Vegetarians experience the rare menu freedom to order from 100 selections, which includes lots of Chinese and Vietnamese options, fruity shakes, noodles, and hot pots. There's a second meat-free location in Brookline.

North End
Restaurants
GREAT ATE

Boston's North End is packed with romantic restaurants and outrageous Italian cuisine. Out of the 100 eateries crammed into one square mile, Phantom picks the 8 GREATEST.

TASTY TIP Resist the tiramisu temptation! In the North End, you should never eat dessert at the same place you have dinner. Pay the check, take a stroll, and grab a cappuccino and a cannoli somewhere else.

THE GREATEST: Late Night

Lucca $$$
226 Hanover St., Boston, Mass., (617) 742-9200,
www.luccaboston.com
Lucca is quite a hot spot, with a solid mahogany bar that stretches from a massive stained-glass mural toward the French doors, framed in ivy. The grappa list will knock your Versace off, and the kitchen keeps firing until 12:15 a.m. Downstairs, the view shifts from the street scene to the glass-encased wine collection framed in stone walls. The fabulous 500-bottle wine list pairs with Lucca's modern Italian menu. Upscale dishes include the goat cheese duck tart and wild boar rigatoni.

THE GREATEST: Undiscovered

Prezza $$$
24 Fleet St., Boston, Mass., (617) 227-1577,
www.prezza.com
Off the main drag, Prezza draws a word-of-mouth crowd for rustic Italian cuisine that's fit for the Phantom. You'll forget the touristy throngs just a couple blocks away when you relax into Prezza's discreet setting of neutral colors and abstract oil paintings. Regulars like to check in at the bar before sitting down to Mediterranean-influenced dishes like balsamic figs bundled with Gorgonzola and prosciutto. The house ravioli are cooked with different exciting flavors like sage brown butter, roasted pears, or spicy sausage and roasted tomatoes.

THE GREATEST: **Mob Scene**

Strega $$$
379 Hanover St., Boston, Mass., (617) 523-8481,
www.stregaristorante.com

Straying from red sauce tradition, Strega gives the North End creative Italian cook-
ing and glittery decor that draws celebrities. The ristorante's name means *witch* in
Italian, and the hypnotizing theme translates into vivid wall murals. The look is
racy and hot, with flirtatious yellow backlighting to illuminate the room's royal col-
ors and stylish black-clad servers. Mob movies like *The Godfather* play on the flat-
screen TV, but all eyes are on the modern Italian dishes like grilled salmon with
capers and mustard sauce. Phantom loves their homemade mozzarella and their
calamari, which comes marinated and grilled or deep-fried.

THE GREATEST: **Mix & Match Menu**

Giacomo's $$
355 Hanover St., Boston, Mass., (617) 523-9026

Giacomo's is a tiny trattoria with straightforward Italian food that won't wear out
your wallet. Lines form outside early in the evening, and customers are rushed in
and out of the charming, crowded little eatery. A huge chalkboard menu covers one
brick wall, with daily specials on the other side of the room. The concept is refreshingly basic; customers mix and match a dish of fresh seafood, pasta, and one
of five flavorful sauces. Phantom recommends sticking to classics, like huge plates
of linguine marinara tossed with succulent shellfish.

THE GREATEST: **Modern Italian**

Sage $$$
69 Prince St., Boston, Mass., (617) 248-8814,
www.sageboston.com

Sage is a wee little bistro that makes a big old impression. The chef-owner grew up
working at his father's butcher shop in the North End, so you can bank on the best
charcuterie in town. The fresh menu is contemporary American rooted in Italian
and French tradition. Phantom loves the potato gnocchi in sage brown butter with
pulled rabbit and edamame. There's also a gorgeous chicken served with potato
foam. No more than 28 linen tables line the clay-colored room, so make reserva-
tions or prepare to wait.

THE GREATEST: Table for 2

Carmen $$$
33 North Square, Boston, Mass., (617) 742-6421
Carmen is a snug, romantic hideout with rough brick walls, wine racks at an arm's length, and low, low lighting. The Italian menu includes small tapas-style plates that are great for sharing or nibbling on at the tiny wine bar up front. Phantom has recurring dreams about the sweet roasted beet salad with red onion, basil, and milky ricotta salata. More substantial dishes include parchment-baked penne marinara with meatballs and the slow-roasted rack of pork.

THE GREATEST: Tailor-Made Meals

Dom's $
10 Bartlett Pl., Boston, Mass., (617) 367-8979
Hidden down a side street, Dom's is perfectly positioned for family dining. The dizzying Italian menu is a whopping 18 pages long, but most customers defer to Dom, who likes to invite himself to the table and ask what you're in the mood to eat. Is there anything the amazing Dom doesn't do? He waits tables, hustles in the kitchen, and sees to it that everyone in the house is happy. Dom's caters to the kiddies, too, offering complimentary spaghetti and a meatball to anyone under 12.

THE GREATEST: Wine Bar

Enoteca Bricco $$$
241 Hanover St., Boston, Mass., (617) 248-6800,
www.bricco.com
Enoteca Bricco is a low-key wine bar with candlelit dining and windows that open onto Hanover Street in the summer months. The wood-burning oven fires away in the exhibition kitchen, and the granite bar is fortified by bins of wine, wine, and more wine. Bricco is exorbitantly expensive, but you'll be gushing over the signature bread pudding all the way to the ATM. The modern Italian menu features innovations like Kobe beef risotto with basil ragu and roasted veal chops with a foie gras crocchette, roasted orange, paprika, and mint.

North End Shops
GREAT ATE

Boston's North End boasts the best Italian finds this side of the Boot. Phantom loves the neighborhood's restaurants, but he especially enjoys snacking in the 8 GREATEST shops and stores.

TASTY TIP **Whether it's a bakery, a coffee shop, or a gourmet grocery, most North End shops offer food samples for good customers. Just don't abuse their generosity by asking for a taste of every cheese in the deli case.**

THE GREATEST: Italian Grocery Store

Salumeria Italiana $$
151 Richmond St., Boston, Mass., (617) 523-8743,
www.salumeriaitaliana.com

Salumeria Italiana is America's best Italian grocery store, selling fabulous salami, Prosciutto di Parma, pasta, and San Marzano tomatoes. The flavor-packed olives are naturally cured in brine for months, and the best selection of artisinal cheeses is available every Friday, when the shipment arrives from Italy. There's also Sicilian sea salt, boar sausage, basil and sun-dried tomato pesto, Mediterranean yellowfin tuna packed in oil, and tomato sauce made with capers and chili peppers. The awesome olive oils range from light yellow to dark green, and slipper-shaped ciabatta bread is available on Saturday only. Counter clerks encourage tasting before buying, so you're sure to be pleased with your purchase.

THE GREATEST: *Sfogliatelle*

Maria's Pastry Shop $
46 Cross St., Boston, Mass., (617) 523-1196,
www.northendboston.com/marias

Maria's Pastry Shop makes the most amazing *sfogliatelle*. The flaky, layered pastry is shaped like a clamshell and filled with cheese, flour, and citron fruit. Sold as standard breakfast fare in Naples, it's sugary sweet and terrifically rich. Maria sells about 400 a week, and every one is cut by hand. Maria's menu also includes cannoli, torrone, and crispelli. They stay true to seasonal Italian specialties like ricotta wheat pie at Christmas, Easter egg bread with hard-boiled eggs baked right into the dough, marzipan lambs, and zeppolo donuts on St. Joseph's Day (March 19).

THE GREATEST: Gelato

Caffe Paradiso $
253 Hanover St., Boston, Mass., (617) 742-1768,
www.caffeparadiso.com

Caffe Paradiso has great espresso, cappuccino, cakes, and cannoli, but the house specialty is homemade Italian gelato in silky, smooth flavors. The sweet, creamy frozen treat is denser and more of a custard than ice cream, made with natural ingredients like wild berries, real cocoa, and even homemade tiramisu. Locals and tourists mingle in the upscale coffee bar, decorated with Roman statues and flags from countries around the world. It's also one of the only places in town where you can catch Italian soccer and European league rugby via satellite. Additional Harvard Square and Lowell locations have the same inviting vibe.

THE GREATEST: Italian Candy

Dairy Fresh Candies $
57 Salem St., Boston, Mass., (617) 742-2639,
www.dairyfreshcandies.com

Dairy Fresh Candies carries the best selection of Italian candies in the neighborhood. The first room is a crowded, tight aisle of goodies by the bag, while the second is stocked with a tempting candy counter of fudge, nuts, and chocolate-dipped pretzels. If hard candies are your pleasure, Perugina flavors include mint, coffee, eggnog, blackberry, lemon, and tangerine. Dairy Fresh also sells licorice chips, gummy candy, Baci chocolates, and candy-coated cinnamon sticks. While anticipating your next sugar craving, stock the baking pantry, too; there's an unbelievable assortment flour, flavored oils, and exotic dried fruits like papaya.

THE GREATEST: Cannoli

Modern Pastry $
257 Hanover St., Boston, Mass., (617) 523-3783,
www.modernpastry.com

One of the North End's oldest pastry shops, Modern Pastry makes the best cannoli. Crispy tubes of deep-fried pastry shell are filled at the last second (so they don't go soggy), dipped in chocolate chips, and dusted with powdered sugar. Other Italian specialties include honey almond nougat called torrone, decadent wedding cakes, rich ricotta pie, and marzipan bomba. Cookie freaks have a heck of a time choosing from delicate Florentines, chocolate biscotti, pignoli cookies, and raspberry-filled bow ties. The store isn't equipped with much seating, which explains the spindles of box string dangling above the counter. There's a second location in Medford.

THE GREATEST: Wine Shop

Wine Bottega $$
341 Hanover St., Boston, Mass., (617) 227-6607
The Wine Bottega houses 500 different wine selections and more than 7,000 bottles. Hardwood floors and antique furniture add to the quaint, rustic atmosphere. The cramped shop deals exclusively in quality wines, though they hardly carry any big brand names. Collectors often discover hard-to-find treasures among the racks, but novices can count on the help of the knowledgeable and friendly staff to find those unsung labels of exceptional value. On Friday evenings from 5 to 8 p.m., they even host free tastings and live jazz.

THE GREATEST: Brick Oven Bread

Boschetto Bakery $
158 Salem St., Boston, Mass., (617) 523-9350
For a quick bite on Salem Street, Boschetto Bakery turns out simple slices of Sicilian-style pizza. The breads are baked in a massive 130-year-old brick oven that can hold as many as 200 loaves. All the hot, right-out-of-the-oven loaves spill over the tabletops, display cases, and shelves that pack the store. There's crusty Tuscan bread, hard little taralline knots, and sesame seed scali from southern Italy. Some loaves are round with a soft, airy center, while others are rough-textured, stretched to three feet.

THE GREATEST: Pastry Selection

Mike's Pastry $
300 Hanover St., Boston, Mass., (617) 742-3050,
www.mikespastry.com
Mike's Pastry has a legendary following and choice real estate on the main drag. With Phantom's favorite selection of Italian pastry, the spacious shop even has enough room for café seating. Their sinful signature is the Lobster Tail of layered, pulled dough that's stuffed with a sinful blend of whipped cream, ricotta cheese, and yellow custard. The boconnotto is a Munchkin-sized cream puff; the baba rum cakes are soft and sweet; and the ring-shaped taralli cookies come plain or sugar-coated. Also available in massive quantities are cookies, cakes, and marzipan. Mike's sells a couple thousand cannoli every day, in flavors like ricotta, yellow cream, chocolate cream, chocolate dipped, and chocolate chip.

South End

GREAT ATE

Boston's South End is a picture-perfect cluster of brownstones, boutiques, and outstanding restaurants. For the city's funkiest atmosphere and most cutting-edge cuisine, Phantom visits the 8 GREATEST South End eateries.

TASTY TIP **Olde Dutch Cottage Candy on Tremont Street is the most mysteriously delicious store in the South End. This candy store/antique shop/florist is open about 12 hours a year, but it's the only place in town where you can find chocolate truffles, Liberace portraits, and silk roses under one roof.**

THE GREATEST: Sleek Scene

Mistral $$$
223 Columbus Ave., Boston, Mass., (617) 867-9300,
www.mistralbistro.com

With the strength of its namesake winds (and exquisite Mediterranean fare), Mistral sweeps high-profile diners off their pedicured feet. Seafood, olive oil, tomatoes, and garlic are used with tremendous results such as the Dover sole with lemons and capers. Thin-grilled pizza is the scrumptious signature appetizer, served with smoky chili oil. Every bite goes down smoothly in this soaring space that's both rustic and stylish. Terra-cotta floors, Provençal fabrics, and mini cypress trees add a European touch, and Boston beauties meet and mingle at bar. For a taste of high society, forget the valet and reserve Mistral's complimentary car service, available to guests in Boston proper.

THE GREATEST: Wine Bar

The Butcher Shop $$$
552 Tremont St., Boston, Mass., (617) 423-4800,
www.thebutchershopboston.com

Barbara Lynch (of No. 9 Park and B&G Oysters) gives the neighborhood a double dose of deliciousness in one tiny storefront. The Butcher Shop is a charcuterie store by day and a trendy wine bar by night. Boeuf snobs unite over high-end noshes like the antipasto plate of artisinal cheese, herb-infused olives, and designer meats like rillettes, foie gras, pâté, and marrow. The wine list is mostly European, and there's plenty of standing room to mingle around the mammoth butcher block table. The elegant atmosphere and A-list crowd make this cured-meat Mecca the most prestigious butcher shop in town.

THE GREATEST: Gourmet Café

Garden of Eden $$
571 Tremont St, Boston, Mass., (617) 247-8377,
www.goeboston.com

Garden of Eden is a sweet little spot that's part café, part bakery, and part gourmet market. The dining room is a collection of antique tables with a stellar street view of Tremont. There's also upscale takeout for those purchasing desserts and picnic provisions like hummus and smoked salmon. Phantom prefers to sit down and dig into a Springfield Salad of beets, walnuts, and goat cheese. Excellent sandwiches include the Grey Street meat loaf on focaccia with spicy apricot ketchup. Just when you think it couldn't get any sweeter, the pastry case hits you in the eye with fruit tarts, chocolate genoise, raspberry crumb bars, and petits fours.

THE GREATEST: Roasted Chicken

Hamersley's Bistro $$$
553 Tremont St., Boston, Mass., (617) 423-2700,
www.hamersleysbistro.com

Hamersley's Bistro is the homey French eatery that Phantom's been looking for all his life. The prices may blow your mind (entrées topping $40), but the food will, too. It's European comfort food that's simple, yet delicious. For starters, the salad of roasted pear, endive, and Roquefort balances bitter leaves with aged balsamic vinaigrette. The house specialty of moist roasted chicken surrenders garlic, lemon, and parsley flavors with every single bite. Pale brick walls, wrought-iron candelabras, and wooden ceiling beams reinforce the refined country setting. You can usually catch Gordon Hamersley working away in the open kitchen, sporting his signature Red Sox cap.

THE GREATEST: Global Menu

Equator $$
1721 Washington St., Boston, Mass., (617) 536-6386,
www.equatorrestaurantma.com

There's something for everyone at Equator, a global concept where Asian, European, and American dishes find themselves on the same menu. You'll feel like you're in a land far, far away while biting into chicken satay with peanut and cucumber dipping sauces. Other favorites include the soft-shell crab tempura, six kinds of curry, prime rib with a baked potato, and crispy tamarind duck. If you're into noodles, they have pad Thai or Cajun chicken pasta. It's all eclectically delicious, including the mix-and-match stir-fries. The global atmosphere incorporates artifacts from all around the world.

THE GREATEST: **Romantic Restaurant**

Icarus $$$
3 Appleton St., Boston, Mass., (617) 426-1790,
www.icarusrestaurant.com

When it comes to romance, Icarus cooks up the perfect recipe of dark wood, dim lighting, and lusty plates that'll have you swapping bites. A statue of Icarus himself, the high-flying mythological figure, is displayed in the two-tiered layout. The contemporary New American menu stresses superlative ingredients that emphasize locally grown produce and farm-raised meat. The signature appetizer is the grilled shrimp with mango-jalapeño sorbet. And at dessert, don't you dare order anything but the chocolate molten soufflé cake with raspberry sauce and vanilla bean ice cream.

THE GREATEST: **Cocktail Lounge**

28 Degrees $$
1 Appleton St., Boston, Mass., (617) 728-0728,
www.28degrees-boston.com

This South End cocktail lounge is named for the proper temperature of a well-made martini, but the atmosphere is much hotter than that. Stylish guests share tapas-style plates while sinking into soft leather seats or mingling at the blue-lit bar. The eclectic menu ranges from raw-bar seafood to bacon cheeseburger sliders and spicy shrimp wontons. Phantom can't resist their rosemary-thyme fries served with lemon pepper aioli and homemade ketchup. But the real reason to hit 28 Degrees is for devilish drinks like the melon martini garnished with prosciutto-wrapped cantaloupe. Be sure to enjoy enough liquids so you can check out the votive-lit, unisex bathroom, where water trickles across a glass ceiling.

THE GREATEST: **Dueling Menu**

Sibling Rivalry $$$
525 Tremont St., Boston, Mass., (617) 338-5338
www.siblingrivalryboston.com

The brothers behind Sibling Rivalry have taken the family feud to a tasty new level. Bob and David Kinkead, both with impressive restaurant resumes, go head-to-head to offer two separate menus from the same exhibition kitchen. You can't help but play favorites as they each take a different spin on the same ingredients. For the "ginger face-off," the spicy root goes into Chef David's tuna tartar with wasabi aioli and Chef Bob's fried squid with papaya-Thai basil salad. The competition gets heated with other standouts like crispy duck in a cherry port reduction. The service can be pretentious, but you'll be too distracted by metallic curtains and lime green sconces to notice.

Theater District
GREAT ATE

If you're anything like Phantom, finding the perfect pre-theater meal is the most important act all night. Phantom curtain calls the 8 GREATEST Theater District eateries.

TASTY TIP Looking for a lickety-split intermission snack? Dominic's (255 Tremont Street) is a total dive with no special menu, but it's perfect for grabbing a quick, cheap slice before the show or between acts.

THE GREATEST: Trendy Italian

Teatro $$
177 Tremont St, Boston, Mass., (617) 778-6841,
www.teatroboston.com

Teatro, which means "theater" in Italian, is a stunning space. The arched, ornate barrel ceiling is gorgeous, cast with soft blue lighting that hangs like heavy applause. The restaurant is a fabulous choice for fine northern Italian dining like thin-crust pizza topped with hot peppers and sea salt. The rigatoni with ragu Bolognese is classic and meaty, and the grilled rib eye comes with Gorgonzola butter. Most of the high decibel buzz comes from the bar, where one-of-a-kind cocktails include the lemoncello-laced Carlini Tini. Even Teatro's Web site is accessible to all the local playhouses; you can link to their sites and even check show times.

THE GREATEST: French Romance

Pigalle $$$
75 Charles St. South, Boston, Mass., (617) 423-4944,
www.pigalleboston.com

At Pigalle, renowned chef Marc Orfaly gets pre-theater dinner applause from Phantom. Stunning dishes reassemble familiar ingredients into something deliciously surprising. The classy menu is seasonal with fine French, Mediterranean, and even Asian influence. Phantom gives a standing ovation to the tuna tartare served on an iced scallop shell. Other specialties include the rib eye steak frites and the bean cassoulet of pork, duck confit, and lamb. Pigalle is a handsome black-and-tan setting with curved leather banquettes, vintage chandeliers, and beaded sconces. Settle into the six-seat bar for inexpensive eats from one of Boston's top kitchens.

THE GREATEST: Pre-Theater Steak

Smith & Wollensky $$$
101 Arlington St., Boston, Mass., (617) 423-1112,
www.smithandwollensky.com

A New York–style steakhouse, Smith & Wollensky has 11 locations across the country. Their four-story Boston powerhouse makes its opulent home in the medieval Armory castle. It's lavished with red velvet, marble fireplaces, animal trophies, and vintage Americana. Portions (and prices) are obscene, including five-pound lobsters and barbaric cuts of beef like the 28-ounce Colorado ribsteak. Also on the picture-framed menu are mountainous portions of onion rings (enough to feed 10!) and 650 selections on the Great American Wine List. Colossal desserts include the ice cream sundae with candy toppings and frozen bananas dipped in chocolate, caramel, butterscotch, or raspberry coulis.

THE GREATEST: Wine Bar

Troquet $$$
140 Boylston St., Boston, Mass., (617) 695-9463,
www.troquetboston.com

Troquet is a smart setting of burgundy walls lined with mirrors. Phantom gives a standing ovation to their rotating selection of fine wines by the glass. Giving unprecedented menu attention to varietals and vintages, four dozen bottles are listed down the center of the spread. Matching dishes are paired off to the sides, with appetizers on the left and entrées on the right. Wines can be sampled in two- and four-ounce pours, and there are 350 available by the bottle. The open kitchen prepares fabulous wine-friendly French and Italian cuisine like foie gras and roasted venison.

THE GREATEST: Happy Hour Menu

McCormick & Schmick's $$
34 Columbus Ave., Boston, Mass., (617) 482-3999,
www.mccormickandschmicks.com

McCormick & Schmick's is a seafood and steakhouse with outrageously cheap happy hour food. Theatergoers can swing by before the show until 6:30 p.m. (weekdays) and afterward from 10 to midnight for the $1.95 social hour menu at the bar. In addition to half-pound cheeseburgers with fries, changing selections include steamed mussels in garlic chili broth, clam shooters, cheese quesadillas, chicken wings, bruschetta, and oysters on the half shell. Phantom likes to position himself at the bar with a stiff drink and put his purple chompers on autopilot.

THE GREATEST: Chinese Chain

P. F. Chang's $$
8 Park Plaza, Boston, Mass., (617) 573-0821,
www.pfchangs.com
P. F. Chang's has successfully transplanted Chinese food into a hip, contemporary
chain. Titanic Chinese lion sculptures flank the entrance, while the chic, faux stone
interior includes earth tones, Mongolian warrior sculptures, and carved wooden
screens. Oversized booths are perfect for family dining, and sauces are whipped up
tableside. Chang's approachable Chinese menu includes tasty chicken lettuce
wraps and orange peel beef. For decadent desserts, check out the six-layer Great
Wall of Chocolate with raspberry coulis.

THE GREATEST: Dessert Course

Finale $$
1 Columbus Ave., Boston, Mass., (617) 423-3184,
www.finaledesserts.com
Defying the mantra of mothers everywhere, Finale insists that dessert comes first.
The elegant desserterie serves light meals and hot toddies, but it's the artfully stunning cookies, cakes, and chocolates that are the main course for most diners.
They're open late for the post-theater crowd, perfecting signature dishes like
molten chocolate cake and crème brûlée. Phantom flips for the Manjari mousse and
the tiny little fruit tartlets. Both locations in Boston's Park Plaza and Harvard
Square are splurge-worthy and have mirrored kitchens so you can watch on as
desserts are assembled.

THE GREATEST: Upscale Burger

The Bristol $$
200 Boylston Street, Boston, Mass., (617) 338-4400,
www.fourseasons.com/boston/dining
The Bristol in the distinguished Four Seasons Hotel may seem like last place you'd
order a burger, but their $17 VIP version takes old-school comfort food to luxury
levels. The juicy half-pound sirloin patty is neatly wrapped in aged Vermont ched-
dar on a toasted poppy seed bun. There's also a double-smoked bacon burger and a
black truffle burger on brioche. The sprawling den-like setting displays red leather
sofas, fireplaces, and a grand piano at the bar.

Cape Cod
GREAT ATE

Cape Cod has long been known for beautiful beaches, cranberry bogs, and summer rentals, but these days it's worth the drive for the restaurants alone. From the Sagamore Bridge to P-town, Phantom reveals the 8 GREATEST Cape Cod eateries.

TASTY TIP There's not a whole lot to do when rainy days douse the Cape. Before the first raindrop hits the ground, bolt for the Cape Cod Potato Chip factory in Hyannis. A quarter million visitors take the free, self-guided tour every year, which concludes with a free bag of Phantom's favorite chips. The factory is open to tours, Monday through Friday from 9 a.m. to 5 p.m. Go to www.capecodchips.com for more information.

THE GREATEST: Wine & Dine

Chillingsworth $$$
2449 Main St./Route 6A, Brewster, Mass., (508) 896-3640, www.chillingsworth.com

Set in a 300-year-old mansion, Chillingsworth is Phantom's favorite spot on the Cape for wining and dining. The exquisite tasting menu guides every guest on a seven-course French culinary adventure. Tasty tidbits like chilled plum soup and grapefruit sorbet are placed between the main dishes, along with amusements and coffee. Featured plates include seared venison with huckleberries and grilled figs and the nectarine tart with whipped mascarpone. Each sloping, squat room of the Colonial manner is appointed with antiques and period wallpaper. Corner hutches and mix-and-match china make the vacationing crowd feel right at home, and six acres of gardens and lawns surround the property.

THE GREATEST: Clambake

Lobster Pot $$
321 Commercial St., Provincetown, Mass., (508) 487-0842, www.ptownlobsterpot.com

The Lobster Pot occupies a harborside, double-decker building that juts out like a long pier. All eyes are on the bobbing boats beyond the fishing village, and the "Top of the Pot" is the perfect place for cocktails as the sun goes down in P-town. The seafood menu ranges from classic shellfish to innovative oysters with pesto to

Portuguese specialties. The traditional clam chowder comes full of briny bivalves, and Phantom's favorite is the pan-roasted lobster in buttery brandy sauce. Be sure to save room for amazing desserts like key lime pie and the mint chocolate chip ice cream sandwich slathered in chocolate sauce.

THE GREATEST: Urban Style Splurge

Twenty-Eight Atlantic $$$
Wequassett Inn, Route 28 Pleasant Bay, Chatham, Mass., (508) 430-3000, www.28atlantic.com

If you've got the bank, roll to Twenty-Eight Atlantic at the Wequassett Inn. The prices are outrageous, but no one seems to bat an eye, unless it's directed toward the gaping view of Pleasant Bay below. Twenty-Eight is exclusive and extravagant with a country club Park Avenue atmosphere of oversized tables and tuxedo-checked chairs. The lofty space is nautically cosmopolitan, and the trendy menu blends American luxury with incredible seafood. Every dish is intricately plated, like the caramelized scallops nested in golden potato webs over pillows of peeky-toe crab. Each course outdoes the last, dripping in delicacies like caviar butter, oxtail ragout, truffles, and foie gras buttons.

THE GREATEST: "Moving" Dinner Experience

Cape Cod Central Railroad $$
252 Main St., Hyannis, Mass., (508) 771-3800, www.capetrain.com

All aboard! The Cape Cod Central Railroad is a truly unique choo-choo experience that combines a scenic ride with a gourmet lunch, brunch, or five-course dinner. The vintage train chugs along a 46-mile, three-hour journey, while the converted kitchen prepares everything on board from an old baggage car. To partake of this unique meal, get your caboose to Hyannis Station and embark on an elegant $60 evening of creamy seafood chowder and entrées like lobster stuffed haddock. As you barrel over the Cape Cod Canal, you'll move on to silky-smooth raspberry chocolate cheesecake. The three-course, $35 lunch is less formal, and there's a Family Supper Train that caters to kids, too.

THE GREATEST: Bar Scene

RooBar $$
586 Main St., Hyannis, Mass., (508) 778-6515, www.theroobar.com

When you want to escape the Cape without leaving the peninsula, RooBar is the perfect place. Nothing about it screams flip-flops and lobster print pants, so be sure to pack your weekend bag full of clubwear. All three locations (Chatham and Falmouth, too) are sleek and sexy with urban atmosphere, yet each one pioneers its own trendy menu. Expect racy concoctions like cinnamon steak, tuna parfait with cilantro lime sorbet, banana-encrusted halibut, or soy-candied spiced ribs. RooBar also does outstanding pizzas with crazy toppings like duck confit, spiced lamb, or a balsamic glaze.

THE GREATEST: Ice Cream Parlor

Four Seas Ice Cream $
360 South Main St., Centerville, Mass., (508) 775-1394,
www.fourseasicecream.com

Four Seas is a darling soda shoppe with parlor chairs, swivel stools, old-fashioned dipping cabinets, and blue flower boxes outside. They have the longest-running ice cream tradition on the Cape, operating out of what was once a blacksmith shop. All of their 34 flavors are churned out of a 10-gallon batch freezer, made with an awesome 16 percent butterfat content and very low overrun. They refuse to top their superior scoops with cheap jimmies, but who cares when you can load up on homemade sauces like butterscotch, blackberry brandy, or crème de menthe. Four Seas is even responsible for inventing several flavors like chip chocolate, penuche pecan, and cantaloupe.

THE GREATEST: Oyster Insanity

Naked Oyster Bistro & Raw Bar $$
20 Independence Dr., Hyannis, Mass., (508) 778-6500,
www.nakedoyster.com

Naked Oyster captures the essence of Cape Cod dining with fresh fish dishes, a chill raw bar, and a dozen different varieties of oysters. Among the oyster choices are "dressed oysters" cooked on the half shell. The Barbecued Bleu is embedded with Great Hill Bleu cheese, caramelized onion, and barbecue sauce, while the Bienville is served with mushrooms, garlic, shrimp, and bacon. There's also the Baked Oishi with pickled ginger and wasabi and the Mediterranean with Gaeta olives, feta, and spinach. The handsome setting is more upscale than the strip mall location implies; united by an ocean theme, the dark wood room gets a cozy glow from candles and oyster lamps overhead.

Red Pheasant Inn $$$
905 Main St., Dennis, Mass., (508) 385-2133,
www.redpheasantinn.com

The Red Pheasant Inn is nestled in a barn that's nearly as old as the nation. The old-world atmosphere is born out in wide plank floors, exposed beams, and two blazing fireplaces. It's a cozy setting complete with rustic pottery and handblown stemware, and the garden out back contributes edible flowers and fragrant herbs for cooking. On the menu, it's classic-meets-creative with New England fare that evolves with the seasons. The kitchen is best known for the rack of lamb cooked in port wine, rosemary, and garlic, but they also prepare a nightly game special along with duckling, local seafood, and aged beef. The impressive wine cellar is well stocked with bottles from Bordeaux, Burgundy, and the Rhone.

Providence
GREAT ATE

Providence is a hot dining scene with authentic Italian on Federal Hill and cutting-edge cuisine for a fraction of what you'd pay in Boston. The best reason to head south? Phantom didn't even pay for parking at the 8 GREATEST Providence restaurants.

TASTY TIP

WaterFire is a "moving sculpture" that takes over downtown Providence all summer long. A few sunsets a month from May to October, the summer series illuminates floating bonfires along a half-mile stretch of three different rivers. Spectators stroll the banks or make dinner reservations at outdoor restaurants along the way. All the details are at www.waterfire.com.

THE GREATEST: Trendsetter

XO Steakhouse $$$
125 North Main St., Providence, R.I. (401) 273-9090,
www.xocafe.com

XO Steakhouse is hot and trendy with provocative sculptures scattered throughout. The exuberant atmosphere includes graffiti walls and random sounds piped into the bathroom. With a motto of, "Life is short, order dessert first," the restaurant promises to break all the norms. The red meat menu kicks off with fluorescent cocktails, followed by a slew of Black Angus steaks. Each cut, including the espresso-rubbed hangar steak, comes with sauces like the tamarind XO. And their French fries are deliciously outrageous, tossed with truffle oil and Parmesan cheese.

THE GREATEST: New-Age Italian

Raphael Bar Risto $$$
1 Union Station, Providence, R.I., (401) 421-4646,
www.raphaelbarristo.com

Raphael Bar Risto is classy and fashionable, and it's carved out of a converted train station that sits waterside. Blond maple wood floors, rich Travertine marble ceilings, a tunnel bar, and colorful paintings contribute to the gorgeous atmosphere. As a pioneer of wood fire cooking, the chef/owner works the element of surprise into his contemporary Italian menu. Phantom likes to start with one of their salads or the daily changing pizza, like the crispy margarita embedded with mozzarella medallions and basil leaves.

THE GREATEST: Italian Wines

Pane e Vino $$

365 Atwells Ave., Providence, R.I., (401) 223-2230,
www.panevino.net

Pane e Vino forms a busy stretch of buttery walls and close-knit tables. The honest
Neapolitan menu gets a lift from an incredible Italian wine list that's even more un-
believable on half-price Mondays. As for the food, it's the classics that are exe-
cuted so well. Roasted red and yellow peppers are heaped over whole basil and
buffalo mozzarella; the rack of lamb sits in a rich cherry demi-glace; and the
golden raisin bread pudding guards the most sweetly saturated center under a crisp
brûléed top.

THE GREATEST: Wood Fired Fare

Mill's Tavern $$$

101 North Main St., Providence, R.I., (401) 272-3331

Mill's Tavern is a classy lattice of dark wood with earthy accents of stone, brick,
and even an oyster shell-embedded bar. Tall oak booths help break up the spacious
room, along with an open kitchen and hurricane lamps. The menu includes a raw
bar but emphasizes rustic wood-fired fare. The tuna Napoleon is a four-tiered tower
with coconut and lemongrass, and for a savory twist on a favorite dessert, try the
Roquefort cheesecake with sides of pear confit and port thyme elixir.

THE GREATEST: Grilled Pizza

Al Forno $$$

577 South Main St., Providence, R.I., (401) 273-9760,
www.alforno.com

Open for five dinners a week, Al Forno is the famous inventor of grilled pizza. The
wood-smoked, paper-thin crust wears a garlicky tomato sauce on pies like the
Provençal, cooked over an open flame with black olive tapenade and goat cheese.
The kitchen also turns out oven-baked dishes like rigatoni with five pepper sauce
and the spicy clam roast. White tablecloth dining takes place on two elegant levels
with an ivory downstairs and a second floor decorated in slate stone tiles.

THE GREATEST: Rustic Fine Dining

New Rivers $$$

7 Steeple St., Providence, R.I., (401) 751-0350,
www.newriversrestaurant.com

New Rivers is a cozy bistro where the modern American cuisine contrasts bril-
liantly with the old-world charm. Intimate, adjoining rooms are painted a deep for-

est green with scarlet accents and pear portraits. Tiny tables and twinkling lights add to the warm, inviting atmosphere. The progressive menu allows for smaller appetites, offering entrées in four- and eight-ounce portions, all with locally farmed ingredients. Waiters in jeans and button-downs jive with the unpretentious atmosphere, while serving charcuterie such as pheasant rillettes with shallot marmalade and rosemary mustard. Other standouts include the juniper-crusted venison loin and wild salmon with beet chips and turnip bisque.

THE GREATEST: Antipasti Bar

Mediterraneo $$$
134 Atwells Ave., Providence, R.I., (401) 331-7760,
www.mediterraneocaffe.com

Mediterraneo offers fine Italian dining and sexy, urban atmosphere. Giant French doors and striking granite and cherrywood bars add to the trendy vibe. Old-world steaks, seafood, and pasta are plated with imaginative presentation, but it's the antipasti bar that makes the biggest impression. The spread changes daily, but includes such items as prosciutto, cipolline onions, provolone, sautéed eggplant, red and yellow peppers, bean salad, potato croquettes, arancini rice balls, olives, or mushrooms. On Friday and Saturday nights, the second level transforms into Club Mediterraneo, a hip Latin dance club.

THE GREATEST: Sandwich Assortment

Geoff's Superlative Sandwiches $
163 Benefit St., Providence, R.I., (401) 751-2248
www.geoffsonline.com

Geoff's Superlative Sandwiches puts a hip spin on the midday meal, with a funky college atmosphere of a checkered floor, 10 raised stools, and exposed brick. There's even a pickle barrel smack in the center of the space; customers are invited to serve themselves as many dill spears as they can stomach. The chalkboard menu lists 100 quirky sandwiches with playful names like Jaws (tuna salad, melted cheese), "Slim" Jim O'Neil (lettuce, tomato, onion, alfalfa sprouts, horseradish), and The Godfather (hot pepperoni, genoa salami, Provolone, pepperoncini oil). Or enlighten Geoff's with your own inventive combination on a choice of seeded rye, wheat, pumpernickel, or a bulky roll.

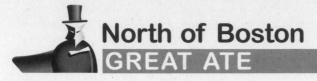

North of Boston
GREAT ATE

The North Shore stands out for its history, rocky coastline, and a growing dining scene of approachable restaurants with affordable prices. Phantom salutes the 8 GREATEST restaurants North of Boston.

TASTY TIP Route 1 in Saugus is the culinary equivalent of the Las Vegas Strip. Take the ultimate tasty tour of plastic cows (Hilltop Steakhouse), the "Leaning Tower of Pizza" (Prince Restaurant), and a Chinese palace (Kowloon).

THE GREATEST: Oyster Bar

Finz $$
76 Wharf St., Salem, Mass., (978) 744-8485,
www.hipfinz.com
Finz takes full advantage of a waterfront location on Salem's Pickering Wharf. Whether sipping colorful martinis out on the patio or slurping oysters by the fireplace, the Atlantic Ocean is never out of sight. The spacious, modern dining room gives the suburban spot a big-city feel, yet the prices are quite moderate for the high quality and creativity. Phantom's favorite dishes include Finz's famous Stoli-wasabi oysters, the spicy Buffalo calamari, and baked lobster stuffed with crabmeat, shrimp, and scallops.

THE GREATEST: North Shore Steakhouse

Gavens $$$
119 S. Main St., Middleton, Mass., (978) 774-0500
Gavens is a stylish suburban steakhouse, offering Prime cuts of meat and an extensive collection of wine. There's nothing "small town" about this fine dining restaurant. It's dark and intimate with plaid curtains and framed mirrors decorating the faint yellow walls. The beefy menu salutes Prime steaks, seafood, and other carnivorous cuts of meat like luscious lamb chops. Phantom likes to preface a New York strip steak with some Alaskan king crab legs. No worries if you ingest some garlicky side dishes; there's minty Listerine by the pumpful in the bathroom. Gavens also has a Beverly location known as G2 Gavens.

THE GREATEST: Greek Cuisine

Ithaki $$

25 Hammatt St., Ipswich, Mass., (978) 356-0099,
www.ithakicuisine.com

France and Spain get all the culinary credit, but Phantom has a soft spot in his belly for Greek cuisine. Ithaki serves some of the finest Greek and Mediterranean food on the North Shore (and all of New England). Named after the smallest of the Ionian Islands, this charming taverna always displays fresh flowers and even fresher flavors. Classic dishes like moussaka (baked eggplant, lamb, béchamel) and dolmadakia (stuffed grape leaves) are updated with modern twists, and the Greek-style roast lamb is impressively large and flavorful.

THE GREATEST: Affordable Seafood

SeaWitch Restaurant & Oyster Bar $$

203 Newbury St. (Rt. 1 North), Peabody, Mass., (978) 535-6057

The SeaWitch is completely casual, comfortable, and affordable. Customers order straightforward seafood dishes at the counter, grab a number and a booth, and wait for the food to be delivered to the table. All selections are served grilled, broiled, or fried. No fancy sauces or sides are necessary when the fresh catch comes straight from the sea. Notable noshes include the delicate fried clams, spectacular swordfish, baked stuffed clams, and broiled haddock.

THE GREATEST: Dinner & Drinks

Brenden Crocker's Wild Horse Café $$

392 Cabot St., Beverly, Mass., (978) 922-6868,
www.wildhorsecafe.com

The Wild Horse Café serves up new American cuisine out of one of the finest kitchens on the North Shore. The eclectic atmosphere is reminiscent of a tasteful living room or parlor. After dining on fresh thyme and onion focaccia, grilled Portobello mushrooms or the renowned brick oven-baked chicken, retire to the Martini Bar area where you can enjoy a Dirty Sicilian or Southwestern Cosmopolitan.

THE GREATEST: North Shore Italian

Donatello $$

44 Broadway (Route 1), Saugus, Mass., (781) 233-9975,
www.donatello-restaurant.com

In an area where spaghetti and meatballs dominate a lot of Italian menus, Donatello stands out for its authentic, inventive cuisine. Equally inviting to both the casual crowd and sophisticated diners, the dining rooms and bar are tastefully decorated, bright, and airy. It's tough to decide on antipasti, but the calamari, carpaccio, and crispy pizzettes are worthy options. The spicy fusilli with lobster is a Phantom favorite, and the double-thick chops (veal or pork) are massive . . . and massively satisfying.

THE GREATEST: Upscale Mexican

Cilantro   **$$**
282 Derby St., Salem, Mass., (978) 745-9436,
www.cilantrocilantro.com
Cilantro serves the North Shore community upscale Mexican cuisine, offering attractive atmosphere to match. The whole red snapper is a rare treat of firm fish locked inside a fully crisped skillet skin, finished in sweet garlic. The filet mignon combines the savory and the spicy with a treasure of medium rare steak draped in chorizo and Chihuahua cheese. The handsome, smallish dining room is dolled up in brick, wood, and terra-cotta-colored walls. For a quick bite, grab takeout from Taste of Cilantro, their more casual sister establishment around the corner.

THE GREATEST: Seafood & Chocolate

Catch   **$$$**
34 Church St., Winchester, Mass., (781) 729-1040,
www.catchrestaurant.com
Catch is . . . well, quite a catch! The cozy bistro turns out incredible seafood like braised Maine lobster towering over a crispy risotto cake or seared scallops with raisins, capers, and almonds. If you're a member of the clean plate club like Phantom, you may not save room for incredible desserts like the blueberry lemon curd tart. In which case, be sure to get John's Box of Chocolates to go. The in-house chocolatier whips up tempting bonbons filled with bright flavors like pistachio, orange, coffee, and passion fruit. The dining room is elegant casual, with an inviting bar where you get a front-row view of the copper pot kitchen.

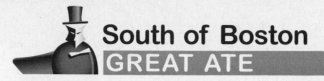

South of Boston
GREAT ATE

South Shore residents used to have to split their time between Boston and Providence to get a decent meal. But the population explosion of the area brought a bunch of awesome restaurants right into their backyard. Phantom strays from the city limits for the 8 GREATEST South Shore restaurants.

TASTY TIP The Village Shoppes at Cobb's Corner in Canton may be the tastiest shopping plaza in New England. In one central location, you can eat spare ribs at Chinatown, steak tips at The Halfway Café, almond toffee crunch at Hilliard's House of Candy, and Oreo cheesecake at White's Pastry.

THE GREATEST: South Shore Sophistication

Coriander $$$
5 Post Office Sq., Sharon, Mass., (781) 784-5450,
www.corianderbistro.com

Coriander prides itself on simplicity, resulting in a truly relaxing experience. An elegant, minimalist dining room plays host to exciting, innovative cuisine and personalized service. A window to the kitchen is barely visible, but the creations from within give every table a decorative presence. Phantom loves the meaty monkfish Provençale and the tender pork roast, which are only outdone by delicious desserts. The pumpkin crème caramel and house-churned plum cassis ice cream are the perfect cap to a sensational suburban dining experience. You can usually expect a personal visit from the chef, too.

THE GREATEST: New England–Style Italian

Tosca $$$
14 North St., Hingham, Mass., (781) 740-0080,
www.eatwellinc.com

Housed in a 1910 Granary Marketplace, Tosca is a dramatic setting of exposed brick, mahogany beams, and lofty ceilings. Using local produce and New England seafood, the open kitchen remains devotedly Italian. The wood oven adds a rustic complexity to many of the pastas, roasts, and cracker-thin pizzas topped with porcini mushrooms and asparagus. Surf-&-turf fanatics like Phantom can get a garlicky shrimp and sirloin version. The hardy lasagna is the richest Phantom has ever tasted, flooded with fontina cheese, smoked chicken, and sweet cipolline onions.

THE GREATEST: Beach Eats

Back Eddy $$$
1 Bridge Road, Westport, Mass., (508) 636-6500,
www.thebackeddy.com

The Back Eddy is a classy clam shack with a light, airy interior. The spacious outdoor patio bar leads to a picturesque pier. Whether you arrive by boat or by car, the Back Eddy is the ideal New England summer restaurant. The atmosphere is comfortable and casual, filled with vacationing city-dwellers and locals enjoying a day on Horseneck Beach. The kitchen takes full advantage of local farms and fishermen, creating dishes like oven-roasted cod loin with Westport littlenecks and applewood bacon-wrapped sea scallops.

THE GREATEST: Middle Eastern Menu

Byblos $$
678 Washington St., Norwood, Mass., (781) 762-8998

Byblos may be the most delicious, authentic, and affordable Middle Eastern restaurant in all of New England, let alone the South Shore. Lebanese music plays in the background, while customers feast on dishes that rely heavily on fresh herbs and olive oil. Named after an ancient Lebanese port city, Byblos keeps the cuisine traditional and flavorful. Hummus and baba ghanoush fly out of the kitchen along with sizzling-hot grilled kebobs. Their tabbouleh is a lemony bulgur wheat salad with ripe tomatoes and parsley, and the fattoush salad combines cucumbers, scallions, radishes, and toasted pitas.

THE GREATEST: South Shore Style

Square Café $$$
150 North St., Hingham, Mass., (781) 740-4060,
www.thesquarecafe.com

Square Café puts way more energy and expense into stylish decor than most suburban restaurants. The masculine look comes from heavy draperies, plaid seats, oversized lampshades, and a dark wood bar. Foodies feel right at home, too, with enticing dishes that lean toward Asian and French influence. Examples include pork and shrimp shumai with coriander dipping sauce. There's also grilled duck with papaya fried rice and Vidalia-stuffed pork chops. Desserts include walnut spring rolls and Vermont maple crème brûlée. The menu caters to all appetites, listing entrées as either small or large plates.

THE GREATEST: Bagel Bakery

Zeppy's Bagel Bakery $
937 North Main St., Randolph, Mass., (781) 963-7022
Since 1925, Zeppy's has been a tradition for Boston bagel lovers. Their secret baking technique results in the area's best New York–style bagels with no flat side to the chewy rings. There's a lot more to Zeppy's than meets the retail shop eye. Even their most loyal bagel buyers don't notice the 33,000-square-foot production facility out back, cranking out one hundred thousand bagels every day. No, Phantom isn't eating them out of their warehouse (although his waistline would suggest otherwise); most are sold wholesale to local supermarkets. The bagels come in tons of flavors like blueberry and cinnamon sugar, and any of their 15 cream cheeses is a perfect match.

THE GREATEST: Ice Cream

Crescent Ridge Dairy $
407 Bay Rd., Sharon, Mass., (781) 784 5892,
www.crescentridge.com
Crescent Ridge Dairy has a picture-perfect dairy bar where families order at the eight windows and then stroll their cones along a white picket fence. Green grass pastures roll away in the background, while headlights and little leaguers flood the parking lot up front. The all-dairy menu has a classic line-up of scoops, sundaes, and frappes, with 31 flavors of ice cream and five frozen yogurts made from farm fresh cream. The sweetest treat is the wild blueberry sundae, swirling concentrated fruit through layers of whipped cream and the creamiest vanilla ice cream Phantom has ever tasted. Plus, Crescent Ridge still offers home delivery from their very own milk man!

THE GREATEST: Greek Salad

Christo's $$
782 Crescent St., Brockton, Mass., (508) 588-4200
Christo's has built its legendary reputation on a world-famous Greek salad recipe. They start with crisp greens, cured olives, ripe tomatoes, and plenty of feta cheese. But what sets Christo's apart is the homemade salad dressing that's so secret that even Phantom doesn't know all the ingredients. On the menu, you'll find other Hellenic favorites like juicy shish kebobs, baked lamb, crispy white pizza, and homemade baklava. Christo's has grown into a massive complex during their 40 years in the business, with five different dining rooms and a seasoned waitstaff that won't flinch when you ask for extra feta.

MetroWest
GREAT ATE

Boston and Worcester are the two largest cities in the New England, and the culinary communities between them are exploding on the restaurant radar. Phantom reveals the 8 GREATEST restaurants in MetroWest Massachusetts.

TASTY TIP If you're looking for a quick, cheap bite to eat in MetroWest, hit the MassPike service stations. But if you have the time for a sit-down dinner, stop along Route 9.

THE GREATEST: Bodacious BBQ

Firefly's Bar-B-Q $$
235 Old Connecticut Path, Framingham, Mass.,
www.fireflysbbq.com
Award-winning pitmaster Steve Uliss has created a barbecue playground where low and slow cooking results in utterly tender ribs, brisket, pulled pork, and chicken wings. Hickory, cherry, and applewood smoke the meats, which are packed with flavor from spice-filled dry rubs. For added zest, the condiment bar includes five saucy sauces, assorted pickles, and 40 radical hot sauces. Check out the all-you-can-eat barbecue buffet on Sunday afternoons. They also do a decadent sweet potato puddin' and incredible desserts like Coca-Cola Cake and white chocolate bread pudding. Firefly's in Marlboro is also home to Dante's, a sports bar and blues club with live entertainment from Thursday to Saturday.

THE GREATEST: Suburban Steakhouse

Coach Grill $$$
55 Boston Post Road, Wayland, Mass., (508) 358-5900,
www.coachgrill.com
The Coach Grill is a fine steakhouse with a dark wood interior of black leather banquettes, mirrored walls, and equestrian art. Stone fireplaces flank the lively rooms, and stately lamps suspend from the recessed ceiling. The meaty menu includes steaks aged for five weeks, plus chops, seafood, rotisserie selections, and a fine wine list. Phantom recommends the masterfully cooked porterhouse steak with excellent marbling on the top loin side and butter knife tenderness on the filet mignon side. Servers in tan butcher jackets deliver a strong, smooth performance with rolling cart presentation of each course.

THE GREATEST: Upscale Indian

Masala Art $$$
990 Great Plain Ave., Needham, Mass., (781) 449-4050

Masala Art is a hip Indian eatery where colored silk cushions light up the window seats and glowing lamps are carved into the wall. The lengthy blue-lit bar features a backdrop of images of mythical Indian characters that pop out in 3-D form. On the menu, regional Indian cuisine draws from the chef's extensive spice library in all kinds of vegetarian, chicken, and lamb dishes. Masala Art also claims to have the nation's only spice bar, where customers can dig into a multi-course adventure while learning about Indian cuisine from the chef. He cooks right before your eyes with spices mixed to your exact specifications.

THE GREATEST: Asian & Italian

Maxwell's 148 $$$
148 E. Central St., Natick, Mass., (508) 907-6262,
www.maxwells148.com

Maxwell's 148 is properly sophisticated for a savvy, suburban clientele. Cream and bronze tones carry a Zen-like vibe, and the room is also marked by a crystal chandelier, thick velvet curtains, and hydro rock gardens. The unfocused, yet fascinating copper-plated menu alternates Italian, French, and Asian dishes loaded with flavor and texture. Every meal starts with a fascinating basket of large Chinese noodles and fresh breads, and it only gets better with dishes like lobster pad Thai, king salmon filet with Chinese broccoli, and pork loin katsu.

THE GREATEST: Sushi Buffet

Minado $$
1282 Worcester Rd., Natick, Mass., (508) 647-0495,
www.minado.com

Phantom is skeptical whenever he see the words "sushi" and "buffet" in the same sentence. However, Minado's all-you-can-eat feast is expansive without compromising quality. The cavernous 360-seat dining room invites seafood lovers to sink their teeth into 100 selections of maki, sashimi, and hand rolls. Along with tuna, eel, and yellow tail, there's crab with avocado, fried salmon, and shrimp tempura. Freshness is guaranteed, with no piece sitting out for more than 15 minutes. The friendly staff is sometimes slow to restock the lobster tail and crab legs, but they're worth the wait.

THE GREATEST: Feng Shui Fusion

Blue Ginger $$$
583 Washington St., Wellesley, Mass., (781) 283-5790,
www.ming.com

Blue Ginger is setting a new standard for quality and style outside of the city. Ming Tsai's inventive "East meets West" cuisine and the celebrity chef buzz make for unforgettable dining. In true Feng Shui fashion, cobalt blue accents enhance the room's bright decor from the front bar to the lively dining room. The delicate foie gras shiitake shumai are rich, delicious dumplings in a dreamy caramelized shallot broth. The house signature, Sake-Miso Marinated Alaskan Butterfish, is intensely sweet and scrumptious with each flaky bite.

THE GREATEST: New American Menu

Fava $$
1027 Great Plain Ave., Needham, Mass., (781) 455-8668,
www.favarestaurant.com

How could a restaurant with flavors this bold be located in Needham's subdued town center? That's what Phantom kept asking himself as he tasted forkful after forkful of their exciting New American cuisine. The intimate neighborhood restaurant is actually located in a former train station. While the conductors are long gone, you can still embark on a spontaneous adventure with dishes like pan-seared scallops over sweet pea risotto. They also do a lovely lobster shepherd's pie and a porcini-crusted rib eye. The food, waitstaff, and the atmosphere are completely unpretentious.

THE GREATEST: Roadside Diner

Harry's $
149 Turnpike Rd., Westborough, Mass., (508) 366-8302,
www.westborough.com/harrys

Harry's is a roadside luncheonette with brown vinyl booths, baby stools at the counter, and some of the area's finest diner food. It's a solid value for breakfast, lunch, and dinner, but Phantom recommends sticking to what they do best: fried clams and ice cream. The Big Belly Plate looks like a mountain of ale-colored coral with deep-fried clams coated in just enough gritty batter to seal in the clam juices. For dessert, order a Big Gulp–sized frappe or a brownie sundae piled high with fudgy cake, piping-hot chocolate sauce, homemade whipped cream, and mini chocolate chips.

Central & Western Massachusetts
GREAT ATE

It's about time Bostonians knew that there's an entirely delicious world west of 495! Phantom gladly goes the distance to the 8 GREATEST restaurants in Central and Western Massachusetts.

TASTY TIP

Belchertown is Phantom's favorite town name in Massachusetts, edging out Sandwich, Orange, and Salisbury. If you know a good dining destination in Belchertown, let Phantom know about it at www.PhantomGourmet.com.

THE GREATEST: California Wine List

Sonoma $$$
206 Worcester Rd., Princeton, Mass., (978) 464-5775
Sonoma is tucked away in the hills of Princeton, but it's worth seeking out for unforgettable global fare and an amazing California wine list. Silver-vested servers are skilled at suggesting an oaky chardonnay or a crisp Sauvignon Blanc, and at the end of the meal, they give every table a tour of the decadent dessert tray. All of the original artwork is for sale, but Phantom suggests saving your pennies for the likes of pumpkin soup served in a hollowed-out gourd or the mushroom-dusted venison chop.

THE GREATEST: Fine Dining

Wheatleigh $$$
Hawthorne Rd., Lenox, Mass., (413) 637-0610,
www.wheatleigh.com
Prepare to be pampered! As you roll into the luxury isolation of Wheatleigh, you're wrapped up in Berkshire beauty and the vintage architecture of the boutique hotel. Dining is an exquisite treat, with artful plates that induce a state of pensive bliss. The fluffy ricotta-stuffed agnolotti is just as unforgettably delicious as the tender, crispy-skinned black bass. The menu is delightfully constrained to ingredients at the perfect peak of harvest, and the six-course chef's tasting makes you feel like a million bucks for just $115.

THE GREATEST: **Pizza by the Slice**

Antonio's Pizza $

31 North Pleasant St., Amherst, Mass., (413) 253-0808

Antonio's Pizza is a late-night favorite for UMass students in search of a hot, cheesy Sicilian slice. Until 2 a.m. on the weekends, college kids mob the counter in the skinny pizza shop, ogling the 20 pies on display. Antonio's serves 200 to 300 kinds of pizza, and about 50 of these exotic varieties are available each day. Outrageous creations include black bean and avocado, lasagna, chicken blue cheese, and even tortellini. There's a second Antonio's in Providence.

THE GREATEST: **Cajun & Creole**

Chef Wayne's Big Mamou $$

63 Liberty St., Springfield, Mass., (413) 732-1011

Chef Wayne's Big Mamou serves awesome Cajun and Creole cuisines in a friendly, fun space decked out in Louisiana murals and stuffed alligators. Enormous entrées include pork loin stuffed with cornbread, sage and sausage over rice. The house specialty blends crawfish, shrimp, and veggies in a lobster brandy cream sauce with puff pastry. Spice it up with one of the hot sauces on the table, and enjoy it with the beverage of your choice, because Wayne's is BYOB. Some customers even bring their own battery-operated blenders for homemade margaritas!

THE GREATEST: **German Restaurant**

Hofbrauhaus $$

1105 Main Street, West Springfield, Mass., (413) 737-4905

For wiener schnitzel, sauerkraut, and strudel, the Hofbrauhaus is the closest to Munich you can get without hopping a plane. There are two dining rooms decorated with German pictures and beer steins. The waitstaff wears German dresses, and the menu covers a wide variety of Bavarian specialties. The sauerkraut *en backtieg* (deep-fried sauerkraut with corned beef and cheese) is simply outstanding. One bite of the sauerbraten with potato dumpling and red cabbage is like taking a trip back to the old country. Outstanding German beers like Schneider Weisse and Paulaner Thomasbrau top off the experience, along with a list of 200 French and German wines.

THE GREATEST: Seafood in Central MA

The Sole Proprietor $$
118 Highland St., Worcester, Mass., (508) 798-3474,
www.thesole.com

The Sole Proprietor is the area's finest seafood restaurant and hippest bar scene.
The incredibly long, varied menu reads like a delicious novel, with tempting chap-
ters devoted to sushi, oysters, and mouthwatering entrées. Wildly inventive specials
include the shrimp macaroni and cheese or roasted mako wrapped in prosciutto.
The seafood motif is tastefully fun, and the vibrant bar is always buzzing. Every
summer, an inflatable crustacean named Buster the Crab commandeers the restau-
rant's roof. He's 75 feet long and 12 feet tall, and during his stay The Sole Propri-
etor offers special crab dishes. If only they had a pot big enough to steam him
in . . .

THE GREATEST: Fairground Food

The Big E $
1305 Memorial Ave., West Springfield, Mass., (413) 737-2443,
www.thebige.com

The Big E is a New England autumn tradition and the ninth-largest fair in North
America. More than one million people pass through the gates every September for
glorious gastronomic gluttony. Phantom goes for the deep-fried dream world,
where everything imaginable gets a hot, golden garb. Corn dogs, Oreos, and veg-
etables all take the fryolator plunge. Phantom's favorites are the deep-fried candy
bars, which emerge with a crunchy seal around a gooey, melted chocolate core.
Check out the Avenue of States for local specialties from Rhode Island, New
Hampshire, Maine, Vermont, and Connecticut.

THE GREATEST: Subterranean Speakeasy

The Tunnel Bar $$
125A Pleasant St., Northampton, Mass., (413) 586-5366

Like the name implies, this ultra-cool bar is located inside a 100-foot-long, 12-foot-
wide railway tunnel that dates back to 1896. The trains stopped running years ago,
and now the only sidecars you'll find here are mixed to order. The wine list reads
like a book, and the mixologists serve about 200 different martinis on weekend
nights. For nibbling, there's shrimp cocktail, a fruit & cheese tray, and warm
toasted nuts. Due to the romantic atmosphere, the dim lighting, and no-cell-phone
access (due to the stone foundation that's six feet deep), this place has earned its
reputation as the "tunnel of love."

Index of Restaurants by Location

Pit Stop Barbeque, 10
Restaurante Cesaria, 57
Ten Tables, 133
Zon's, 43

Downtown

Ándale!, 102
Anthem, 45
Café Fleuri, 51
Locke-Ober, 65, 124
Parker's, 51
Peking Tom's, 39
Pizza Oggi, 113
Pressed Sandwiches, 60
Sam LaGrassa's, 59
Silvertone, 140
Spire, 84
Sultan's Kitchen, 57

East Boston

Santarpio's Pizza, 112
Taqueria Cancun, 4

Faneuil Hall

Durgin Park, 44
Houston's, 137
Plaza III, 106
Seasons, 66

Fenway

El Pelón, 77
Fenway Park, 81
Tiki Room, 48

Ladder District

blu, 135
Chacarero, 118

Newton

Buff's Pub, 34
Cabot's, 87
Sweet Tomatoes, 78

North End

Billy Tse, 37
Boschetto Bakery, 164
Bova's Bakery, 94
Caffe Paradiso, 163
Caffe Vittoria, 42
Carmen, 161
Daily Catch, 134
Dairy Fresh Candies, 163
Dino's, 79
Dom's, 161
Enoteca Bricco, 161
Fiore Ristorante, 105
Galleria Umberto, 33, 91
Giacomo's, 89, 160
Lucca, 159
Marco Cucina Romana, 114
Mare, 136
Maria's Pastry Shop, 162
Mike's Pastry, 164
Modern Pastry, 163
Nebo, 136
Neptune Oyster, 120
Pizzeria Regina, 111
Polcari's Coffee Shop, 40
Prezza, 159
Sage, 160
Salumeria Italiana, 162
Strega, 160
Taranta, 96
Wine Bottega, 164

Somerville

Blue Shirt Café, 76
Dali, 5, 114
Diesel Café, 41
Johnny D's Uptown, 16
O'Naturals, 75
Out of the Blue, 121
Petsi Pies, 7
RedBones, 9

R. F. O'Sullivan's Pub, 19
Rosebud Diner, 53
Sabur, 55
Sound Bites, 14
Tu Y Yo, 101
Vinny's at Night, 77

South Boston

Café Polonia, 56
Jasper White's Summer Shack, 148
Salsa's, 101
Terrie's Place, 13

South End

Addis Red Sea, 41
Aquitaine, 69
B&G Oysters Ltd, 134
Bob's Southern Bistro, 10
The Butcher Shop, 165
Caffè Umbra, 35
Charlie's Sandwich Shoppe, 12–13
Chicken Lou's, 35
Code 10, 81
Delux Café, 134
The Dish, 47
Equator, 166
Flour Bakery, 6
Franklin Café, 93
Garden of Eden, 166
Hamersley's Bistro, 34, 166
Icarus, 116, 167
Masa, 32
McCormick & Schmick's, 33
Metropolis Café, 132
Mike's City Dinner, 12
Mistral, 48, 165
Pho Republique, 93
PICCO, 88
Polka Dog Bakery, 8
Sibling Rivalry, 167
Skipjack's, 131
Stella, 135
Tremont 647, 15

28 Degrees, 167
Union Bar and Grille, 5

Theater District

The Bristol, 21, 170
Davio's, 128
Finale, 49, 170
P. F. Chang's, 170
Pigalle, 168
Smith & Wollensky, 169
Sorriso, 108
Teatro, 168
Troquet, 139, 169

Waterfront

Barking Crab, 105
Chart House, 29
Intrigue Café, 105
Meritage, 138
No Name Restaurant, 122
Sel de la Terra, 46

Watertown

Deluxe Town Diner, 68
KnowFat! Lifestyle Grille, 74
La Casa de Pedro, 95
Strip T's, 133
Wild Willy's, 20

Beyond City Limits

Cape Cod & The Islands

Cape Cod Central Railroad, 172
Chillingsworth, 171
Four Seas Ice Cream, 173
Hearth 'n Kettle, 26–27
Kream 'N Kone, 72
Lobster Pot (East Wareham, Mass.),
   99
Lobster Pot (Provincetown, Mass.),
   171–172
Naked Oyster Bistro & Raw Bar, 173

Woodman's of Essex, 71
Ye Olde Pepper Companie, 24

Northwest of Boston
Harrows Chicken Pies, 35
Kimball Farm, 86
Nancy's Air Field Café, 141
Papa Jim's Exotic Hot Dogs, 82

Rhode Island
Al Forno, 176
Angelo's Civita Farnese, 90
Costantino's Venda Ravioli, 107
Dave & Busters, 29
Geoff's Superlative Sandwiches, 177
Haven Brothers Diner, 94
Julian's, 17–18
Mediterraneo, 177
Mill's Tavern, 176
New Rivers, 176–177
Nordic Lodge, 100
Pane e Vino, 176
Pastiche Fine Desserts, 51
Raphael Bar Risto, 175
The Spiced Pear, 65–66
10 Steak & Sushi, 130
22 Bowens Wine Bar & Grille, 143
XO Steakhouse, 175

South of Boston
Arthur & Pat's, 13
Ascari Café at F1 Boston, 47
Back Eddy, 182
Byblos, 182
Chinatown, 38
Christo's, 183
Coriander, 181
Crescent Ridge Dairy, 183
Delfino, 109
50s Diner, 54
G. H. Bent Co, 119
Halfway Café, 32–33

Henry's Root Beer Stand, 60
Hilliard's House of Candy, 23–24
Hingham Lobster Pound, 73
Lynwood Café, 113
Memphis Roundhouse, 10
Quan's Kitchen, 39
Red Lion Inn, 116
Ron's Gourmet Ice Cream and 20th
    Century Bowling, 87
Saporito's Florence Club Café, 91
Square Café, 182
Tosca, 181
Tutto Italiano, 117
Wendell's Pub, 78
White's Pastry, 8
Zeppy's Bagel Bakery, 183

Vermont
Al's French Frys, 68
Curtis Bar-B-Que, 142

West of Boston
Bison County, 69
Blue Ginger, 122, 186
Campania, 90
Carl's Steak Subs, 60
Casey's Diner, 52
China Sky, 39
Coach Grill, 184
Domenic's Italian Bakery and Deli,
    89
Fava, 186
Firefly's Bar-B-Q, 184
Harry's, 186
Il Capriccio, 115
Ma Glockner's, 36
Masala Art, 55–56, 185
Maxwell's, 148, 185
Mendon Twin Drive-In, 32
Minado, 130, 185
Rainforest Café, 28
Taqueria Mexico, 103

Alphabetical Index

The Castle, 41
Catch, 180
Central Kitchen, 155
Chacarero, 118
Charlie's Sandwich Shoppe, 12–13
Chart House, 29
Chauncey Creek Lobster Pier, 98
Cheesecake Factory, 50
Chef Wayne's Big Mamou, 188
Chez Henri, 97
Chicken Lou's, 35
Chillingsworth, 171
China Pearl, 17
China Sky, 39
Chinatown, 38
The Chocolate Dipper, 24
Christina's Ice Cream, 87
Christina's Spice & Specialty Foods,
    133
Christo's, 183
Chunky's Cinema Pub, 48
Cilantro, 180
The Clam Box, 72–73
Clio, 64–65, 85
Coach Grill, 184
Code 10, 81
Cold Stone Creamery, 88
Coolidge Corner Clubhouse, 70
Coriander, 181
Cosi, 61
Costantino's Venda Ravioli, 107
Craigie Street Bistrot, 154
Crescent Ridge Dairy, 183
The Crystal Quail, 143
Cuchi Cuchi, 154
Cuffs, 85
Curtis Bar-B-Que, 142

D

Daily Catch, 134
Dairy Fresh Candies, 163

Dali, 5, 114
Darwin's Limited, 119
Dave & Busters, 29
Davio's, 128
Delfino, 109
Delux Café, 134
Deluxe Town Diner, 68
Diesel Café, 41
Dino's, 79
The Dish, 47
Dok Bua Thai Kitchen, 31–32
Domenic's Italian Bakery and Deli,
    89
Dom's, 161
Donatello, 179–180
Dream Diner, 52
Dunkin' Donuts, 40
Durgin Park, 44

E

Eagle's Deli & Restaurant, 20
East Coast Grill & Raw Bar, 122
Edible Arrangements, 74
Eldo Cake House, 158
El Pelón, 77
Emma's Pizza, 113
Enoteca Bricco, 161
Equator, 166
Excelsior, 139, 149

F

Fava, 186
Federalist, 139
Fenway Park, 81
50s Diner, 54
Figs, 26
Finagle A Bagel, 26
Finale, 49, 170
Finz, 121, 178
Fiore Ristorante, 105

Firefly's Bar-B-Q (Framingham, Mass.),
    184
Firefly's Bar-B-Que (Marlborough,
    Mass.), 11
The Fireplace, 44
Flatbread Company, 5
Flo's Steamed Hot Dogs, 80
Flour Bakery, 6
Fore Street, 141
Formaggio Kitchen, 4
Four Seas Ice Cream, 173
Franklin Café, 93
Frank's Steakhouse, 127
Fresh City, 59
Friendly Toast, 94
Fuddruckers, 20
Fugakyu, 129

G

Galleria Umberto, 33, 91
Garden of Eden, 166
Gavens, 178
Geoff's Superlative Sandwiches, 177
George's Coney Island Hot Dogs, 82
G.H.Bent Co, 119
Giacomo's, 89, 160
Gilley's, 79
Gingerbread Construction Co, 78
Ginza, 131, 157
Golden Lamb Buttery, 143
Golden Temple, 37
Great Bay, 83
Grill 23 & Bar, 126–127
Grotto, 150

H

Halfway Café, 32–33
Hamersley's Bistro, 34, 166
Harbor Sweets, 23
Harraseeket Lunch, 72

Harrows Chicken Pies, 35
Harry's, 186
Haven Brothers Diner, 94
Hearth 'n Kettle, 26–27
The Helmand, 56
Henrietta's Table, 15
Henry's Root Beer Stand, 60
Hilliard's House of Candy, 23–24
Hingham Lobster Pound, 73
Hi-Rise Bread Company, 153–154
Hodgie's, 88
Hofbrauhaus, 188
Houston's, 137

I

Icarus, 116, 167
Iggy's Bread of the World, 8
Il Capriccio, 115
Intrigue Café, 105
Ithaki, 179

J

Jasper White's Summer Shack, 99,
    148
Johnny D's Uptown, 16
Johnny Rockets, 21
Jose's Mexican Restaurant, 103
J. T. Farnham's, 72
Julian's, 17–18
Jumbo Seafood, 157

K

Kane's Donuts, 58
Kashmir, 147
Keith's Place, 14
Kelly's Roast Beef, 117
Kenmore Diner, 54
Kimball Farm, 86
King Fung Garden, 33, 156

KnowFat! Lifestyle Grille, 74
Kowloon, 38
Kream 'N Kone, 72

L

L.A. Burdick Chocolate, 22–23
La Casa de Pedro, 95
Lala Rokh, 57, 151
La Morra, 108
Legal Sea Foods, 120, 123
L'Espalier, 65, 149
Les Zygomates, 92
Lobster Pot (East Wareham, Mass.), 99
Lobster Pot (Provincetown, Mass.),
    171–172
Locke-Ober, 65, 124
The Loft Steak and Chop House, 45
Lucca, 159
Lynwood Café, 113

M

Maggiano's Little Italy, 109
Ma Glockner's, 36
Maine Diner, 53
Marco Cucina Romana, 114
Mare, 136
Maria's Pastry Shop, 162
MaryAnn's Diner, 54
Masa, 32
Masala Art, 55–56, 185
Matt Murphy's Pub, 124
Maxwell's 148, 185
McCormick & Schmick's, 33, 169
McDonald's, 62
Mediterraneo, 177
Memphis Roundhouse, 10
Mendon Twin Drive-In, 32
Merengue, 96
Meritage, 138
Metropolis Café, 132

Metropolitan Club, 128
Meze Estiatorio, 56–57
Michael's Deli, 119
Middlesex Lounge, 136
Midwest Grill, 95
Mike's City Dinner, 12
Mike's Pastry, 164
Mill's Tavern, 176
Minado, 130, 185
Mistral, 48, 165
Modern Pastry, 163
Moogy's Breakfast and Sandwich
    Shop, 118
Morton's, 127
Muddy River Smokehouse, 11

N

Naked Fish, 121
Naked Oyster Bistro & Raw Bar, 173
Nancy's Air Field Café, 141
Nebo, 136
Neptune Oyster, 120
New Bridge Café, 128
Newburyport Lighthouse, 115
New England Soup Factory, 123
New Rivers, 176–177
News, 93
Ninety Nine Restaurant & Pub, 27
No Name Restaurant, 122
No. 9 Park, 66, 151
Nordic Lodge, 100
Not Your Average Joe's, 25
Novel, 148

O

Oak Room, 127
Ogunquit Lobster Pound, 100
Oishii Sushi Bar, 3, 129
Oleana, 4, 50
Olé Mexican Grill, 103